Delmar's Handbook for Health Information Careers

Delmar's Health Information Management Series

Shirley A. Anderson, Ph.D., RRA

Karen Jody Smith, MS, RRA

Shirley Anderson
Series Editor

Delmar Publishers

an International Thomson Publishing company I(T)P®

Albany • Bonn • Boston • Cincinnati • Detroit • London • Madrid
Melbourne • Mexico City • New York • Pacific Grove • Paris • San Francisco
Singapore • Tokyo • Toronto • Washington

NOTICE TO THE READER

Cover Design: Brucie Rosch

Publishing Team:
Publisher: Susan Simpfenderfer
Acquisitions Editor: Marlene McHugh Pratt
Developmental Editor: Jill Rembetski
Project Editor: William Trudell

Art and Design Coordinator: Rich Killar
Production Coordinator: Cathleen Berry
Editorial Assistant: Sarah Holle
Marketing Manager: Darryl L. Caron

COPYRIGHT © 1998
By Delmar Publishers
a division of International Thomson Publishing Inc.

The ITP logo is a trademark under license

Printed in the United States of America

For more information, contact:

Delmar Publishers
3 Columbia Circle, Box 15015
Albany, New York 12212-5015

International Thomson Publishing Europe
Berkshire House 168-173
High Holborn
London, WC1V7AA
England

Thomas Nelson Australia
102 Dodds Street
South Melbourne, 3205
Victoria, Australia

Nelson Canada
1120 Birchmount Road
Scarborough, Ontario
Canada M1K 5G4

International Thomson Editores
Campos Eliseos 385, Piso 7
Col Polanco
11560 Mexico D F Mexico

International Thomson Publishing Gmbh
Königswinterer Strasse 418
53227 Bonn
Germany

International Thomson Publishing Asia
221 Henderson Road #05-10
Henderson Building
Singapore 0315

International Thomson Publishing - Japan
Hirakawacho Kyowa Building, 3F
2-2-1 Hirakawacho
Chiyoda-ku, 102 Tokyo
Japan

1 2 3 4 5 6 7 8 9 10 XXX 03 02 01 00 99 98 97

Library of Congress Cataloging-in-Publication Data

Anderson, Shirley A.
    Delmar's handbook for health information careers / Shirley A.
Anderson, Karen Jody Smith.
        p.   cm.— (The health information managment series)
    Includes bibliographical references and index.
    ISBN 0-8273-8083-6 (alk. paper)
    1. Medical records—Management—Vocational guidance—United
States. I. Smith, Karen Jody. II. Title. III. Series.
RA976.A78   1997
610.69′5—dc21   97-13364
                                                  CIP

JOIN US ON THE WEB: www.DelmarAlliedHealth.com
Your Information Resource
• What's New from Delmar • Health Science News Headlines • Web Links to Many Related Sites
• Instructor Forum/Teaching Tips • Give Us Your Feedback • Online Companions™
• Complete Allied Health Catalog • Software/Media Demos • And much more!
Visit www.thomson.com for information on 35 Thomson publishers and more than 25,000 products!

Contents

Preface

Now more than ever as students approach graduation they must market their skills and abilities to the ever-changing healthcare industry. In the past, it was assumed that there would be numerous positions in hospitals. Managed care, rightsizing, consolidations, systematic delivery systems, team approaches, and paperless documentation were a few of the trends that changed this assumption. From an acute-care job market familiar with the skills of health information management professionals, new avenues are burgeoning. To secure positions internal and external to the healthcare industry, developing a resume that will result in interviews is essential. Interviews provide the opportunity to market skills. These skills are not for jobs. Rather, they are applied to positions that are part of a career path. Securing a job at times can be relatively easy. Developing a career, one that allows an individual to use unique skills, abilities, and education, takes planning. Career planning incorporates the goals, values, and needs of the individual.

The concept of a text that assists health information management professionals in career management was exciting; writing the book was invigorating.

In Chapter 1, health information management is identified as a profession. Career opportunities, as outlined in the literature, are discussed. Traits of a professional and ways to create a good impression that will assist in establishing a strong career foundation are presented. The importance of specifying goals, needs, and values as the foundation for career management is included.

Chapter 2 provides valuable information for searching the job market manually and electronically. Career opportunities are identified and the distinction between a job and a career should help the reader in the development of a career path. Self-assessment is introduced to facilitate development of a job search action plan. Executive search firms, employment agencies, and outplacement firms are described. References and resources beneficial in the job search are included.

Chapter 3 contains sufficient information to assist in the development of a portfolio. The principal use for the portfolio is as a companion to the resume. In addition, the portfolio is an important component of career planning and advancement. Mentoring and networking are also important components and these are discussed.

Chapter 4 was perceived by the reviewers as a great idea. The assumption that everyone knows how to write a business letter is no longer valid. The various types of letters that are associated with searching and securing a position are discussed with examples included.

Chapter 5 explains that the goal of resume writing is to secure a job interview. Uses for a resume and the various formats are discussed. Action verbs are provided as well as a worksheet to assist in the development of a personal resume.

Chapter 6 provides categories of questions that have and could be asked on interviews. The different types of interviews are discussed. The settings, preparation, formats, and strategies are covered as well as techniques to assist with self-confidence.

Chapter 7 incorporates postinterview strategies. The importance of documenting facts and feelings surrounding each interview is emphasized. Helpful hints on reimbursement and contacting references are provided. First month on-the-job do's and don'ts will help you get off on the right foot.

Chapter 8 includes information relating to graduate school, employment, international, entrepreneurial, and intrapreneurial opportunities.

Chapter 9 provides a realistic touch to a career path by including information on burnout, stress, and stages in a career.

Appendix A includes a listing of nearly 100 different titles and responsibilities frequently associated with various health information management positions.

Appendix B is a listing of approved programs in health information administration and health information technology.

Appendix C will assist new graduates and seasoned professionals in the development of a professional resume. The examples provided can be used for comparative purposes.

The Glossary provides definitions that will assist in understanding the contents of this textbook and other publications. Refer to this Glossary frequently. The terms included are those used by health information management professionals in a variety of settings.

Features

Delmar's Handbook for Health Information Careers was developed specifically to advance the career of health information management professionals. This textbook is currently the only one available for those seeking this career path. Readers who would benefit from the contents are:

- Students in health information administration and technology programs
- Accredited record technicians
- Registered record administrators
- Certified coding specialists
- Healthcare professionals employed in information management
- College graduates interested in information systems, informatics and health information
- High school students researching a career in health information management

With the HIM profession rapidly changing and roles and functions being restructured more frequently, this book is essential for everyone interested in shaping a career future in health information management.

Portfolio development, covered in Chapter 3, is new to most health information management professionals. Those outside the profession will find the contents helpful in providing insights into the profession. This is the only textbook that includes this newest trend for securing positions in the rapidly advancing health information industry.

The sample resumes in Appendix C and the cover letters in Chapter 4 are health information management specific. Details for conducting electronic job searches are included in Chapter 2.

At the beginning of each chapter, learning objectives are provided to facilitate identification of key concepts.

Throughout the text, bullets, figures, and tables were used to enhance understanding of the major points covered. Each chapter is summarized. Review activities provided after the summary are to reinforce ideas and concepts.

Position Titles and responsibilities in Appendix A will assist the reader in searching the job market and in becoming familiar with skills needed for the profession. For the student, the importance of course content is readily seen. For the employed graduate, the skills that must be acquired or validated for a particular position are identified. For both, this is a resource to advertised positions, many of which could be overlooked without the awareness provided by this appendix.

The American Health Information Management Association's Vision 2006 has been incorporated as deemed appropriate by the authors. The two authors have had over forty years of combined experience in working with college students and graduates. Assistance has been provided in securing entry-level positions and in career advancement.

Acknowledgements

Several individuals facilitated the development of this textbook and we want to acknowledge their contributions. We are grateful to our husbands, Marion M. Anderson and Michael Smith, for their encouragement, advice, and assistance. Jill Rembetski, development editor for Delmar, provided valuable counsel, focus, and direction. Marion Waldman encouraged us to write the book as part of the Series in Health Information Management.

Two of our co-workers at Saint Louis University deserve special recognition for taking extra time to assist with manuscript preparation and review and for supporting our efforts. Our thanks and appreciation to Jeanne M. Donnelly and Nancy L. Gaines.

We acknowledge the efforts of our reviewers. They had constructive suggestions for improvement and they also provided positive feedback. We were grateful for their comments. The reviewers were:

O. Ray Angle
Assistant Director
Career Center
Saint Louis University
St. Louis, MO

Sue Ellen Bice, MS, RRA
Coordinator
Health Information Technology
Mohawk Valley Community College
Utica, NY

Marjorie H. McNeil, MS, RRA
Assistant Professor
Division of Health Information Management
School of Allied Health Sciences
Florida A&M University
Tallahassee, FL

Carol E. Osborn, PhD, RRA
Assistant Professor
The Ohio State University
School of Allied Medical Professions
Health Information Management Division
Columbus, OH

Rachelle Stewart
Health Information Management
University of Illinois at Chicago
Chicago, IL

Glenda A. Terry, RRA
Instructor
Health Information Technology
Spokane Community College
Spokane, WA

Mary E. White, MA, RRA
Health Information Management
Sinclair Community College
Dayton, OH

At this writing, four books have been developed for the series in Health Information Management, and from these authors we drew enlightenment and direction. Our appreciation to Rozella Mattingly, Merida L. Johns, Dana C. McWay, Beth Anderson, and Kimberly A. Suggs.

Chapter 1

Health Information Management as a Profession

Goals

After reading this chapter, you should be able to:

1. Discuss potential career opportunities for health information management professionals.
2. Identify emerging roles as incorporated into Vision 2006 of the American Health Information Management Association (AHIMA).
3. Select at least one characteristic of a professional and discuss the importance of this to you.
4. Explain the importance of making a good impression and its impact on your success in a profession.
5. Sketch the success cycle.
6. Discuss the relationship between needs and values for a successful career.

Introduction

Of all the allied health professions, health information management is one of the most exciting, with a variety of opportunities in the healthcare industry as well as in other areas. There are hundreds of jobs that need the skills of health information management professionals. These skills are not as well established as those for a nurse, accountant, or lawyer. In order for health information management professionals to obtain jobs that will develop into careers, two conditions must be present. They must know their skills and must be able to market those skills to employers.

This chapter will start you on your way to marketing your skills and securing a position in this dynamic field. An understanding of *health information management (HIM)* as explained in this chapter, will assist you in researching the job market. Several job opportunities will be mentioned. Vision 2006, which has implications for the future of the health information management profession, is introduced in this chapter and visited later in Chapter 8.

Understanding your needs and values can assist you in securing the right job. For new graduates of health information technology and administration programs, the information in this chapter will be valuable for securing the right job. For those who have backgrounds in medical record documentation, computers, management, and other areas, this chapter has information for commencing a career as a health information management professional. For the seasoned professional, the information can assist in changing positions and advancing in a career.

Health Information Management Background

For centuries there have been nurses and physicians. As a profession, health information management is relatively new, and only since 1991 has it been associated with a national organization, the American Health Information Management Association (AHIMA). Health information management developed as information systems assumed greater importance in the processing and analyzing of patient-care documentation. Generally, health information management is considered a combination of skills involving computers, business, medical sciences, medicolegal aspects, and systems for reimbursement and data processing. *Health information management* is a general term with applications to a variety of settings. Any workplace involved with health care and information management can use the knowledge, skills, and abilities of a health information management professional. Among the potential employers are insurance companies, hospitals, managed-care groups, home health agencies, hospices, ambulatory surgery centers, clinics, group practices, subacute-care facilities, rehabilitation centers, computer companies, consulting firms, and behavioral healthcare facilities. In addition to numerous employment locations, there are hundreds of job titles used by health information management professionals. A study by the authors (1989) of 66 positions indicated that 358 different titles were used for these positions. For example, 10 additional titles were associated with the job title diagnosis-related group coordinator/validator as shown in Figure 1-1.

Educational Programs

The American Health Information Management Association (AHIMA) is a sponsor of the Commission on Accreditation of Allied Health Education Programs (CAAHEP). *Essentials* refer to the minimum standards of quality used in accrediting programs that prepare individuals to enter health information management and other allied health programs accredited by CAAHEP. AHIMA establishes, maintains, and promotes appropriate quality standards for educational programs in health information management. Through AHIMA's Council on Accreditation, recognition is given to those educational programs that meet or exceed the minimum standards that are outlined in the document, "Essentials and Guidelines for an Accredited

---

Additional titles used for performing similar functions:

DRG Manager

DRG Specialist

Director of DRG Operations

Coordinator of Review Activities

Utilization Review Coordinator

Concurrent Chart Reviewer/Analyst

Medical Information Coordinator

Statewide Director, Medical Records

Manager, Data Entry

Review Process/DRG Specialist

Figure 1-1.   Diagnostic-Related Group (DRG) Coordinator/Validator

Educational Program for the Health Information Technician and the Health Information Administrator." There are approximately fifty programs throughout the United States that are accredited in health information administration (HIA), although colleges vary on the name given to the degree awarded, for example, health information management, health information administration, and medical record science. The majority of these programs award bachelor's degrees with a few offering master's degrees and some offering certificates. There are more than a hundred two-year postsecondary school programs that are accredited as programs in health information technology (HIT). These programs exist at community and technical colleges and other sites as shown in Appendix B. The listing of programs in Appendix B is subject to change. The latest information can be obtained by contacting the American Health Information Management Association headquartered in Chicago, or accessing their web site at http://www.ahima.org.

Allied Health

The primary functions of allied health professionals and practitioners are to promote health and to provide services associated with healthcare. Some allied health professionals, such as physical therapists and occupational therapists, have considerable patient contact associated with their responsibilities. Health information management professionals are like clinical laboratory specialists in having little or no direct patient contact. Educational requirements for those considered allied health practitioners and professionals range from certifications to postdoctoral training in a science related to healthcare. For example, medical office assistants can complete a postsecondary program in one year and obtain a certificate. A career as an audiologist or speech pathologist requires up to six years of study after high school, leading to a master's degree.

Career Opportunities

According to the Bureau of Labor Statistics (1996), more than 47,000 additional health information management professionals will be needed by the year 2005. Nurses, social workers, and even physicians are among those who compete for the available positions in health information management.

Through experience and additional education, a variety of healthcare professionals may have acquired skills relating to this field.

Frequently employers do not realize that the biomedical component of the curriculum for many health information technology and health information administration programs includes courses in anatomy, physiology, pathology, pharmacology, and clinical medicine. The depth of coverage can extend beyond nursing care into the medical science areas of diagnoses and treatments.

In the business area, many programs require students to take courses in accounting, marketing, management theory and practice, management information systems, and economics. Listing these courses on your resume as shown in Appendix C can facilitate marketing your skills in these areas for a variety of positions, including some outside the healthcare industry.

Since each curriculum has unique features to meet the program's goals, you should be aware of your program's components and emphasize them to employers. The position titles described in Appendix A range from an account representative to a medical records administrator in veterinary medicine. If you are starting your studies in health information technology or management, peruse the position titles and descriptors. The list in Appendix A can be expanded. As you acquire knowledge, skills, and abilities, relate them to a specific position. You can do this in a separate notebook or in a computer file. You can also add to the list of position titles. As you review journals, news magazines, and other publications, make note of the jobs advertised and the skills that are requested. Add them to the list you are compiling. If the position is one you would like when you graduate, start acquiring the skills, and record the details as the skills are achieved.

If you are already working in health information management, you can follow a similar process. To add to your skills, you can volunteer for various teams or special projects that will relate to the job you are seeking. You can also attain additional knowledge, skills, and abilities by taking courses at the undergraduate or graduate level.

Vision 2006

Appendix A identifies some of the existing roles that have been advertised and performed by health information management professionals. New roles are being envisioned because of the rapid changes occurring that will influence health information management. These changes involve the following:

- The health care industry with the shift from hospitals to the nonacute-care setting.
- The documentation of patient-care and billing processes through electronic systems.
- The labor market with about one-quarter of all new jobs being in health-care.

A Venn diagram as shown in Figure 1-2 was developed by AHIMA. With the patient at the center, six emerging roles are in three clusters:

1. Data management analysis with the roles being clinical data specialist, data quality manager, and research analyst.
2. Patient health information coordination with the role being patient information coordinator.
3. Information systems management with the roles being security manager and document and repository manager.

The seventh role, that of the HIM manager, is an enterprise or facilitywide responsibility that includes working with a chief information executive and system users.

Career scenarios for these roles are covered in Chapter 8. For now, the important consideration is that there are existing and emerging opportunities. The healthcare industry is changing and you can monitor these changes by reading job advertisements and appropriate articles to keep in tune with knowledge, skills, and abilities needed for various positions.

Positions in Times of Change

The prevalence of managed care with capitated forms of payment is one of the many changes occurring in the healthcare industry. Organizational, environmental, and technological changes are taking place in healthcare that will influence health information management. Team approaches are being used for problem solving. Consumers are being involved and even managing their own health information. Job opportunities that are anticipated to be in demand as a result of the changes are coding specialist, clinical data

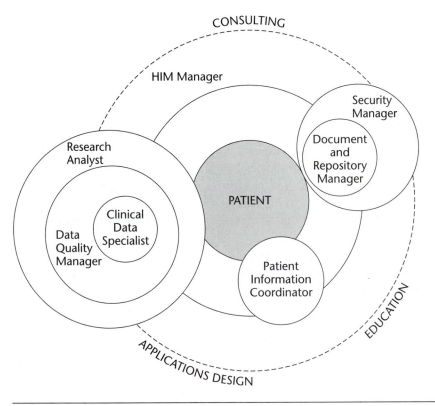

Figure 1-2. Emerging HIM Roles (Reprinted with permission, © the American Health Information Management Association)

analyst, educator/trainer, clinical data systems manager, director of health information management, and management consultant. These are developed further in Figure 1-3.

Professionalism

Upon graduation, you will start your career as a health information management professional. The transition from college student to professional requires that you have certain characteristics. Six important steps are explained next.

Coding Specialist: With the anticipated integration of traditional and ambulatory-care services, coders may be coding a continuum of care rather than one specific episode of care. A broader range of complaints, symptoms, diagnoses, and treatments would need to be coded.

Clinical Data Analyst: The future will be driven by data. Therefore, job opportunities will surface for individuals who can identify trends, display the trends, and communicate responses.

Educator/Trainer: When change occurs, education or additional training is needed to meet the challenge of the change.

Clinical Data Systems Manager: As health information systems begin to integrate, clinical data systems managers will be needed to establish procedures for these systems and the services they support as well as to ensure they provide accurate and timely information to decision makers.

Director of Health Information Management: The ability to design, implement, direct, and control will continue to be in demand. These skills coupled with experience will take you into the future.

Management Consultant: A wealth of job opportunities await the risk taker! It is anticipated that the number of firms offering services in management, consulting, training, and development companies will continue to increase.

Figure 1-3. Job Opportunities as a Result of Change

Making a Commitment to Lifelong Learning

The knowledge acquired in college provides you with entry-level skills and competencies. As a professional you are expected to possess knowledge and skills beyond entry level. Knowledge related to health information management alters with technological advances. To keep current, you will need to continue your education either formally or informally. In addition to having general knowledge, developing an area of specialization can assist in advancing your career. Read everything you can that relates to your specific topic of choice. This may be accreditation, classification systems, the budgeting process, procedure manuals, position descriptions, quality improvement, work sampling, group dynamics, motivation, or any topic that is of interest or may be required for your current job or advancement. Keep notes that you can review and use as needed.

As a professional, you are expected to possess state-of-the art knowledge. With the rapid changes in technology and information management you will need to continue to read, attend conferences, take courses, contact vendors for updates on the latest equipment, and benchmark by comparing what you do with those who are leaders in certain areas. These are just a few ways you can continue to learn.

Demonstrating Credibility in Job-Related Activities

Credibility means that others can trust you to do your job in the best way possible. As a professional you strive to invest whatever time and effort is needed to produce a quality product. A professional will do the best possible job adhering to the highest standards for quantity and quality.

Gaining Maturity

As a professional, you are expected to demonstrate composure in stressful situations. You should think through the consequences of your actions before responding. An event that seems overpowering may appear completely different after a restful night of sleep or a conversation with a friend or mentor. At best, waiting can help to validate the course of action that should be taken. Maturity means that your decisions are made based on careful consideration of the alternatives and not on the emotions of the moment.

Developing a Winning Attitude

Throughout this book, the need for a positive attitude will be emphasized. As a professional, you should believe in yourself. Be aware of your areas of strength and how these relate to the organization that has employed you. Assess your knowledge, skills, and abilities in relation to the goals of the organization. In this way, you are aware that the organization needs you to achieve their mission. You can and should be a valuable person to the organization, making a difference, whether you are performing routine tasks or deciding on policies.

You can create your own definition of a winning attitude in terms of success. What does success mean to you economically, emotionally, and

AAMT: American Association for Medical Transcription

AHIMA: American Health Information Management Association

HIMSS: Health Information Management Systems Society

HFMA: Healthcare Financial Management Association

NAQAP: National Association of Quality Assurance Professionals

Figure 1-4.   Professional Organizations Related to Health Information Management Professions

spiritually? Gossiping, nitpicking, and being uncooperative are behaviors that should not be exhibited by a professional person.

Demonstrating a Stable Work Ethic

As a professional you should adhere to a code of ethics. AHIMA has developed a set of ethical principles to safeguard the public and to contribute within the scope of the health information management profession to the quality and efficiency of healthcare. The ten principles are summarized in Chapter 8.

Belonging to a Professional Organization

There are several organizations that have activities related to the profession of health information management. These may be national organizations with component state associations or they may be local and regional groups formed to support and encourage members for a specific topic. A few of the national associations that contribute to the advancement of health information management are shown in Figure 1-4.

Good Impressions

As a student, you may have attended professional meetings, taken field trips, or represented your college at a recruitment event. Did you dress differently? For internships, practicums, clinical experiences, and management experiences, generally explicit instructions are given regarding a dress code. Creating a good impression, however, involves more than clothing. Throughout your career you should want to leave others with good impressions that endure. Being competent in your job is expected. Being a person with whom others like to associate is important. You can create good impressions in many ways. The following list of traits is not inclusive. Add your own to this list. The traits identified here can contribute toward improving yourself, making others enjoy associating with you, and developing your career.

1. Exert extra effort to complete tasks in a timely manner.
2. Be flexible and adapt to changes in a positive manner.
3. Be respectful of the skills and abilities of others.
4. Listen to others.
5. Be prepared for meetings.
6. Conduct yourself professionally at all times.
7. Maintain a positive attitude.
8. Use information appropriately and ethically.
9. Be on time.
10. Return everything you borrow with a thank you.
11. Cultivate good hygiene and manners.
12. Learn from the past, plan for the future, and each day do something nice for another person.

The Success Cycle

Success—everyone seems to desire it. Success conjures up ideas of wealth, power, fame, and great achievements. For most of us, success can be defined in relation to career, family, and spirituality. Successful career management involves taking charge of your future by determining your personal goals, values, and needs and selecting a job that is compatible with these. The success cycle, as shown in Figure 1-5, is a way of helping you find the right job that can be the beginning of a career.

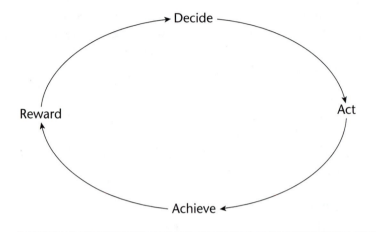

Figure 1-5.   The Success Cycle

The first step in the success cycle is deciding on a goal. For example, your goal following graduation may be to obtain a position as a data coordinator. Once the goal has been decided, act on the goal.

Acting on the goal is the second step. You will need to determine the course to follow. This could include:

Identifying facilities that employ data coordinators.

Looking through journals and newspapers to see if there have been vacancies advertised for a data coordinator or for skills related to such a position.

Talking with your instructors to see if they have information regarding agencies, pharmaceutical companies, or others who hire data coordinators.

Attending professional meetings and talking with people regarding career opportunities.

Having researched the position, you will be ready to apply for a job as a data coordinator. The data you have collected should provide leads regarding employers who may be eager to review your resume.

The third step in the success cycle is achievement of your goal. Your resume was reviewed by an employer, you were asked to interview, and you were hired. You are now ready for the final step—a reward. Celebrate the event by enjoying a special lunch, shopping, or going to the movies. As shown in Figure 1-5, the success cycle is never ending. You should be ready to repeat the cycle. As a goal is achieved, a new one should be established. This will encourage your career progression.

Values and Needs

Satisfaction from your work can be attained by finding a job and ultimately a career that is consistent with your values. Values are those feelings that guide us toward the way things ought to be. Our value system evolves from our interactions over time with the environment in which we live. Lawrence Kohlberg, a theorist in value development, has constructed a model showing the three stages of value orientation:

* *Stage 1: Preconventional (ages 2 to 7).*   In this age group, one becomes responsive to the culture values of right and wrong, good and bad. In the younger child the meaning of the value is not understood but accepted from whatever the authority figure says.
* *Stage 2: Conventional (ages 7 to 12).*   In this age group, the person conforms to the expectations of society, family, and peers to win the approval of the authority figure. Fixed rules, social order, and respect for authority typify this stage.
* *Stage 3: Postconventional (age 12 and older).*   Individuals begin to draw on their own conscience to determine what is right or wrong. The individual starts believing in principles such as justice, humane treatment of others, and respect for the dignity of others (Edge and Groves, 1994).

Other theorists believe that 90% of our value system is firmly in place by age 10. Morris Massey stated that we are shaped by events that occurred around us as we were growing. If these events happen to a group of people and shape an entire generation, they are referred to as a *generational value cohort*. For example, individuals who were young during the Great Depression of the 1930s grew into security-conscious adults. This level of security consciousness is not a trait of those individuals who were born during the 1940s and later (Edge and Groves, 1994, p. 7).

Whatever theory you may follow, the important fact to remember is that your value system is shaped by your exposure to events that have occurred during your life. When your employer's values parallel yours, you are well on your way to being satisfied in the workplace. Values are instrumental in attaining a sense of well-being in the workplace. The ability of an employer to meet your needs is also important. It is the desire to fulfill your needs that motivates you to work.

Understanding Your Needs

Abraham Maslow is a behaviorist who developed the hierarchy of needs to support his theory on why people work. Maslow illustrated his theory using a pyramid model (see Figure 1-6). The base of the pyramid represents *physiological needs*, including the basic survival factors such as food, clothing, and shelter. These needs must be fulfilled before moving up the pyramid to the next level, which is *security*. It can include numerous factors such as seeking housing in a neighborhood that is perceived to be safer than the one in which you are currently living, or replacing your broken-

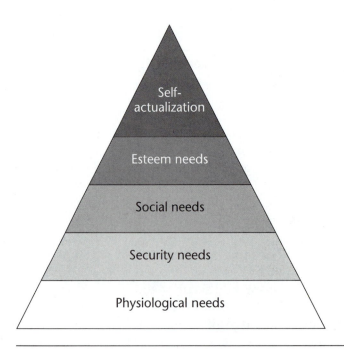

Figure 1-6.   Maslow's Hierarchy of Needs

down car with one that is more dependable. Once you feel secure, the third level in the pyramid is the need to belong or to *socialize* with others. Humans need to have a sense of belonging to someone. Unfortunately, this particular level is not easily obtainable for some and may result in an entire lifetime of having this need unfulfilled. As you progress up the pyramid, satisfying needs become more difficult. The need for *self-esteem* must be identified on an individual basis. Not only does it incorporate your personal value system, but self-esteem also is affected by peer pressure and society in general. There are those who are always desiring the bigger, better, or more expensive. Some people are never satisfied.

At the top of the pyramid is *self-actualization*, which is the motivating factor that drives individuals to achieve their maximum potential. Maslow contends that people will continue to be motivated as long as a need has not been met. Once the need has been met, then it ceases to be a motivator.

Maslow's hierarchy of needs serves as a foundation for understanding what you desire from a career and why you may find yourself dissatisfied at times. Meeting your needs encompasses your personal life and your professional life.

Application of Maslow's Hierarchy to Health Information Management

To assist you in thinking along the lines of career management, Figure 1-7 is an application of Maslow's hierarchy to health information management. The model used is circular whereas Maslow's model is vertical. The rationale for this choice is to indicate that the needs process is ongoing.

In today's volatile healthcare environment, an individual who has "moved up the ladder" in the organization can become displaced. For this person, the drive to meet the physiological and safety needs returns after being at the self-actualization level. In the diagram you are at the center with your needs around the periphery.

By determining goals, values, and needs, the new graduate can obtain insights into the type of position that would provide satisfaction. Figure 1-8 is a values and needs self-assessment instrument to assist you as you reflect on the values and needs you desire.

After you have identified your values, rank them in order of importance. Now, having completed the values and needs self-assessment, you can move on to developing career goals that harmonize with these. To support

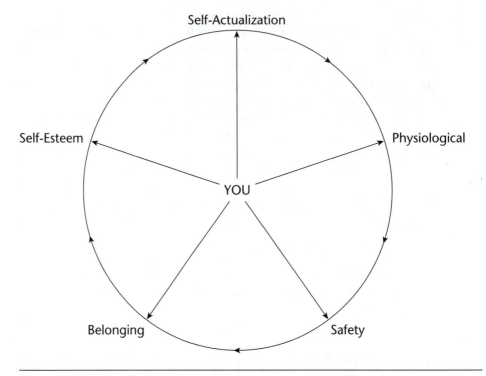

Self-Actualization

Self-Esteem

Physiological

YOU

Belonging

Safety

Figure 1-7.   The Health Information Management Hierarchy of Needs

attainment of your goal, you can establish specific objectives and a timetable, for example:

Objective 1: to search for advertisements for a DRG coordinator in the local newspaper.

Timetable: Begin now and continue searching each weekend issue from March 1 onward.

Objective 2: to attend local meetings to talk with professionals in various hospitals regarding opportunities available for a DRG coordinator.

Timetable: Started in January and continued until hired.

Objective 3: to develop my resume with DRG coordinator as the specific career objective.

Timetable: Completed by March 15.

Develop your value statements and indicate their importance to you by circling the number most reflective of your feelings (1 = not important; 4 = very important).

Value Statement	Rating
1.	1 2 3 4
2.	1 2 3 4
3.	1 2 3 4
4.	1 2 3 4
5.	1 2 3 4

Rank the following statements in order of their importance to you (1 = lowest; 5 = highest).

_____ Recognition

_____ Salary

_____ Job security

_____ Opportunity to be the best you can be

_____ Ability to work with people you enjoy

_____ Other

Your most important value is _____.

Your most important need is _____.

Use this assessment to guide you as you begin job searching and defining your career path.

Figure 1-8.   Values and Needs Assessment

DRG coordinator is an example of one goal. As you review Appendix A and continue to read the chapters, additional information will be available to assist you in considering and deciding from the alternatives which specific entry-level position or advancement opportunity is right for you at this stage in your career.

Summary

- Because the *health information management professional* concept is relatively new, there is a need to market your skills to prospective employers.
- Health information management professions are considered the component of allied health with minimal direct patient contact.
- Changes in healthcare will result in new career paths. Seven have been identified in Vision 2006.
- To continue to maintain status as a professional, six important skills are lifelong learning, credibility, maturity, a winning attitude, ethics, and organizational identity.
- Although your outward appearance can facilitate a good impression, there are several traits that assist in making you a respected associate.
- Identification of a goal, your values, and needs provides insights into jobs that lead to a satisfying career.

Review Activities

1. From a recent journal, newspaper, or other trade publication, select two advertised positions for an HIM professional.
2. For the two positions selected in #1, state two reasons why the job would or would not be a career choice for you.
3. Review the positions in Appendix A. Name five other positions to add to this list.
4. Surf the Internet to locate the curriculum for another HIA or HIT program, compare your curriculum, and list similarities and differences.

5. Look up the word *skill* in a dictionary and write the definition. Make a list of the skills in HIM that you have already acquired. Compare your list with your classmates.

References

American Health Information Management Association, Council on Accreditation (1994). Essentials and guidelines for an Accredited Educational Program for the Health Information Technician and the Health Information Administrator. Chicago: American Health Information Management Association.

Anderson, S. and Smith, J. (1989). *Manpower resource guide for roles and functions of the medical record practitioner in the health care industry.* St. Louis, MO: First Class Solutions.

Borges, E. (1994). Transforming Yourselves: Pathways from Medical Records to Health Information Management. *Journal of the American Health Information Management Association*, 65 (3), 36–38.

Bureau of Labor Statistics, Office of Employment Projections (1996). Employment projections: fastest growing occupations, 1994–2005. http://stats.bls.gov. empta01.htm. May 14, 1997.

Drafke, M.W. (1994). *Working in health care: What you need to know to succeed.* Philadelphia: F.A. Davis Company.

Edge, R., and Groves, J. (1994). *The ethics of health care: A guide for clinical practice.* Albany: Delmar Publishers, Inc.

Fuller, R. (1988). *The new management*, 4th ed. New York: Macmillan Publishing Company.

Holton, E. (1991). *The new professional.* Princeton, NJ: Peterson's Guides.

Jones-Burns, M. (1997). Seeing Your Way Through to AHIMA's Vision 2006. *Journal of the American Health Information Management Association*, 68 (1), 30–33.

MacDonald, E. (1997). Vision 2006 Is a Hit at Winter Team Talks. *Journal of the American Health Information Management Association*, 68 (1), 6, 8.

Purtilo, R., and Haddad, A. (1996). *Health professional and patient interaction.* Philadelphia: W.B. Saunders Company.

Rudman, W., Watzlaf, V., Abdelhak, M., Borges, E., and Anania-Firouzan, P. (1996). Career Paths, Mobility, and Advancement for Health Information Managers. *Journal of the American Health Information Management Association*, 67 (7), 67–71.

Chapter 2

Searching the Job Market

Goals

After reading this chapter, you should be able to:

1. Conduct a successful job search.
2. Differentiate between a job and a career.
3. Perform a self-assessment to target suitable jobs or careers.
4. Use job search resources.
5. Determine resources that will assist in the job search.
6. Discuss the importance of developing a job search action plan.

Introduction

Remember your first job hunting experience? If this occurred during your teenage years or as a student to supplement the cost of education, probably little attention was given to potential career advancement opportunities, organizational mission and goals, traits of the boss, or the benefits package offered. Acceptance of the position was driven primarily by the need for money to pay bills and for spending. Unfortunately, many individuals still take this approach when seeking an entry-level position following graduation from college. In today's workplace, employers desire employees that are not only qualified for the job, but also "fit" into the organization. To "fit," employees must believe in the mission and goals of the organization, as well as the products or services being offered. For this reason, it is essential for job seekers to know themselves prior to initiating a job search. This is accomplished by assessing your personal needs, goals, and objectives.

Once the personal assessment is completed, the next step is to identify organizations that are compatible with your needs and desires. Knowing your personal parameters will assist you in targeting the job market, maximizing your attributes, and minimizing job search frustration.

For health information professionals, the healthcare industry offers a wealth of opportunity. In acute-care facilities, opportunities include:

- Coder of inpatient and/or ambulatory health records
- Medical transcriptionist
- Registrar, the most common being tumor registrar or trauma registrar
- Risk management
- Utilization review
- Quality review
- Management positions in departments such as health information services, admitting, finance, and education

Careers in health information are not limited to acute-care facilities. Nontraditional career paths can be found in:

- Managed care
- Physician offices
- Insurance companies
- Accounting firms
- Law firms
- Sales
- Research
- Education

With such a wide variety of employment opportunities, there is no reason a job or career that meets your needs cannot be found. Initially you must decide if you are seeking a job or a career. Making this decision first will determine how much time, effort, and preparation will be involved in the search. A successful job hunt involves:

Determining if you are seeking a job or a career.
Assessing yourself.
Evaluating past experiences.
Identifying attributes desired in the workplace.
Determining geographic boundaries.

A Job or a Career?

What is the difference between a *job* and a *career*? Many use the terms synonymously; however, they do not have the same meaning. A *job* is a position that allows for a steady source of income but does not lead to achieving a career goal. A *career* implies that you will progress through life with your work while earning a living in your chosen career path. For example, you desire to become the supervisor of coding. However, to attain your ultimate goal, experience is necessary. The career path leading to your goal might look something like this:

Outpatient coding for one year.
Inpatient, non-Medicare coding for two to three years.
Inpatient, Medicare coding three to five years.
Supervisor of coding possible after five years of coding experience.

For this reason, you accept an entry-level coding position that will begin your career path. Often, especially for the new health information graduate, it is difficult to determine a career path since the graduate's experience in the field of health information is minimal. Therefore, a job is often the first step. Once experience is gained, career options become more apparent and career paths can be developed.

To summarize, a job is for a period of time whereas a career is the lifelong pursuit of a goal. Once you have decided whether you are seeking a job or a career, the next step is to assess yourself to determine the attributes and values that you would not sacrifice for a job or career. Performing a self-assessment will further assist you in targeting the type of position you are seeking.

Who Are You?

Self-assessment involves taking an in-depth look at your values, personality, interests, and skills (see Figure 2-1). Also, it is important to look at what you liked and disliked about past work experiences and to consider your geographic boundaries. The end result of the self-assessment process is to gain insight into your needs, likes, and dislikes. Applying what you know about yourself in selecting a job or career will enable you to make better choices. Much has been written about how to perform self-assessments and many instruments are available for this purpose. It is important to

Exhibiting loyalty to the company	Dealing with organizational change
Being at work on time	
Evidencing a desire to learn	Managing time
Taking pride in details	Exhibiting discipline in work habits
Showing flexibility, adaptability	Thinking creatively
Seeing the big picture	Solving problems
Organizing work	Making decisions
Dressing appropriately	Understanding organizational dynamics
Adapting to diversity of tasks and people	
	Learning new skills and duties
Working cooperatively with others	Persevering until job completion
Participating as a member of a team	Prioritizing work
	Handling multiple priorities
Exhibiting a good attitude	Dealing with stress

Figure 2-1. Employability Skills

remember all assessments require two steps: You complete the assessment and then analyze the results. Answering each question honestly will maximize its usefulness. For this reason, some individuals prefer to administer the assessment to themselves rather than seeking the assistance of another individual or service. Our approach to self-assessment will be to first perform a personal inventory, then evaluate past experiences, and finally address geographic boundaries.

To get started on self-assessment, the example that would lend itself to self-administration is in Figure 2-2, which is an adaptation of a Career Orientations Inventory developed by Edgar H. Schein and published in his booklet *Career Anchors: Discovering Your Real Values.*

After completing the assessment, analysis of results is accomplished as follows:

1. Take a sheet of paper and list the italicized words in the statements that you have checked. Those are the characteristics you would like in a job.
2. Write down the entire statement you checkmarked.

The intent of this instrument is to identify the type of career for which you might be best suited. Place a checkmark next to the characteristics that reflect your preferences.

_____   1.   *Helping* others is important to me.

_____   2.   I prefer a *structured environment* where there is very little variation in daily activity.

_____   3.   I consider myself a *risk taker*.

_____   4.   Recognition by peers is more important to me than *recognition* by management.

_____   5.   I like knowing several functions rather than *specializing* in one specific function.

_____   6.   Salary should be based on *skill* level as acquired through work experience.

_____   7.   *Monetary stability* is not important to me.

_____   8.   If I am to feel successful, I must succeed in *creating* something that is entirely my own.

_____   9.   The ability to define work, select tasks, and establish my *own schedule* is important.

_____   10. I seek out opportunities to use my *special skills*.

_____   11. I thrive on *solving problems* that are complex.

_____   12. I prefer a job that has a *daily routine*.

_____   13. *Benefit packages* are important to me.

_____   14. I need to feel that I am *contributing to the workplace and society*.

_____   15. I do not like an environment with *strict rules and policies*.

_____   16. I desire a position that affords me *financial security*.

_____   17. Having the opportunity to *analyze and evaluate* must be part of the job.

_____   18. As long as I am receiving *pay commensurate with my contribution*, I am happy.

_____   19. I desire *power and freedom* to advance my career.

_____   20. I prefer work that is *detailed*.

Figure 2-2.   Job Characteristics

3. Compare your checklist to the following list for an indication of the type of career for which you might be best suited.

Please remember that this is not an exact science, but only an indicator to assist you in focusing on the type of career that might provide you with the greatest probability of satisfaction.

Checkmarked Statements	*Type of Career*
2, 4, 6, 10, 12, 13, 16, 20	Technically oriented
1, 4, 14, 18	Service oriented
3, 7, 8, 9, 15, 19	Entrepreneurial
5, 8, 9, 11, 13, 17	Managerial

Now that you have an indication of the type of career for which you might be best suited, let's look at the type of positions in the field of health information that fall into each category or have some or all of the characteristics important to you.

• *Technical career:* A technical career is one that allows application of a specific competency. Coding and transcribing medical reports are two careers in health information that are considered technically oriented. Individuals desiring a technical career are fulfilled by striving to perform their skill at the highest level possible. Technically oriented individuals tend to experience frustration if they are asked to learn another function, for example, a coder being asked to learn how to assist physicians in the completion of health records or the transcriptionist being asked to learn how to respond to a request for patient records. Although learning other functions can be frustrating for these individuals, they achieve satisfaction in assisting others in their technical area of expertise. Normally, technically oriented individuals are not interested in management opportunities.

• *Service career:* This type of career is for individuals who have a commitment to a cause, for example, improving the environment or finding the cure for a disease. Workers in service careers strive to attain their values and will move organizations to achieve their goal. Service careers provide the health information management professional with an avenue to enter nontraditional fields as found in research and humanitarian-type environments. In these areas, health information management professionals can utilize their expertise in data gathering, analysis, and display. For example, the health information professional can gather data from patients for drug protocols for the purpose of curing diseases, or for research being performed on public health issues such as the effect of secondary smoke or discontinuation of free breakfast and lunch programs for economically disadvantaged school children. In an acute healthcare facility, these individuals could work in the oncology department or in the tumor registry.

- *Entrepreneurial career:* This is definitely the risk taker's career path. These individuals initially work in organizations, but as soon as they feel ready, they will leave the organization to form or acquire a business. They are driven to create a product or offer a service. Over the past few years, this has been a growth area for health information management professionals. Today, there are numerous opportunities to establish your own company or join another in providing services in coding, management, reimbursement, transcription, law, and systems analysis, to mention a few. Also, careers in sales and technical support have increased. Examples include working for corporations with transcription services, optical disk systems, office equipment, computers, and software.

- *Managerial career:* Individuals choosing a managerial career desire a position where total accountability and responsibility rest within their scope. Management positions can be found in all aspects of healthcare, whether in a hospital, clinic, or corporation. Be creative if you are seeking a management career. Do not limit your job hunt to positions strictly in healthcare. Your education in health information has prepared you for many fields including information systems, business, finance, and law.

Figure 2-3 shows some areas where health information management professionals have been employed in a hospital setting.

Now that you have an understanding of the type of career for which you might be best suited, it is time to evaluate past experiences.

Evaluate Past Experiences

Evaluating past work experiences provides insight into what you liked or disliked about previous jobs. Knowing these elements will hopefully enhance your chances of not repeating a bad experience. As mentioned in the discussion on personal inventory, there are many instruments available that will assist you in assessing past work experiences. Figure 2-4 is a very simple way to complete the task.

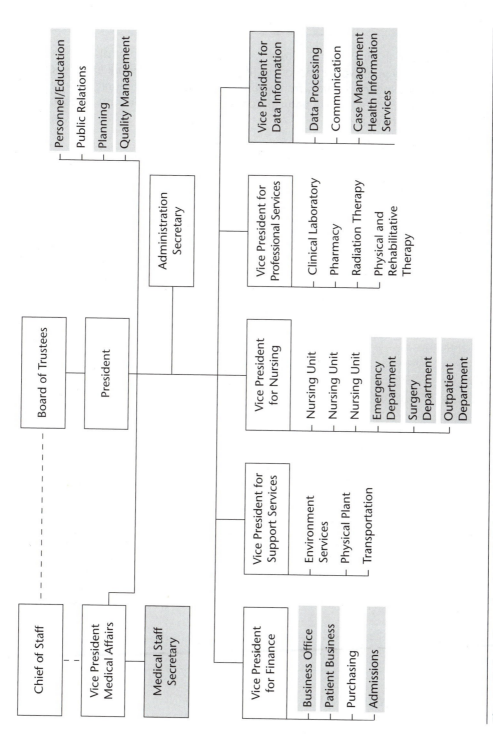

Figure 2-3. Organizational Model, Community Hospital (Adapted from Mattingly, R. (1997). *Management of health information functions and applications*. Albany, NY: Delmar Publishers)

The intent of this instrument is to document what you liked or disliked about each of your work experiences. If you have minimal work experience or no work experience, draw from volunteer service or community service activities in which you have participated. Complete the following for each position you have held:

Position: _____

Likes	Dislikes	Why?
_____	_____	_____
_____	_____	_____
_____	_____	_____
_____	_____	_____
_____	_____	_____

Position: _____

Likes	Dislikes	Why?
_____	_____	_____
_____	_____	_____
_____	_____	_____
_____	_____	_____
_____	_____	_____

Figure 2-4. Inventory of Previous Work Experience

By completing the inventory of previous work experience, you have identified characteristics that will serve as the foundation for defining your ideal job or career path. If you could not find likes or dislikes, then you probably have not had sufficient work or life experiences to establish personal priorities. As experience is gained, this assessment is worth repeating as it helps you isolate the real reason you are contemplating a job change.

More in-depth testing and analysis about possible career paths based on your personal inventory and evaluating past work experiences can be achieved by contacting the career placement office at colleges, universities, and employment or outplacement firms. There is one more component in the self-assessment process: determining geographic boundaries.

Determine Geographic Boundaries

Geographic boundaries are the geographic areas in which you desire to work and live. Early in the job search process it is essential to ask yourself if you are willing to relocate. If yes, then where? You might start by asking yourself how far you want to live from family and friends. Is a three-hour drive or a one-day drive okay? Once this has been determined, take a map and draw a circle around those geographic areas that meet your distance needs. This exercise will help you focus on your target market.

Researching locations prior to initiating your job search will refine the market you are targeting. When your geographic boundary has been determined, investigate elements important to your everyday life, including:

Cost of living

Proximity of affordable housing to work

Commuting time from home to work

Taxes—state and community

Educational system

Cultural activities

Accessibility to libraries

Climate

Primary industry

Healthcare systems

As a graduate of a health information technology or health information administration program, consideration should be given to these general observations:

1. There are more career opportunities in cities that do not have colleges or universities offering programs in health information technology or health information administration.
2. Rural communities are underserved by health information professionals. Thus, individuals practicing in rural areas may find a variety of consulting opportunities in long-term-care facilities, residential centers, and physician offices, to mention a few.
3. Cities with a variety of healthcare systems not only provide more career opportunities but allow career or job changes without relocating.
4. Employment in acute-care facilities located in cities outside a major metropolitan area often allows a faster track to management positions.

Demographic information about cities can be found in a variety of resources located in public libraries. Newspapers are a wonderful source of information. If you do not want to subscribe to the newspaper, check with the public library to see if it subscribes to one from the city you are interested in targeting. Assuming you have Internet access, the World Wide Web is another option. To search the Web for a specific city, enter the name of the city and state in the search box. Yahoo and InfoLink are two search engines that can be used for this purpose. Contacting the chamber of commerce in the city you are considering is another excellent resource. It can provide items such as brochures, maps, descriptions of the city as well as surrounding areas, a listing of realtors, and other services that would assist you in making a decision about a particular location. For more specific information regarding the cost of living, the educational systems, and availability of housing, a realtor is an invaluable resource.

Determining acceptable geographic boundaries is an integral part of a successful search. In doing so, you will maximize your time, effort, and opportunities as you begin the search for a job or career. Having completed the third component in the self-assessment process, you are now ready to develop a plan to search for a job or career.

Develop a Job Search Action Plan

Now that you have a better understanding of the type of career in which you are interested, the kinds of organizations, and the geographic location, it is time to develop an action plan that will provide for an effective job search. A job search can be a very tedious process. A positive attitude is imperative for the search to be successful. How long should the search take? The rule of thumb is one month for every $10,000 earned. With a salary of $60,000, expect the job search to take a minimum of six months. In a "normal" economy, the following time frames can be anticipated:

- Six to twelve months to obtain an executive-level position.
- Three to six months to obtain a middle-level position.
- Two to three months to obtain a professional position.
- Two months to obtain an hourly position.

Searching for a position is a full-time job. The following tips are to assist you during the search process:

1. Maintain an income throughout the job search. If you are currently employed, stay that way until you have found a new position. Having a steady income not only removes the need to accept a position just for the paycheck, but provides an opportunity for you to continue the search until you find a job that matches your goals. If you are unemployed, try to find a job that can help sustain you during the search process.

2. Organize the search process by designating work space in your home. During the search process, it is important not to share the work space with others. This space will become the office from which appointments are scheduled, files are maintained, letters are written, and follow-up calls are made. You need to have a place where all search materials are maintained in order to coordinate the process.

3. Purchase a telephone answering machine to facilitate communication between you and the individuals with whom you have interviewed or desire an interview. Although they may cost more, an answering machine that automatically records the date and time of the message may be money well spent. Make sure your outgoing message is professional, not cute. For example, an acceptable message would be: *You have reached (your name). I am unable to come to the telephone right now. Please leave your name, message and telephone number at the tone and I will return the call as soon as possible. Thank you for calling.*

4. Maintain a log of all telephone conversations made as well as those received. The log will document to whom you have spoken and the topic of conversation, and will remind you of any necessary follow-up activities. Record the following in the log:

Date the call was made or received.

Name of the individual called or name of the caller.

Reason for the call and/or a brief note about the conversation.

Action to be taken.

5. Purchase an appointment book that has plenty of space to schedule appointments and follow-up calls. Although you may prefer to use one of the software programs with an appointment scheduling component, you still need to take an appointment book with you to facilitate the scheduling of meetings or interviews.

6. Select simple classic stationery and envelopes for thank-you notes. Use white or soft tones only.

7. Evaluate your wardrobe. Do you have clothes appropriate for the type of position you are seeking? If you are uncertain, and the organization with whom you are interviewing is within driving distance, it may be time well spent to go there and observe employees in the workplace or going to and from work. Spruce up your wardrobe if necessary and do not forget to polish the shoes! In today's work environment, some businesses have chosen a casual mode of dress. If you are faced with this situation, do not dress casually for the interview. Always look and act professionally. Suggestions on dress and grooming will be discussed in greater detail in later chapters of this book.

8. Familiarize yourself with the reference department in the public library. To broaden your career outlook, review these resources:

U.S. Industrial Outlook: lists job prospects for more than 350 industries.

U.S. Dictionary of Occupational Titles: contains more than 22,000 different job descriptions.

Encyclopedia of Careers and Vocational Guidance: a four-volume collection of careers.

Gale Directory of Databases: an extensive two-volume reference with volume 1 containing online databases and volume 2 containing a listing of databases on CD-ROM, diskette, magnetic tape, and handheld and batch database products.

Excellent references specifically for the health information management professional include:

Journal of the American Health Information Management Association

Advance

For the Record

9. Subscribe to newspapers, professional journals, and publications as needed.

10. Visit a bookstore and purchase books needed to become knowledgeable in job searches, resumes, and cover letters.

11. Depending on your potential employment level, list with appropriate search firms, employment agencies, alumni associations, professional organizations, and all other referral services. Try to select search firms and employment agencies where the employer pays the related fees. Identifying search firms and employment agencies that are knowledgeable about the field of health information management can be a challenge. A starting point would be those that advertise in professional journals such as the *Journal of the American Health Information Management Association, Advance,* or *For the Record.* Also, if you know someone who had a positive experience with a search firm or employment agency, ask for the name of the firm or agency and the name of his or her contact. Finally, you can contact the program from which you graduated and someone may be able to provide you with guidance.

12. Recent graduates or seniors in health information educational programs should attend campus job fairs. Do not just browse; have your resume in hand. Job fairs directed specifically toward health information students are rare. Companies are going to direct their efforts toward programs with a large number of graduates. Therefore, attend job fairs in other programs such as business, computer science, and information systems. Be prepared to explain the field of health information management and how you can fit into their company. Obtain a list of companies that will be represented at the job fair from the program sponsoring the fair. If a list is not available, contact the college or university career planning office, or the student organization for the program sponsoring the job fair (see Figure 2-5).

13. Be prepared for your interview by researching the organization with whom you are interviewing. Again, the reference department in the public library is an invaluable resource. The following references provide the historical performance of an organization along with analysts' comments providing the anticipated future outlook:

Moody's

Standard and Poor's

Annual reports are also available at the public library for many companies.

Do your research and be prepared to ask appropriate questions during the interview. For example, after reviewing the annual report you notice an increase in the number of outpatient surgeries. You might ask if this trend

Figure 2-5. Using School Employment Offices

is anticipated to continue or will the facility need to expand to meet the demand for services. Being knowledgeable about the organization indicates that you are sincerely interested in the position.

Networking

The oldest and best method for securing a job is through networking. Networking involves contacting individuals with whom you are acquainted either directly or indirectly who can assist in your job search. These acquaintances might be able to inform you of job possibilities within their organizations or provide information such as names and telephone numbers of persons at other organizations who might be aware of employment opportunities. For networking to be successful, it is necessary to list all individuals you want to contact. The larger the list, the more interviewing possibilities, for example, consider classmates, co-workers, friends, relatives, and neighbors.

Agencies

There is usually some confusion regarding the difference between an executive search firm, an employment agency, and an outplacement firm. Each has a definite place in the job search process. Understanding the differences will assist you in selecting the one that will match your needs.

Executive Search Firms

Characteristics of executive search firms include:

- Identifying and appraising candidates for a specific position. This requires a contract between the employer and the search firm.
- Receiving payment from the organization to which it is contracted.
- Being either generalists or specialists. If you are searching for an executive position in healthcare, then you will need to use a firm specializing in that area.
- Not always acknowledging receipt of resumes.
- Face-to-face interviewing and reference checking of all prospective candidates prior to presenting the candidate to the organization for an interview.

Employment Agencies

Characteristics of employment agencies include:

- Finding jobs for people and also for companies.
- Having fees paid by the individual seeking a job. Payment does not usually occur until the individual has been gainfully employed. This sometimes results in a mismatch of individual to job. Do not take the payment issue lightly. Most employment agencies receive one percent for every $1,000 of the first year's annual salary. Know up front if you are responsible for the fee or if the employer will absorb the cost (see Figure 2-6).

Research employment agencies and prescreen them on the telephone. Do not be pushed into an interview with an agency that does not appear to meet your needs.

Outplacement Firms

Characteristics of outplacement firms include:

- Assisting you in packaging your resume presentation to perspective employers.

- Providing assistance to individuals who are seeking employment due to being phased out of their positions. In recent years, due to mergers, right-sizing, or reengineering of the workplace, companies have absorbed the cost of the outplacement firm for employees who have been displaced. Individuals in management positions are most likely to be offered this benefit as part of their termination package. Services provided by outplacement firms include:

Assessment of the terminated employee's background.

Psychological testing and feedback session with employee.

Career suggestions.

Resume preparation.

Interview training.

Providing office space from which participants can make telephone calls.

Secretarial support for typing resumes and letters.

Support groups comprised of individuals who have been displaced and are in the job search process.

Figure 2-6.   Read the Contract Carefully before Signing

Computerized Job Searches

The ability to perform computerized job searches has revolutionized the job hunting process. Although job bank databases have been around since the 1970s, access was primarily limited to professional job search firms. Today, however, accessibility to these databases is open to anyone with a personal computer, a modem, and a dial-up connection through an on-line service. An on-line connection means you have access to a database through the use of a computer via telephone lines. Service providers such as America OnLine, CompuServ and Prodigy charge a fee for the access they provide to newspapers, bulletin boards, libraries, and the Internet. The Internet is comprised of computers from the public and private sector that network to exchange information worldwide. Through the Internet the World Wide Web can be accessed, which is where companies store information. As one author links to another, a *web* of information is created. To go from one web page to another a software product called a *navigator* is needed, for example, the Netscape Navigator.

Through the World Wide Web, you have access to vendors that offer services supporting job searches. These services include placing your resume in their resume database, searching job postings, locating information on companies, and entering chat rooms or news groups to converse with others on job search or job-related issues. Services provided vary by company, so it is important to find one that meets your needs. One web site that might be a starting place is HeadHunter (http://www.headhunter.net). This service provides job hunters access to 1,400 job openings and can be searched according to job title, skills, or location. Another site is the Monster Board (www.monster.com), which is a much larger site than HeadHunter. At the time of this writing, both services were free.

It should be noted that companies also access computer job banks to search for individuals with specific qualifications to fill vacancies. Computer job banks use a resume as the source document for the database. Key words are abstracted from the resume and placed into the database. A recent trend in human resource departments is to use applicant tracking systems to screen internal candidates for job openings within the organization. In-house applicant tracking systems ease the storage problems created by paper resumes as well as provide managers with the opportunity to survey resumes of applicants more quickly than wading through stacks of paper. Filling positions from within the company provides a cost savings to the organization since fees for search firms, employment agencies, and advertising are not incurred. Other benefits of in-house applicant tracking systems include decreased human error and bias in the handling and classifying of resumes since computer systems support objective recruitment for positions. Sensitive data such as date of birth, gender, and race are not to be entered into the system.

For the employee, mobility within the organization is enhanced, affording the opportunity to gain seniority while pursuing a satisfying career. Identification of available positions is expanded as key words from your resume may match positions you were unaware were vacant.

Although in-house tracking systems are beneficial, for every positive there is a negative. Key words can be a problem area. For example:

1. If the person entering the data or the software itself selects the key words from your resume, the words selected may not be entered correctly into the database.

2. The individual hiring can weigh the key words to enhance the selection process. As a result, your resume and qualifications may not match those desired by the individual and your resume may not be chosen from the database.

3. If you are qualified for a job, but it is below your skill level and salary, the computer may not identify you as a potential candidate even if you are willing to accept a lesser position. If you are aware this happened, use personal contacts to get considered. Although skill level and salary are not included on a resume, this information can be accessed through the human resource system already in place within the organization.

4. If a scanner is being used to input data into the system, review your resume to make sure there is nothing that will cause the scanner problems such as the color of ink, intricate graphics, a personal photograph, or the color of paper on which your resume is printed.

Whether the resume database is an internal tool used only by your current employer or you are using a computer job bank external to the organization, it is important to validate data entered into the system to ensure quality and accuracy. This can be accomplished by asking for a printout of your file. When selecting an external computer job bank service:

- Ask for a specific list of what will be abstracted from your resume.
- Request the names and addresses of companies that use the job bank service.

- Request specific information on the number of searches that are made of the database.
- Inquire about how many placements have resulted.
- Ask for a demonstration of the system using the live system and your resume.
- Determine how often the database is updated.
- Request names of individuals who have used the system.
- Get a fee schedule.

Remember, if it sounds too good to be true, it probably is, and you need to continue the search for a company.

Sites specifically targeted toward health information management professionals are minimal. Therefore, you must be creative when entering key words to search the database. For example, you may search for information systems rather than health information systems, or enter health careers instead of health information. Other key words that might be helpful:

Career development
Career planning
Employment opportunities
Information management
Information technology
Jobs
Job listings
Job postings

Each database is unique, so you will want to use at least two search engines, for example, Yahoo and InfoSeek. If you are using a web navigator, you will be able to designate the search engine you want accessed.

The following is a list of addresses compiled from a variety of resources to assist you as you begin to explore the vast amounts of information available through the World Wide Web. The resources printed have been verified; however, the Internet is constantly changing, with resources added and dropped routinely and web addresses changing on a frequent basis.

For New Internet Users

The Riley Guide by Margaret F. Riley, http://www.jobtrak.com/

This is a great resource on how to use the Internet, incorporating the Internet into your job search and finding jobs via the Internet.

Searching for Jobs in Health Care

- http://www.medsearch.com

  Job listings from a variety of sources with affiliations to health maintenance organizations, insurance companies, and pharmaceutical companies, to mention a few. There is also a section for business and management, which is another possibility for locating positions in health information.

- http://www.careermosaic.com/cm

  The largest national recruitment agency, Hypertext Links, contains information about employers, companies and job opportunities, career advice, and cost-of-living index. Go into the Health Care Connection to secure career information, employer profiles, and jobs for physicians, nurses, therapists, pharmacists, administrators, financial specialists, and information experts.

- http://www.gvpub.com

  Great Valley Allied Health Opportunities is a resource for allied health professionals searching for careers in the healthcare industry.

Job Bank Specifically for Health Information Professionals

- http://www.ahima.org

  This new site allows the user to access Job Bank or HIM Practice Forum on career management. To access the Job Bank from AHIMA's home page, click on the AHIMA Online logo.

General Job Search Resources

- http://www.jobweb.org

  JobWeb is a listing of web sites for various employment opportunities. Employment opportunities for hospitals is located under the heading "not-for-profit."

- http://www.jobbankusa.com/search.html

  America's JobBank can be searched via key words to find positions in healthcare.

- http://www.collegegrad.com

  College Grad's home page is an interesting site for new college graduates. This site provides information on entry-level jobs, resumes, job searches, interviews, and how to negotiate an offer.

- http://www.yahoo.com/

  Yahoo is the largest site or search engine for searching the World Wide Web. Jobs in health information can be found by doing a search on the key words *health information employment*.

- http://www.espan.com

  E-span Jobsearch will give you several employer and job databases; interested employers can upload your resume directly for viewing; includes a salary guide at http://www.espan.com/is/ref/salary/salary.html.

What Is Needed to Do Computer Searches

If you do not have a computer but would like to use the computer for job searches, colleges, universities, libraries, copy service centers, and community agencies are resources you can contact. If you have a computer, it must have a communication card and a modem with a speed of at least 14,400 bits per second (bps) with 28,800 bps preferred. You will also need a communication program, access to a telephone line, and an account with an on-line service such as America OnLine, CompuServe, or Prodigy. Now that you are ready, there is one more area that needs to be discussed: netiquette, or Internet etiquette.

When communicating via the network, pretend you are communicating face-to-face. Be as professional on the network as you would during an interview. Here is some advice:

- Check your spelling, grammar, and punctuation.
- Do not type your messages in all capital letters. This is the same as shouting.
- Keep communication direct and to the point.
- Do not put anything on the Internet that is private. Remember, the Internet is not a totally safe environment.

Bibliography

The Internet is a complicated place. It is important to identify resources that may be of benefit to you. The best place to start is your local bookstore, public library, or career center. To jump-start your quest for information, the following list is provided:

Be Your Own Head Hunter Online, by Pam Dixon and Sylvia Teirsten, Random House

The Complete Idiot's Guide to the Internet, by Peter Kent, Osborn McGraw-Hill, Prentice Hall

Connecting to the Internet, by Susan Estrada, O'Reilly & Associates, Inc.

Electronic Resumes for the New Job Market, by Peter D. Weddle, Impact Publications

Hook Up, Get Hired! The Internet Job Search Revolution, by Joyce Lain Kennedy, John Wiley & Sons, Inc.

How the Internet Works, by Joshua Eddings, Ziff-Davis Press

The Internet Companion: A Beginner's Guide to Global Networking, Second Edition, by Tracy LaQuey, Addison-Wesley

The Internet Navigator, by Paul Gilster, John Wiley & Sons

NetPractice: A Beginner's Guide to HealthCare Networking on the Internet, Opus Communications

Other Resources

There are many resources to aid your job search. For instance:

National Ad Search: a weekly tabloid compilation of employment want ads from seventy-two key newspapers from across the United States. This can be ordered from National Ad Search, Inc., P.O. Box 2083, Milwaukee, WI 52101 (800/992-2832).

National Business Employment Weekly from the *Wall Street Journal* is available at newsstands and drugstores.

Directors of Executive Recruiters lists 2,300 search firms in the United States, Canada, and Mexico by area of specialization. Addresses and phone numbers are given. The directory contains salaried positions starting from approximately $40,000. This can be ordered from *Directors of Executive Recruiters*, Templeton Road, Fitzwilliam, NH 03447 (603/585-6544).

Book of Lists is available in most major cities. Large firms and major industries in the city are listed. Check with the public library or chamber of commerce to locate a copy of the reference.

Federal Jobs Digest is a biweekly publication covering the federal job market. This digest is available at newsstands or can be ordered at *Federal Jobs Digest*, 310 North Highland Avenue, Ossining, NY 10562 (800/824-5000).

How to Get a Federal Job, by David Waelde, Fedhelp Publications, Washington, DC.

Corporate Jobs Outlook! is a newsletter about career opportunities at 500 leading corporations. The newsletter includes salaries, benefits, advancement opportunities, research and development, growth plans, financial stability, and industry outlook. This can be ordered from Corporate Jobs Outlook, Inc., P.O. Drawer 100, Boerne, TX 78006 (210/755-8810).

Newspaper ads are the best-known source, but not the most effective (see Figure 2-7). According to Richard H. Beatty (1992), "Between 10 and 14 percent of all jobs are filled as a result of newspaper advertising." In his book he offers guidelines to get the most out of the newspaper:

- Read the classified ads for specific positions that are of interest to you, and respond by sending a copy of your resume along with an appropriate cover letter.
- Read the business section. Look for firms that are expanding in some way.
- Carefully read announcements of internal promotions as well as new appointments from sources outside the company. When someone is promoted, there is a vacancy created.

Professional associations may offer members job hunting services such as computer job banks or coordination of employment opportunities during local, regional, or national meetings.

Alumni associations at colleges and universities may offer placement services to alumni, including matching alumni resumes with job listings

Figure 2-7. Carefully Review Classified Sections of Newspapers

and forwarding the names of qualified alumni to the listing employer. There is usually a nominal charge for this service.

Religious organizations have evolved in recent years, offering major support systems to those who have been displaced from their employment.

Summary

- Searching for a job or a career can be a challenge. A successful job hunt involves:

    Determining if you are seeking a job or a career.

    Assessing yourself.

    Evaluating past experiences.

    Identifying attributes desired in the workplace.

    Determining geographic boundaries.

- Developing an action plan to give direction to your job search.
- Recognizing that a job search is a full-time endeavor. Give it your full attention.
- Identifying available resources in career planning centers, public libraries, universities, and colleges.
- Networking which is the best resource in locating job opportunities.
- Maintaining a positive attitude.

Review Activities

1. Describe factors that should be considered when determining the type of job or career on which to direct your search.
2. Determine the type of job or career that meets your needs.
3. Identify three positions that fit into the job or career type determined in #2.
4. Of the resources mentioned in this chapter, select two that would assist you in performing a job search. Explain why these were chosen.
5. Locate two job opportunities using the World Wide Web.

References

Beatty, R.H. (1992). *The new complete job search*. New York: John Wiley & Sons, Inc.

Kennedy, J.L. (1995). *Hook up, get hired!* New York: John Wiley & Sons, Inc.

Latas, M. (1993). *Job search secrets: 301 that can work for you!* St. Louis: Job Search Publishers.

Miller, M.F. (1996). *NetPractice: A beginner's guide to healthcare networking on the Internet*. Marblehead, MA: Opus Communications.

Nolan, K., and Miller, K. (Eds.) (1996). *Gale directory of databases*. New York: Gale Research.

Schein, E.H. (1990). *Career anchors: Discovering your real values*. San Diego: Pfeiffer and Company.

Chapter 3

The Portfolio

Goals

After reading this chapter, you should be able to:

1. Discuss the purposes for developing a professional portfolio.
2. Identify the benefits of maintaining a portfolio.
3. Organize the contents of a portfolio.
4. Discuss the uses of a portfolio.
5. Recognize the importance of confidentiality in the use of the portfolio.
6. Determine the value of self-assessment.
7. Assess the advantages of a mentor.
8. Discuss the value of networking.

Introduction

The word *portfolio* may bring to mind a briefcase for carrying drawings or papers, or a list of stocks, bonds, and other investments. In this chapter, portfolio pertains to documentation of various projects compiled from college courses and during work experiences. The contents of the portfolio provide a display of the scope and quality of your education and experiences. Throughout your education and work experiences, when you make presentations, produce graphs, or develop a new procedure, for example, these documents can become part of your portfolio to showcase your different skills and abilities.

Why Develop a Professional Portfolio?

A portfolio is a factual description of your strengths and accomplishments. The portfolio that you compile as an undergraduate should be designed to meet a variety of jobs. The entry-level initial position that you will obtain following graduation is rarely the exact one you planned for when you started school. In planning your portfolio, try to include documentation for several positions that you would consider to start your career path. If your portfolio contains a variety of good examples applicable to several functions in information processing and management, you are prepared to apply for various positions that might be available upon graduation. Adaptations can be made at various stages as you seek to advance your career.

Employers hire people who can perform specific tasks and functions. The portfolio provides concrete evidence of performance. Many courses during the college experience will incorporate group or class projects. These indicate that you have been an active member of a team. *Teamwork* is an important component of most entry-level positions. Your effectiveness working with teams can be documented in the portfolio through projects and through statements from classmates and instructors.

As the portfolio gains greater acceptance in health information management, some employers may even request that it be previewed before a person is offered a position. Use discretion when deciding who should and should not view the contents. Do not make your portfolio a companion document to your resume for every employer. Your portfolio contains creative information that is valuable in marketing yourself. You may decide after an initial interview that the position is not the one you want. Use your portfolio for the select few places where you want to be employed. When the interview is especially promising and you are invited for a second interview, that is when you may want to introduce your portfolio.

Benefits

By developing a portfolio, you will be able to:

1. Examine your progress in your educational program by comparing portfolio contents over a period of time.
2. Evaluate your growth and development instead of viewing only single accomplishments.

3. Compare achievements in light of your career goals.
4. Provide prospective employers with concrete examples of work-related experiences performed during your college years and in work settings.
5. Support with specific examples the statements made regarding your knowledge, skills, and abilities.
6. Indicate that you have had experience as a member of a team when the documentation is from a group or class project.
7. Provide evidence that you have had experiences that are work related.

Organization

The content of the portfolio will depend on your course of studies and on the part-time and full-time work experiences that you have had. Projects and visuals can be organized in a variety of ways. Select one that best showcases your knowledge, skills, and abilities and reflects your personality. Use tabs to divide the contents into major headings and subheadings. Examples of major categories that can be used for organizing projects and visuals are subject, year, function, and location. An explanation of each follows.

Subject Categories

If you decide to use a subject approach in presenting your achievements, two or more of the following could be used to divide sections of your portfolio:

Clinical Medicine
Coding
Computers
Health Information Systems
Human Resources Management
Quality Assessment
Record Retention and Retrieval
Release of Information
Research

Statistics/Data Analysis and Display

Transcription

Utilization Review

Figure 3-1 shows examples under each of the subject headings of items that could be included. Include only the materials that prove your superior performance. Since the purpose of the portfolio is to showcase your skills and abilities, your aim is to include items that surpass ordinary accomplishments. For the college student, organizing the results of assignments by subject can enrich the educational experience. This provides an opportunity to monitor your growth and progress in certain subject areas. Later, it will provide documentation of accomplishments when interviewing for an eagerly sought position.

Year

To arrange the portfolio by year, the associate degree–seeking student would include specific examples of achievements during the freshman and sophomore years; the baccalaureate degree–seeking student would include examples from four years of study; and the graduate-degree student, seeking either a master's or doctoral degree, would include examples mainly from the graduate program with a few good examples from work experience and/or the undergraduate experience. Actual years could be used for tabs when dividing chronologically.

Function

Arranging your portfolio by functions could include categories such as planning, organizing, leading, controlling, and representing. Examples of projects that could be included under the function of planning might be:

A Program Evaluation Review Technique (PERT) network developed for moving files from one area to another.

Policies and procedures developed for a particular function or selected samples from a revised or newly created policy and procedure manual.

A list of objectives to be achieved by a work area team.

The following are projects or visuals by major subject areas that could be included in a portfolio. Videotaping of a presentation as listed for clinical medicine may appropriately appear in other categories such as computers or health information systems. Headings, such as Clinical Medicine, are changed to correspond to your course work. For example: Clinical Medicine could be Pathophysiology, Pathology, Pharmacology, or other.

Clinical Medicine

Final examination having a grade of 93 or higher

Term paper on particular disease or operation

Videotape of a presentation on a specific disease or surgical procedure made to a class

Computer disk of an in-service conducted during the practicum.

Coding

Examples of coding using ICD-9CM, CPT, DSM-4, etc. for unique or difficult diseases and operations

Computers

Flowcharts, graphics, presentations using specific software

Health Information Systems

Reply to a request for proposals (RFP)

Diagrams developed for installation of new systems

Human Resources Management

Results of productivity studies

Self-evaluation of time management skills

Quality Assessment

Quality improvement studies

Record Retention and Retrieval

Comparative studies covering filing and numbering systems

(continues)

Figure 3-1.   Portfolio Contents by Subject

Release of Information

Statements from clinical supervisors on skills

Examples of policies and procedures developed on an individual basis or as part of a class project

Paper copy or videotape of in-service given to physicians, new employees, or others on confidentiality during your practicums or at other times

Research

Statements of participation and skill in research from clinical supervisor, physician, or other

Analysis of research study/article

Statistics/Data Analysis and Display

Final examination showing skill in applying formulas

Pages or photocopies of pages from statistics workbook

Printout of computer-generated statistical data

Census table created with software

Edit check using formulas

Graph displaying discharge statistics

Transcription

Transcribed reports for various operations and body systems

Listing of types of operations and diseases that you have transcribed

Utilization Review

Description of participation during clinicals in prospective, concurrent, and/or retrospective reviews

Figure 3-1. *Continued*

For the management function of organizing, the items presented in the portfolio could include:

A position description.

A revised organization chart.

An outline of qualifications needed by a person for a specific position.

Location

Organizing the portfolio by location could include examples of performance for different departments or work areas. To illustrate, for appropriate work areas the subdivisions could be: Admitting, Data Processing, Emergency Department, Human Resources, Information Services, Quality Improvement, Radiology Department, and Utilization Management. Each work area would include a project completed appropriate to that area.

Location could also be by types of care and facilities, for example, Managed Care, Home Health, Long Term, Subacute, Mental Health, Acute, Hospice, and Health Maintenance Organization. When applying for a position in a full-service consulting firm, having a portfolio that includes examples of projects in a variety of facilities would definitely complement the resume and strengthen your qualifications for a consulting position.

The portfolio does not contain everything you have done. You should include examples of successful past performance that provide evidence of the skills and abilities listed on your resume.

Appearance

Think of your portfolio as a professional document. If you conceive of the portfolio as a scrapbook, your attitude will result in a collection of memorabilia. The following guidelines should facilitate the development of a professional document:

Cover should be soft and rich-looking.

Page size is 8½-by-11 inches, with each encased in a transparent acetate jacket.

Table of contents and tabs are included for easy reference.

Contents are clear, concise, and professionally presented.

Print is dark and laser quality.

Key words and phrases are highlighted and bolded.

Graphs and charts are incorporated when possible. "A picture conveys a thousand words."

Examples should consist of successful past projects.

Presenting your achievements in a well-organized professional way may help you attain the position for which you have applied. The time and energy you expend to develop the portfolio are well worth the effort when your career goal has been achieved.

Contents

The sections of a portfolio are flexible. Generally, a portfolio will have some or all of the following:

Cover sheet

Table of contents

Resume

Management philosophy statement

Personal statement/summary

Projects*

Visuals: presentations, charts, and graphs*

Continuing education certificates and statements regarding application of learning

Diplomas and results of certifying examination

Statements from instructors, clinical supervisors, employers, officers of organizations

Goals for the next five years

References on one page, followed by actual letters of reference when available

The two sections that were identified with asterisks (*) can be organized by subject, year, function, or location as described previously. Additional details regarding the other sections that could be included in the portfolio are as follows.

Cover Sheet

The cover sheet of the portfolio should include the word *portfolio* followed by your name boldfaced and capitalized, address, and telephone number. For example:

Portfolio

of

MARY SMITH

345 Clayton Road

Oakland, California 11111

(000) 000-0000

The identifying information should be centered and should be the first page on the right as the cover is opened. The table of contents is the next page.

Table of Contents

There are several ways of organizing the portfolio, reflected in the table of contents. Two examples are shown in Figure 3-2.

Management Philosophy

Writing your management philosophy gives direction to the leadership style you will take with you to the work world. Through your philosophy you indicate how you perceive and judge the world around you, how you

Example 1	Tab	Example 2	Tab
1. Resume	Green	1. Section 1	1
2. Management Philosophy	Red	Resume	1.1
3. Personal Statement	Blue	Management Philosophy	1.2
4. Projects by Location	Orange	Personal Statement	1.3
Home Health	HH	2. Section 2	2
Mental Health	MH	Project Summaries	
Subacute Care	SA	Projects by Subject	
5. Visual Presentations	Yellow	Quality Improvement	2.1
Board of Directors	BD	Risk Management	2.2
Medical Staff	MS	Utilization Review	2.3
Nursing Administration	NA	3. Section 3	3
or		Visual Presentations, Charts,	
Confidentiality	C	and Graphs:	
Quality Improvement	QI	Quality Improvement	3.1
Systems Improvements	SI	Risk Management	3.2
		Utilization Review	3.3
Continue with other sections following the format.		Continue with this format until all sections have been tabled.	

Figure 3-2.   Portfolio Organization

gain a sense of personal satisfaction and competence, how you would handle conflict, and how you would use power.

Some of the considerations in developing your management philosophy include:

Will I be a team player doing what is best for the company and my boss?

Will I be a great negotiator willing to give up something in order to receive?

Do I plan to be a compassionate supervisor? If not, why?

Do I plan to volunteer to coordinate activities, lead groups, serve on committees?

Will I seek advancement opportunities; be open to new risk-taking challenges?

Will I participate in continuing education and community service activities?

Do I plan to be an autocratic, participative, situational, or other type of manager? Two extreme examples might be the styles of General George S. Patton and Mother Teresa.

Will the information management functions be departmental, or will I strive to reach out, to work with the entire organization, cultivating relationships through lunches and other meetings with personnel?

Will I emphasize quantity or quality or both?

Will I aggressively go after what I want? What will I do if I lose?

Will I confront the boss for incorrect or unethical policies?

Will I encourage creativity, problem solving, and critical thinking from the employees and be an example to them?

The Myers–Briggs type indicator provides assessments of your personality type. For some employers, completion of this is required before hiring for management positions. The indicators are extroversion versus introversion, sensing versus intuition, thinking versus feeling, and perception versus judgment. The Myers–Briggs and other assessments can be of assistance in writing your management philosophy and determining what your style of management will be.

An assessment of needs can be another useful instrument in obtaining data to guide you in the development of your management philosophy. Data include indicators for achievement, dominance, affiliation, deference, autonomy, nurturance, succorance, abasement, change, order, endurance, intensity, introspection, aggression, and exhibition.

Other resources that assist in the development of your management philosophy are inventories that enable you to reflect on various assumptions about the use of power and other traits. As you seek the cooperation of others to accomplish tasks, what do you perceive as necessary to influence those with whom you will associate? Will your power base be grounded in authority, reward, discipline, expertise, information, a combination, or other?

By assessing your personality needs and considering the questions provided in this section, you are better able to develop the management philosophy that can guide you in being an effective and efficient supervisor, manager, and leader. Figures 3-3 and 3-4 are samples of student-developed management philosophies.

By defining management and sharing that definition with my co-workers, the process of activities being accomplished with and through other people commences. A manager needs to be an integral part of a team. The team is effective and efficient when goals are attained and resources are kept to a minimal cost. A good manager is skilled in planning, organizing, leading, and controlling.

My management beliefs include the nine steps of the strategic management process: identifying the current mission, objectives, and strategies of the organization; analyzing the environment; identifying opportunities and threats; analyzing the resources of the organization; identifying strengths and weaknesses; reassessing the mission and objectives; formulating strategies; implementing strategies; and evaluating results.

I strongly believe in delegation of responsibilities. I will encourage creativity and interaction among my employees. Creativity will test their abilities. Interaction will contribute to a harmonious and positive work environment. Standing up for what I believe will be practiced even when it hurts. Critical and logical thinking will be used for problem solving and, when appropriate, gut feelings will be considered. Advancement will be sought because it provides new challenges. Certainly, the more effort put into management, the more satisfaction achieved.

Figure 3-3.   Management Philosophy 1

To say you are a certain type of leader seems easy enough. I have found upon further consideration that knowing oneself and the values and principles you choose to live and work by can be quite a task. I have based my personal management philosophy on my values, beliefs, and experiences. I believe that being a manager means more than accepting the title. In my opinion, a manager of any sort is first and foremost a leader. A leader is someone people want to follow and whose example they respect. As a manager, my aspirations are to set the example for the team, to encourage a positive attitude, and to develop an atmosphere of excellence in the workplace. I believe in leading by listening and learning from others. I will be a risk taker using my personal education and experience as a guide. The expertise of my peers will be applied when appropriate.

Through the emphasis on teamwork, traits such as honesty, sincerity, hard work, dedication, and commitment to the organization's mission will be reinforced. Each member of the team will be encouraged to use their talents and abilities to do the best job possible while looking for ways to improve.

Setting goals and accomplishing these will be encouraged and practiced. My philosophy is to lead the team.

Figure 3-4.   Management Philosophy 2

Personal Statement/Summary

Through your personal statement, you want the reader to conclude that you stand out from the competition. You want to be seen as special. Your personal statement helps the reader visualize you as an individual. Information contained in this statement should not be found elsewhere in your portfolio. In developing your personal statement, you need to consider the attributes an employer wants in an employee.

For example, a person who married after high school and later returned to college could include a description of the motivation and steps taken to return to college as an adult. Another example would be someone who volunteered throughout high school to tutor children in reading. The personal statement would include a description of how this occurred and the contribution this made to a career in health information management, health services, or other. Descriptive statements could be made on how you became comfortable with computers, software, and solving problems. How you achieved the ability to work successfully with people or as a member of a team would be another area to describe in the personal statement. If you worked while attending college to pay for your tuition while maintaining a high grade-point average, a statement or two regarding this can highlight your academic achievement while securing job experiences. In Chapter 4 additional topics are provided that can be considered as you develop your personal statement.

Projects and Visuals

As mentioned earlier, the projects and visuals sections can be organized by function, location, and in various other ways. In these sections, your projects and visuals are evidence of outcomes, achievements, and results.

Projects can be summarized in a narrative outline such as shown in Table 3-1. Visuals such as charts, graphs, and figures can be presented in this section or a separate one. When there is a need for confidentiality, identifying information can be removed.

Continuing Education

For those who have been in the profession for several years, this section could include a summary of continuing education experiences. For the recent graduate, certificates of workshops and conferences attended should be placed in transparent acetate jackets. To enhance this section, a description of key points learned and statements regarding the application of these key points in the work setting should be included. Results and outcomes achieved should be described also.

Table 3-1.   Project Summary

Project	Organization	Year	Outcome
1. Designed and conducted customer satisfaction survey	Our Lady of Peace Retirement Facility	1996	70% return rate; see Tab 1
2. Conducted in-service on confidentiality	Orthopedic Group Practice	1996	Physicians, Nurses (18) in attendance; see Tab 2

Diplomas/Results of the Certifying Examination

Copies of undergraduate and graduate-school diplomas provide evidence for the statements made in the resume. When scores for the certifying examination place you in the eighty-ninth or higher percentile, these can be included. Also, if a perfect score was achieved in the coding component, this could be provided to the reader.

Statements

Instructors may throughout your education write special notes regarding your accomplishments. Inclusion of these in the portfolio supports claims made in your resume and during the interview process. Performance assessments made by clinical supervisors can be included in the portfolio as well as letters thanking you for volunteer service; commendations received as an officer or committee chair of an organization; letters awarding you a scholarship; or other statements of excellence or achievement.

During your education and again in the work setting, notes thanking you for special effort may be received. Frequently, these are read and tossed. Such recognition from peers, supervisors, instructors, and others is an unsolicited expression of accomplishment. If the note is not dated, you can add this and additional identifying information. As a courtesy, you may want to request the person's permission to include the letter in your portfolio.

Goals

As part of career mapping and planning, you will want to identify your goals. An important section of the portfolio is a list of your goals for the next five years. Will position, money, or both be important? Is your intention to remain in a specific type of healthcare or to seek diversity? Do you intend to specialize or to generalize? Is your goal to be an entrepreneur or intrapreneur? When presenting these to a prospective employer, you want to make sure there is a match. The employer's needs should be consistent with your goals.

To obtain the job you love, you should envision what you perceive as your ideal job (Rogers, 1996). List the characteristics about that job that appeal to you. What do you enjoy doing? What excites and stimulates you to achieve? What activities make you feel confident and successful? Such considerations will assist you in deciding your career and within that framework what your goals will be.

References

Three to five references can be listed in the portfolio. Include name, organization, complete address, and telephone number. You may want to include fax number, e-mail address, and details such as the fact that your reference has an answering machine or the best time to reach the person.

If actual letters of reference have been prepared, these can be included in the portfolio.

Uses

The principal use for the portfolio is as a companion to the resume. You do not show your portfolio to every prospective employer. When the interview indicates this is the job you want and the place you really want to work, the portfolio can contribute to your success in achieving the position. Many applicants will not take the time or the extra effort to showcase their talents. By presenting a portfolio, you will impress and influence.

A corollary use for the portfolio is as an important component of career planning and advancement. Through the portfolio, your career becomes focused; your growth and development can be monitored; and your strengths and accomplishments are highlighted. Bits and pieces of your education and subsequently your career are organized. In the process of preparing the portfolio, your goals become easier to identify and a logical career progression should occur. Through the process, you will see if you are ready for promotion, a change to another organization, or a salary increase request. In each situation, the portfolio can provide the evidence needed to indicate to your employer why you are ready.

For generations, educators have used portfolios to advance in rank. Today employers in fields other than education are recognizing the value of a portfolio.

Confidentiality

There are two aspects of confidentiality to be considered: (1) content and (2) reader.

In regard to content, if the project was a class assignment, the organization may have been simulated, and including it in a portfolio does not breech confidentiality. If an actual organization was involved, the student should ask permission to include this information in the portfolio. You may want to append at the bottom of the document that permission was obtained from (specify person) on (specify date). This serves as a reminder to you and the reader that careful consideration has been given to confidentiality.

Generally, there will not be objections to including projects in the portfolio when the use is internal for promotion or salary raises. When use is for external purposes, such as securing a position with another organization, care should be exercised to eliminate patient, financial, and other confidential information. At times, removal of confidential data should be a consideration for internal use as well.

From the employer's perspective, prudent use in processing the portfolio information is part of the professional code of conduct. Copies of components of the portfolio, such as diplomas, should be made only with permission from the owner of the portfolio. In addition, the reader should be prudent when discussing the contents and should do so only with those who have a right to know. The portfolio can be a valuable resource that will be provided to a prospective employer when the owner is confident that it will be used discreetly and professionally.

Self-Assessment

Self-assessment, the process of identifying and analyzing your strengths and weaknesses, is referred to throughout this book. The checklists provided in various chapters are a resource for self-assessment. The process of self-assessment is a component in the development of the portfolio.

Employers are interested in what you know. Equally important is what you can do for the organization with what you know. In your portfolio, proof of past accomplishments is included to indicate potential future achievements. As the portfolio is developed, you should see a progressively fuller profile of your gifts, skills, and abilities that transform you into an independent, lifelong learner. Through portfolio development, you can take control of your education, making it truly a preparation for the career you envision and seek. The evidence of past achievements in your personalized portfolio enables you to see where you are and what steps remain in the attainment of your career goal. "After all, what is education but a process by which a person begins to learn how to learn" according to

Peter Ustinov (Noble, 1995). The ability to judge one's performance and to improve should be a component of both formal education and the professional career. Portfolio development provides a visible means to focus on progress toward a goal.

Having a vision is much better than letting your future go where it will. By targeting projects that are to be included in the portfolio and having a definite focus for each assignment and course, you will be ready for the job market upon graduation and later to advance to the next step in your career progression.

Through self-assessment, one can become a self-directed learner, planning appropriate experiences that will lead to growth and to a definite career goal. Through self-assessment, formal education becomes more efficient and effective.

The portfolio takes shape as the learner self-assesses and applies learning to a definite career plan.

Advantages of a Mentor

The word *mentor* is of Greek origin. Mentor was the loyal friend and wise advisor of Ulysses and the teacher and guardian of Ulysses' son Telemachus. Thus, a mentor today is an advisor. A mentor can be a college professor or an experienced professional. Clinical supervisors frequently become mentors for students. The mentor can assist in providing answers to questions such as (1) why the portfolio is being developed; (2) what kinds of information should be included; and (3) how the information can be improved. In regard to improving information, when certain class projects do not result in an "A" or in achieving a denotation of "Excellent," the mentor can assist in improving the document until it is deserving of inclusion in the portfolio.

An effective way of mentoring the development of the portfolio is to have three spaced appointments. During the first meeting, the purpose of the portfolio is articulated, the contents are planned, the organizational arrangement to be followed is discussed, and proposed contents are outlined. During the second meeting, the mentor reviews the contents and offers suggestions on additional materials that would enrich the portfolio. The mentor also comments on areas for quality and quantity improvement. At the final meeting, the portfolio is polished and ready to be offered to prospective employers.

Having someone as your mentor who has developed his or her own portfolio would be the ideal. However, this is not always possible. A professional who hires employees can be a valuable mentor because that person usually has a keen sense of the skills needed for a particular position. Another way of selecting a mentor is by position. If your goal is to be a long-term-care consultant, you could request someone who has this position to be your mentor in your preparation for an entry-level position or a lifelong career in this specialized field.

College professors can be excellent mentors since many have had experience in developing personal teaching portfolios that provide a factual description of teaching strengths and accomplishments. The teaching portfolio includes documents and materials that collectively suggest the scope and quality of teaching performance. Instructors who have had experience with a teaching portfolio frequently can apply the principles to assist you in the development of the professional practice portfolio.

In the process of selecting and organizing your portfolio, you will need to reflect, self-assess, and review your goals and accomplishments. The process will, in itself, provide focus and positioning for entry-level or career advancement opportunities.

Networking

Obtaining a position through networking has been in existence for decades. In real estate, it is location, location, location. In the employment game, Logue (1993) has said it is contacts, contacts, and more contacts. What used to be called the "old-boy network" is aptly referred to as networking. This career-building technique may be formal or informal.

Informal networking consists of building bridges throughout your career. Each person may someday be one who can be of assistance to you or you to them. Formal networking is established by building a list of contacts to help with specific situations and to provide assistance in meeting career goals including specific problems that can occur in the job setting.

Research of nonacute-care positions indicated that 46 percent of the respondents had used acquaintance networking during their career to find new positions (Anderson and Smith, 1989). Knowledge of vacancies in the healthcare industry can be obtained through recruiters, advertisements in journals and newspapers, telephone hot lines, and electronic searches. However, the best resource for learning about position vacancies is through personal contact with those who are in your network.

You may think you do not know anyone in the city where you would like to work. Or, you may know persons in acute care but not in home health. Through your network of instructors, clinical supervisors, or officers in professional organizations for which you hold membership, the network expands. Recruiters known to persons in your network are identified to you. Positions that were unadvertised become known. Names of professional contacts are provided to you. Networking can assist with finding the first position, advancing your career, developing professional relationships for mentoring, and providing encouragement for those times in your career when you need to talk to someone who has experienced a similar situation. At other times, you may want a mentor just to listen. By explaining a problem to another person, the solution seems easier. Lifelong friendships can be established through career networking.

Start early in your career to develop a circle of acquaintances who can assist you in advancing your career. Various ways can be used to organize networking contacts. Collecting business cards is one method that facilitates filing information in alphabetical order. Office supply outlets have folios for maintaining business cards.

Figure 3-5 provides an example of a form that could be used to maintain a network listing. Having this form on your personal computer makes it easy to arrange the data alphabetically and to cross-index from firm to name contact. The list could be developed by categories. A major category would be contacts from professional organizations. As your career develops you could have a separate listing for each organization to which you belong, such as the American Health Information Management Association, American Association of Healthcare Executives, and American Management Association.

Other categories for listings are contacts from the community, social groups with whom you associate, other professions, and personal contacts through religion, politics, hobbies, or the like.

The volunteer assistance, throughout your career, that you give to professional organizations is important. Working with leaders provides name and skill recognition. When a position is available, who do you think will be contacted? Of course, those who are already known and have shown their talents and abilities in various areas. This is a good example of the saying, "It's what you know and who you know."

Prospecting

When you send your resume to a wide range of companies and associates without knowing if any jobs are actually available, this is referred to by

Last Name	First	Company	Telephone	Date(s) Contacted	Outcome

Figure 3-5. Networking Contacts

some as *prospecting*. Prospects can come from instructors, family, fellow classmates, an alumni group, recruiters, and a mass mailing to a particular industry such as all hospitals in a particular area. In this era of downsizing, you may have received a resume and cover letter from a church or synagogue member or a former professional colleague requesting your assistance in finding a job. Sharing a job hot-line telephone number or data regarding new markets is one way of helping a job searcher.

The informational interview covered in Chapter 5 is a form of prospecting that is especially helpful for entry-level positions. Informational interviews are less formal than regular interviews. A major purpose of this type of interview is to provide a contact for the type of position or industry in which you will be looking for a position.

Career fairs are another form of prospecting. By attending these, you can learn of positions available in healthcare. At a fair, buyers and sellers of jobs come together. The event may be held on a college campus or an off-campus site such as a hotel. Some are organized for all college students; others for students in a particular discipline, for example, health information management, management information systems, accounting, health administration, or finance students. When organized by the campus career placement center, you can inquire if your resume should be brought to the event. Generally, a business card is sufficient. Having your own name card to circulate widely is important. During the semester before graduation, about 100 to 200 name cards can be printed for use as you search for and interview for positions. Make sure your telephone numbers—home and office—are correct. When you distribute your card to various representatives from companies or healthcare organizations, do not wait until you are contacted. If you learn of a position vacancy for which you are qualified and interested, be sure to obtain a specific name and other information needed to follow up with a resume, cover letter, and telephone call.

Your dress for these events does not need to be the same as you would wear to an interview. You should wear comfortable walking shoes and be neat and not outlandish. Career fairs are arranged for the exchange of information between students, who are buyers of jobs, and company representatives, who are seeking the brightest and best for the positions that will be available in their organizations.

Through the various types of prospecting mentioned, you can gather information regarding realistic job expectations and opportunities that may be available to you in the near and distant future. You too are looking for gold in the form of a job that meets your goals and that is in harmony with your values.

Name Cards

Earlier mention was made of the importance of collecting name cards as part of the system of networking. It is important to have your own name card and circulate your card widely. Make sure your telephone numbers, home and office, are correct. Be sure to include your e-mail address. Distribute your card to instructors, classmates, clinical supervisors, family members, contacts at church or synagogue, and elsewhere. By making it easy for the right people to reach you, you are facilitating the process of career advancement.

Job Banks

Listings of positions available in certain fields are maintained as job banks. Groups such as AHIMA charge a fee to include your resume in the bank and to allow access to the listing of positions available. The charge is minimal, and if you are willing to locate outside the area in which you are living, such resources can be helpful. When relocating is not an option, using local networks is usually more effective and efficient.

To make sure positions that are maintained in job banks and those advertised in journals and newspapers are still open, you should first telephone human resources or another contact you have in the organization. During the conversation, additional details regarding the position could be elicited to assist in tailoring your letter and resume.

Portfolio development, self-assessment, and networking are key components in career planning. By using them appropriately you can secure the right positions to achieve your career goals.

Summary

- Start early in your career to develop a portfolio to display the scope and quality of your education and experience, strengths and accomplishments.
- Organize your portfolio to best showcase your successful past performance. Arrangements used can be by subject, year, function, location, or other.
- Develop a management philosophy to give direction to the leadership style you will bring with you to the work world.

- Show your portfolio to a select few. Use it as a capstone for that important interview.
- Apply self-assessment techniques to identify strengths and weaknesses at various stages of your career.
- Secure the assistance of a mentor to facilitate professional growth and development.
- Establish a network of contacts that can contribute to your career advancement.

Review Activities

1. Based on the college courses you have had and your work or volunteer experiences, list the projects, tests, and other visuals you could include in your portfolio. Then develop a table of contents for your portfolio.
2. Write your own management philosophy. State a problem that could occur in the work world. If you were team leader, outline how you would resolve the problem within the framework of your management philosophy.
3. Construct your own personal statement. Ask another to critique it, listing ways you are unique as indicated by your personal statement.
4. Identify by position three persons who could serve as mentors to assist you in developing a portfolio.
5. Write the names of ten people you already know who would be contacts in your network for procurement of information regarding jobs that are available.

References

Anderson, S., and Smith K. (1989). *Manpower resource guide for roles and functions of the medical record practitioner in the health care industry.* St. Louis, MO: First Class Solutions.

Assessment at Alverno College (1985). Milwaukee, WI: Alverno College.

Fry, R. (1996). *Your first resume* (4th ed.). Franklin Lakes, NJ: Career Press.

Grappo, G. (1994). *Get the job you want in thirty days.* New York: The Berkley Publishing Group.

Gross, P., and Paskill, P. (1991). *Want a new better fantastic job?* Lake Oswego, OR: RightSide Resources.

Hart, S. (1991). *How to find your first job out of college.* Mission Hills, CA: Burning Gate Press.

Kotter, J.P. (1995). *The new rules.* New York: The Free Press.

Krannich, R.L., and Krannich, C.R. (1989). *Network your way to job and career success.* Manassas Park, VA: Impact Publications.

Latas, M. (1993). *Job search secrets: 301 that can work for you!* St. Louis, MO: Job Search Publishers.

Logue, C.H. (1993). *Outplace yourself.* Holbrook, MA: Bob Adams, Inc.

Noble, K.A. (1995). The International Education Quotations Encyclopaedia. Philadelphia: Open University Press.

O'Brien, J. (1996). *The complete job search organizer.* Washington, DC: The Kiplinger Washington Editors, Inc.

Ramos, B. (1995). *Win the job search battle.* Sherman Oaks, CA: Somar Press.

Rogers, R. S. (1996). *Get a job you love.* Chicago: Dearborn Financial Publishing, Inc.

Seldin, P. (1993). *Successful use of teaching portfolios.* Bolton, MA: Anker Publishing.

Weinstein, B. (1993). *Resumes don't get jobs.* New York: McGraw Hill.

Additional Resources

Myers, I.B., and McCaulley, M.H. (1985). *A guide to the development and use of the Myers–Briggs type indicator.* Palo Alto, CA: Consulting Psychologists Press, Inc.

Myers, I.B., and Myers, K.D. (1993). *Myers–Briggs type indicator, form G self-scorable (revised).* Palo Alto, CA: Consulting Psychologists Press, Inc.

Chapter 4

Professional Correspondence

Goals

After reading this chapter, you should be able to:

1. List considerations that will improve business letters.
2. Identify by paragraphs the organizational arrangement of a business letter.
3. State at least five style guidelines for professional writing.
4. Identify ten major sections of a business letter.
5. Write a request for organizational information.
6. Outline major items to include in a request for an informational interview.
7. Describe the content to be included in a resume cover letter.
8. Relate the information to be included in an interview confirmation letter.
9. Discuss the interview thank-you letter.
10. Identify important details of a job rejection letter.
11. Write a job acceptance letter.
12. Compose a letter of resignation.
13. Critique professional correspondence offering suggestions for improvement.
14. List at least five items that would be appropriate to include on an employment application.

Introduction

In this chapter, guidelines for writing letters and examples of various types of professional correspondence will be provided. Specific letters included are:

- *Requests for information:* either asking for organizational information or for an informational interview.
- *Cover:* the letter that accompanies the resume.
- *Interview confirmation:* a letter to verify that the date and time of interview are correct.
- *Interview thank you:* words of appreciation for the first and subsequent interviews.
- *Job rejection:* letter written when you have been offered a position and decide that it is not for you.
- *Job acceptance:* letter stating that you accept the offered position and the benefit package.
- *Resignation:* a formal and official notification to the appropriate person that you are leaving a position.

Every business letter that you write is a selling letter. The words you select and the appearance of your letters will be a way of marketing yourself. The various techniques to create a positive impression on your reader will be discussed in this chapter.

The final section of this chapter provides guidelines to assist you in developing a job application that can be effective. Having an application that is professional in appearance can facilitate an interview.

Guidelines for Professional Correspondence

The letters you write will either leave a positive or negative impression. Although there are no specific rules to guarantee that your letter will be effective, using the techniques for good letter writing will assist in preparing a letter that is professionally worded as well as visually pleasing.

Six important considerations are subject, audience, purpose, organization, style, and appearance as summarized in Table 4-1.

Table 4-1.   Six Considerations for Business Letters

Consideration	Description	Attention Focused On
Subject	What	Theme; intent
Audience	Who	Reader and wider audience
Purpose	Why	Reason you are writing; reason reader should respond
Organization	Content	Briefly telling the reader what you are going to say and what you said
Style	Structure	Words being readily understood
Appearance	Impression	An effective positive outcome

Subject

As you prepare to write your letter, one of your first considerations should be the subject. What will be the theme of this letter? For some letters a subject line is included to clarify the intent of the letter, for example: **Subject:** Job Interview.

For the letters discussed in this chapter, a subject line is generally not used. The subject of your letter will be the type of letter you are writing. From the situation, the subject originates. For example, the request letter can have as its subject a request for organizational information or a request for an informational interview. In both you are asking for a favor. Effective business letters do not occur by accident. One way to start is to think about the subject of the letter you are writing.

Audience

Considering your audience is important. One problem that can occur is that you misjudge who your audience will be. Your letter may be read by a wider audience than the person to whom it is addressed. As you write, remember that you are marketing yourself to all those who will and could possibly read your letter. Ultimately, the letter could be retained in your permanent personnel file for future reference. Do not take for granted that the audience has the same knowledge or background as you. Consider all others who may read it. For example, if you send a cover letter and resume to the director of human resources, they may be circulated to the director of health information management, the healthcare administrator, the director of quality improvement, and others. By considering your audience, you will be careful to explain technical terms and acronyms, and will use an effective tone to capture attention.

Purpose

To determine the purpose of the letter, first answer the question: Why am I writing? If your letter is to accompany your resume, you may have an answer with several parts. For example, you are writing

- To establish that you are the best person for this job.
- To indicate that you have researched the company.
- To induce the reader to peruse your resume.
- To obtain an interview.

You can summarize your purpose by stating, "I am writing to convince the employer that I have the qualifications to accomplish the job; that I am familiar with the company; and that after reading my resume, the company will want to interview me."

Now, ask yourself: Why should the employer respond? To answer, summarize your qualifications listed in your resume. Be sure your qualifications match the advertised job requirements: "I am sending my resume and cover letter to secure an interview, because through education and experience, I can perform the job to meet and possibly exceed the employer's expectations." The cover letter should compel the employer to read your resume. Your resume is proof that you can meet the company's needs.

Organization

The first three considerations relate to the what, who, and why, that is, subject, audience, and purpose, respectively. Organization addresses the contents, the part of the letter called the body. When organizing the body of your letter, the following can serve as a guide:

Part 1: State the reason for the letter, that is, your purpose. This is usually short.

Part 2: Explain what you want to happen or describe the information you have. Include all of the information that the reader needs.

Part 3: Provide supporting evidence or request action.

Part 4: Establish a positive response through a thank you, offering assistance, providing a telephone number, and/or suggesting what the reader may do or your action plan.

The organization of a business letter allows the content to flow logically and in an orderly manner.

Style

Style is the way you structure your words. The rules of communication change with trends and time. *The American Management Association Style Guide for Business Writing* (1996) is arranged alphabetically from "Abbreviations" to "Word Processing." Rules, principles, and examples are provided in this book for using words, expressing thoughts, and writing for the business world. This reference and others can assist you when specific information is needed. The following guidelines will facilitate clarity in writing your business letters:

1. Present paragraphs in logical order with one main idea. Vary the length of each to eliminate monotony. Avoid exceptionally long paragraphs.

2. Economize on words. Choppy or exceedingly long sentences can promote vagueness (seventeen words to a sentence is the average).

3. To be effective, eliminate passive voice. To achieve power with your words, structure each sentence with subject, active voice, action verb, and object. A list of action verbs is provided in Chapter 5.

4. When possible, be specific, using names, numbers, dates, and terms that can be readily understood.

5. Select words that convey a positive tone. An example of a negative tone would be: "I cannot meet with you until January 6." To create a positive, you could say: "I would be pleased to meet with you on January 6 or later at your convenience.

6. Structure your sentence to put your reader first by using "you." Avoid overuse of "I" and "me."

7. Read the letter out loud. Check your spelling. Have an eagle-eyed student or instructor proof your letters for accuracy in grammar and other details.
8. Make sure the letter is complete with important details included.

Guidelines on style have been summarized with seven words starting with C. The style of a letter should be conversational, clear, concise, complete, concrete, constructive, and correct (Dugger, 1993).

Literary writing can differ from business writing in several ways. Long and complex sentences are common in literature. Uncommonly used words and colorful expressions are sometimes encouraged. The contrary is true for a business letter. Your sentences should be concise, clear, and well constructed. Words should be readily understood on a first reading. Clarity is essential.

Appearance

A good letter obtains the results you intended. The reader will have a first impression of your letter even before reading it. The paper quality and general appearance will have something to say about you.

When selecting paper, use as a minimum 20-pound bond with 25-percent cotton-fiber content. A 24-pound bond with from 50- to 100-percent rag content is more expensive but gives an executive appearance. The standard size is 8½-by-11 inches.

White is frequently the preferred stationery color. Avoid flashy colors or odd shapes and sizes. Light tints of ivory, blue, and gray may be used. You will need to assess your audience. Your envelope generally should match the stationery. The envelope can differ when you use a large envelope so that the resume and cover letter need not be folded.

There are a variety of formats for a business letter. The two mentioned here are modified block and full block. Blocked style, in which the paragraphs are not indented, is the simplest and is commonly used. The full-blocked style occurs when everything in the message is flush with the left margin. In the modified block, the date, signature, and closing are placed to the right to allow them to stand out. The block style looks professional. Sample letters using full block and modified block are included in Figures 4-3 and 4-4.

Word processing software is readily available today in most college computing centers. A quality letter is relatively easy to produce by using software such as Microsoft Word, WordPerfect, or MacWrite Pro. Files can be added to the software to check spelling and grammar and to search for appropriate words with a thesaurus.

Ten Major Sections of a Business Letter

Most business letters are single spaced with one blank line between paragraphs. There should be at least a 1-inch margin on the left and right. If the letter is short, side margins can be 2 inches or more. The top and bottom margins are usually one and one-half times that of the side margins. Mainly, you want the information to look balanced and aesthetically pleasing. Select a typeface that is easy to read.

There are required and optional sections to a business letter. The ten discussed here are included in most letters.

1. *Letterhead.* At the top of the page you can enter your name, address, and phone number on one line. This information can be flush with the left margin or centered. Although not common in business letters, boldfacing your name and using a larger type size may be acceptable for cover letters (Parker, 1988).

Another style frequently used for cover letters is eliminating the letterhead at the top of the page and entering this information after your typed name. In this format, after typing your name, your address is supplied on the next two lines, and your phone number is on the fourth line. Both styles are used. As you type your letter, make a draft using both styles and determine which one appeals to you.

2. *Date.* Skip a line or two and enter the date (month, day, and year) the letter is written.

3. *Inside address.* This is the name of person to whom you are writing. Be sure to include all the details: the person's name, title, the name of the company, and the company's complete address including the zip code.

4. *Attention line.* As a rule, you should obtain the name of the person who is to receive your letter. When you cannot obtain a name, and have only the company's name, you can use the attention line to send your letter to the appropriate department. For example: Attention: Director of Health Information Services.

5. *Salutation.* Use the reader's name. If you are uncertain, try to obtain the name and correct spelling. There are times when you may have to use: Dear Personnel Director *or* Dear Director of Health Information Management. As a last resort, you could use: Dear Reader. Never write "to whom it may concern." If you want your letter read, using the person's name is one of the best ways to accomplish this.

When you are not sure of gender, for example, the name Marion Smith, you may use for the salutation: Dear Marion Smith.

6. *Body of the letter.* In three to four paragraphs your message is conveyed to the reader. Be sure to use the style guidelines mentioned previously.

7. *Complimentary close.* The wording is your choice. Formal closures are: Very truly yours *or* Respectfully. Less formal are: Sincerely, Sincerely yours, *or* Cordially.

8. *Signature.* Four lines are usually allowed between the complimentary close and your typed name. A woman can sign her name: Mary Smith *or* (Ms.) Mary Smith. If a man's name could be confused with that of a woman, he can sign his name: (Mr.) Terry Jones.

9. *Typed name.* Your typewritten name can include credentials as follows: Mary Smith, A.R.T.; Helen Jones, R.R.A.; Mary Jones, A.R.T., C.C.S. Frequently, the periods are eliminated and the credentials are entered as follows: Mary Jones, ART, CCS. Academic degrees at the master's and doctorate levels may be included, for example: Helen Jones, M.B.A., R.R.A. Advanced degrees should be placed before credentials.

10. *Enclosure.* When your resume or other information is enclosed, you should add: Enclosure. Enclosure should be used even when you have already mentioned in the body of the letter that there is an enclosure and it should be spelled out.

Having discussed the what, where, whom, why, and how of a business letter, the next section will cover the letters you will write to market yourself.

Request Letter

When asking for a favor, you want to have a tone that will make your reader responsive. Keep the letter short. Start with a sentence that states your purpose. Explain why you are making the request. Emphasize the valuable service the reader would be rendering by cooperation. End the letter by clarifying the action that should be taken. Remember to try to make it as convenient as possible for the respondent. In Figure 4-1, the request is for organizational information. In Figure 4-2, the request is for an informational interview.

Mary Smith
38 N. Ballas St.
St. Louis, Missouri 63141
(314) 977-5555

January 25, 199X

Helen Bathcel, R.R.A., Manager
Health Information Services
National Health Systems
2222 Cross Street
Omaha, Nebraska 68111

Dear Ms. Bathcel:

In May, I will graduate with an associate's degree in health information technology from St. Charles Community College. Having read about your company in the publication *For the Record*, I am interested in learning about future opportunities with National Health Systems.

Based on this information, I plan to structure my career accordingly. A self-addressed envelope is enclosed for your convenience in sending to me an annual report and other information.

I am eager to hear from you. If you have questions or I can further assist you with this request, please call me at (314) 977-5555. A message can be left if I am not available. Your assistance with this request would be appreciated.

Sincerely,

Mary Smith

Enclosure

Figure 4-1. Request for Organizational Information

MARY HENDERSON, R.R.A.
226 Grand Avenue
Montello, California 93944
(408) 666-4444

February 3, 199X

Mr. Ted Wilson, RRA, Manager
Health Information Services
Community Hospital of Montego
P.O. Box HH
Montego, CA 93941

Dear Mr. Wilson:

At your convenience, I would like to schedule a brief informational
interview to discuss career options in information systems. Next
year, I will graduate from California Technological University
(CTU) with a bachelor's degree in health information management.
Dr. Mary Fields, a professor at CTU, stated that you were a
visionary leader applying ultramodern technology and systems,
and that I should network with you.

This informational interview will provide you with an
exemplification of the curriculum at CTU and of the entry-level
skills of the 199X graduating class. You would be rendering a
service to your hospital in determining how the abilities of CTU
graduates meet your needs.

On Thursday of next week, I will telephone your office to schedule
an appointment. If you prefer to contact me, I can be reached at
(408) 666-4444. Thank you for considering this request. I look
forward to talking with you about the exciting opportunities in
information systems.

Sincerely yours,

Mary Henderson, RRA

Figure 4-2.   Request for Informational Interview

Since initially these request letters are almost solely to your benefit, you should be courteous while convincing the reader that you are worthy of an affirmative response.

Cover Letter

The cover letter can be identified by several different terms. Among those used are:

- Letter of introduction.
- Transmittal letter.
- Routing slip.
- Bridge, that is, one that is constructed between you and a prospective employer.

Whatever term is used, the purpose of the cover letter is to say enough about yourself to secure the reader's attention. Once you have the attention, the words should compel the reader to review your resume and to interview you for a position. A well-written cover letter is brief and focused with the following included:

- Highlights of your accomplishments, an introduction of yourself.
- Information to indicate that you have researched the company.
- Indications that you have the right skills and experience for the job.
- Reasons that will motivate the employer to interview you.

An unsolicited resume will in most cases be discarded if not supplemented by a cover letter. Whenever you send a resume, a cover letter should be included. Your letter should make you stand out from the others who are interested in this job. There are two types of cover letters:

1. The *letter of application* is used when you are applying for a specified vacant position as shown in Figure 4-3.
2. The *letter of inquiry* is used when you want to learn if there are employment opportunities related to your career objective as shown in Figure 4-4.

Mary Henderson, RRA
226 Grand Avenue
Chicago, Illinois 60624
(312) 788-2608

April 27, 199X

Ms. Patricia McPherson, MPA, ART, CCS
Healthcare Associates
2400 River Boulevard
Ashland, Ohio 44004

Dear Ms. McPherson:

This letter is in response to the health information manager position that was advertised in the April 21 issue of *ADVANCE*. Having attended the Ohio National University, relocating to Ashland would be welcomed. I am confident that my qualifications in management merit your consideration.

For the past year, I have supervised the coding section in a governmental hospital accredited recently by the Joint Commission on Accreditation of Healthcare Organizations (JCAHO). As an active participant in the self-study process, I assisted in the achievement of accreditation.

Having been involved in various aspects of information management, I possess excellent knowledge of chart processing and case-mix systems. As indicated on the enclosed resume, I was employed part-time during college by Solutions, Inc. My major responsibility was total quality management and the application of computers to quality improvement.

I would appreciate the opportunity to discuss your needs and my qualifications. Within the next week, I will contact you by telephone. The second week in May, I will be visiting friends in the Ashland area. To schedule a time to discuss further how I can contribute my skills to your organization, please contact me at (312) 788-2608.

Sincerely,

Mary Henderson, RRA

Enclosure

Figure 4-3. Cover Letter of Application, Full-Block Style

MARY JANE SOLTIS, A.R.T.
330 Bennett Street • Mobile, AL 36603-5893
Telephone (334) 661-3445

May 20, 1997

Frances Vott, M.D.
Carra Medical Group
1600 Carra Avenue
Birmingham, Alabama 35234-1990

Dear Dr. Vott:

Thank you for discussing with me on the telephone the possibility of joining your group as an office manager. As mentioned, I am seeking a position that will expand my skills in ambulatory information systems. A former instructor, Jody Marris, contacted me regarding your possible need for an information manager.

With two years of experience in the largest health maintenance organization in Alabama, I am ready for new challenges. A copy of my resume is enclosed. You will notice that I graduated from Bishop State Community College. Currently, I am taking management courses through the external degree program offered by St. Mark's College.

With my experience and education, I am confident that I can implement the computer technology needed by your group. One of the projects I completed was assisting programmers in designing an information system that generated management reports for administration. After I tested the system, I documented problem areas needing revisions.

I will telephone you during the week of June 2 to discuss in more detail your needs and those of the group and to arrange an appointment. Thank you for your consideration of my qualifications.

Sincerely,

Mary Jane Soltis, A.R.T.

Enclosure

Figure 4-4.   Cover Letter of Inquiry, Modified Block Style

The difference between the two letters occurs mainly in the opening paragraph. In the application letter, you will state the position for which you are applying and indicate where you learned about the opening. In the inquiry letter, you will define the position you are seeking and explain why you are interested in the organization.

Studying Figures 4-3 and 4-4, you should be able to see the following in each paragraph:

First paragraph: the reason for which the person is applying or inquiring, how the person learned of the position, and why the person is interested or qualified for the position.

Second paragraph: summary of qualifications, an aspect of the person's background that is not on the resume, and how the person's experience would benefit the company.

Third paragraph: supporting evidence of qualifications by describing a specific accomplishment.

Fourth paragraph: a flow of action that produces a positive response from the reader.

When you write a cover letter, remember that you want to convey what you can do for the company. Avoid concentrating on what the company can do for you. Address your letter to someone who has the authority to initiate the hiring process or the person specified in the job vacancy notice. Strive for enthusiasm and professionalism in your choice of words.

Be brief and focused on the subject, audience, and purpose.

Interview Confirmation Letter

Throughout your professional career, there will be opportunities to write confirmation letters. Such letters are written when the subject involves a serious commitment. Making appointments, offering services, or changing procedures and policies are examples of confirmation letters. In a confirmation letter, you want to clearly state what you are confirming.

In the interview confirmation letter you should include the place, date, and time of the appointment. Mention what you may be bringing with you, for example, your portfolio, or a copy of your resume. If you are coming from out of town, provide the place where you will be staying and when you expect to arrive, in case your host has to change the arrangements and needs to notify you.

The purpose of the interview confirmation letter is to keep your name before the potential employer. You want to avoid the danger of "out of sight, out of mind." By confirming the interview, you achieve the purpose of being visible while reducing any confusion that could occur regarding appointment details. In Figure 4-5, the interview confirmation includes a thank you, confirmation, agenda, and statement of intent. All are important components of the interview confirmation letter.

Thanks for Interview Letter

Manners are demonstrated in part through thank-you letters. Evidence of manners can be a persuasive tool for obtaining a job. Writing a thank-you letter for an interview is one indication of professional behavior. The interview thank-you letter is also a way of keeping your name on the potential employer's desk.

Etiquette columnist, Ann Chadwell Humphries, has said, "In a market where business and individuals spend fortunes to differentiate themselves, a simple thank-you note makes a lasting impression. It's noticed when it's received, and it's noticed when it isn't" (Clark, 1997).

The appreciation expressed in your letter should be warm and sincere without being gushy. The interview appreciation letter generally includes three to four paragraphs as follows and as illustrated in Figure 4-6.

First paragraph: a thank-you statement that includes where the interview was conducted, the position for which you interviewed, the day and date of the interview, and a recall of something that occurred during the interview to trigger the reader's mind specifically to you.

Second paragraph: a few sentences expressing continued interest in the position and briefly matching your qualifications to the position.

Third paragraph: a few sentences providing support by indicating your willingness to render additional information to validate your qualifications, plus a closing sentence that is professional.

Job Rejection Letter

Once you have decided against a job offer, a courteous letter to the company is appropriate. In writing the letter, consider how you would feel if you

Thomas Green
375 East Vaughn Street
Lafayette, Louisiana 75555
(318) 222-6666

July 7, 199X

Mr. Samuel Shorer
President
Health Information Associates
1400 Ezack Street
Ruston, Louisiana 71270

Dear Mr. Shorer:

Thank you for scheduling me to interview with you in your office at 1400 Ezack Street on Monday, July 21, at 9 A.M.

Sunday afternoon, July 20, I will arrive in Ruston, and will be staying at the Holly Inn on Fairmont Street; the phone number is 329-5555. I will bring my portfolio, which contains various projects completed during college. Several of the projects relate to the computer associate position for which I have applied.

I am qualified through education and experience for computerized health information systems. As you may have noticed on my resume, during summers and part-time during semesters, I marketed computers and trained others to use a variety of software packages. With my education in health information technology and my knowledge of information systems, I am confident I could effectively meet your needs.

Thank you for providing me an opportunity to discuss how my abilities can benefit Health Information Associates. I look forward to meeting you on July 21.

Sincerely,

Thomas Green

Figure 4-5.   Interview Confirmation Letter

Thomas Green
375 East Vaughn Street
Lafayette, Louisiana 75555
(318) 222-6666

July 22, 199X

Mr. Samuel Shorer
President
Health Information Associates
1400 Ezack Street
Ruston, Louisiana 71270

Dear Mr. Shorer:

Thank you for the exciting and enriching interview with you on July 21 in your office. Hearing about your goals as president of the Louisiana Systems Society was especially interesting. I would like to extend my appreciation to your entire staff for the gracious welcome extended to me.

The computer associate position seems like it was made for me.

My interest in your company increased as a result of the visit with you and your associates. Preparing and presenting training for clients throughout the Southwest would apply the oral and written communication skills developed during college while I worked part-time marketing computers and training others in software applications.

Should you need additional information concerning my qualifications or want a list of references, please contact me at the number above. I look forward to hearing from you again and becoming an integral member of Health Information Associates.

Sincerely yours,

Thomas Green

Figure 4-6.   Thanks for Interview Letter

were receiving a refusal. Would you like to receive a letter stating that another applicant has been offered a position for which you applied? Turn this around. You are writing this type of letter to an employer. The employer has offered you a position. You are writing to say you reject the offer because of a better opportunity or you are no longer interested in the position.

In rejecting a job offer you should express appreciation for being considered. Briefly mention the better opportunity that you have accepted. For example: "I am unable to accept your offer because I accepted a similar position with another company." Do not mention that the salary is larger or other details. End with a thank you and a warm closure.

After the interview, you may find that there is a mismatch. Either you do not like the company and/or your skills do not harmonize with the position. State in your letter a reason as simply as possible. For example: "I have had no experience with Excel software." Then keep the door open by stating what you plan to do about this. Your comment could be either that you are scheduled to take an Excel course or that you are seeking a similar position that uses other software. If in the future the company needs someone for Excel or other software, you could be contacted. When you know of someone who is qualified for the position or can help the company in its search, you may want to suggest this. Close with a gracious thank you. Figure 4-7 is an example of a refusal response to a company's job offer.

Acceptance Letter

The offer you have been waiting for has been received. It may come at the end of the first or second interview. The response may come to you through personal contact, by letter, or by telephone. The information generally provided includes: you are hired with a certain title; you are to report to a certain person; you will start on a certain day; and you will receive a certain salary and benefit package, such as comprehensive health and dental insurance. Additional details might include: "When you attain credentials as a registered record administrator, an additional $500 will be added to your gross salary." Postinterview strategies are found in Chapter 7. In this section, the acceptance letter will be discussed.

You should put your job acceptance in writing, confirming the important details of the position. As you peruse the letter in Figure 4-8, you should see an enthusiastic response to the good news; acceptance of the position and salary offered; confirmation of the place, date, and time of starting; and an eagerness to be with the company.

Christine Johnson
2222 South Street
Sioux City, Iowa 50584
(718) 111-9999

April 4, 199X

Mr. John Kline
Holy Angels Hospital
Recruitment Division
4444 S. Washington Highway
Ft. Lauderdale, Florida 33308

Dear Mr. Kline:

Thank you for considering me for the position of medical records supervisor. At this time, I cannot in good conscience accept the offer.

The quality improvement experience required for this position exceeds my background in this specialized area. I want to do an excellent job. To prepare myself for future opportunities such as yours, I have accepted a position in Sioux City.

I have contacted my former instructor, Walter Webb, at St. Mary's College (402) 777-9999. He may be able to provide the names of graduates who are now prepared to accept the responsibilities needed for the medical records supervisor position at Holy Angels.

Your consideration has been the incentive I needed to obtain additional training in quality improvement. Thank you for the confidence you had in me.

Sincerely,

Christine Johnson

Figure 4-7. Job Rejection Letter

Karen McBeth
1111 Main Street
Philadelphia, PA 19101
(215) 333-6666

June 30, 199X

Carol Gannon, Director
Health Information Management
New Port Hospital
340 Spring Street
Philadelphia, PA 19104

Dear Ms. Gannon:

With pleasure I accept the position of medical information specialist. I am enthusiastic regarding this new assignment and will plan to be in your office by 8 A.M. on August 1, 199X.

As outlined in the letter from Human Resources, my starting salary will be $14 an hour with a $500 bonus when credentials as an accredited record technician are obtained. The benefit package outlined in the letter seems appropriate to an entry-level position.

Thank you for your confidence in me. I will make every effort to exceed your expectations. I am eager to start working with the health information management team.

Sincerely,

Karen McBeth

Figure 4-8. Job Acceptance Letter

Resignation Letter

You are changing employment. You could be leaving a part-time position held while you were a college student, or it may be another full-time position. When you are moving on, the letter you write should be short, honest, and positive. If your tenure with the employer was not pleasant, keep your letter professional. You may need a reference from this employer in the future.

Letters of resignation are written for various reasons. You may have had a job requiring considerable travel and now you want to be able to go home each night. You may wish to resign because your current position does not allow for growth. Most times, it is better to have a job offer from another company before resigning from your present position. Having been bypassed for promotion, receiving a better job offer, or starting your own business are other reasons for resigning.

The resignation letter may include an expression of appreciation to the company or to your supervisor. You may state that it was not an easy decision and give your reason for having to resign. You could offer to stay to train a replacement or to stay until a replacement is found. When you have already agreed to start another position on a specific date, you may not be able to wait. Usually, two weeks' notice is sufficient. Circumstances can lengthen this time, for example, if you hold a position for which few people have the specialized training. The closing paragraph should include a thank you and a personal note may be added. For example, "I will miss the quality improvement team with whom I was closely associated during the past three years." The major components of the resignation letter are included in Figure 4-9.

Letter Maintenance

During a job search, you could send out up to a hundred letters. These could be filed on disk or on hard copy. Develop a system that suits you with the resources you have available. Always make sure you have a copy of the letters you send. These are necessary for making notations, such as the date and type of response. Maintaining a log of letters that you have sent can be especially helpful. An example is shown in Table 4-2.

Another reason for saving your letters is to avoid having to create a completely new letter. Use past letters as prototypes for future letters. By

JoAnn Carr, ART, CCS
555 South Eighth Street
Jersey City, New Jersey 07305
(201) 444-8888

February 1, 199X

Natalie Clifford, MBA, RRA
Director, Health Information Services
United Medical Center
2039 Kenney Street
Jersey City, New Jersey 07305

Dear Ms. Clifford:

With regret and with some excitement I must resign as clinical
information manager, effective March 1, 199X. My husband will
be relocating to California to pursue an offer in a law firm. This is
an opportunity for both of us as it will allow time for me to
complete the requirements for a bachelor's degree.

If you have a replacement prior to my leaving, I would be glad to
assist in the training. The procedure manual for my section has
recently been revised and will be helpful to the new manager.

Your encouragement during the past two years has contributed to
my success. Thank you for allowing me to take on additional
responsibilities and to develop the position. I will leave with fond
memories of United Medical Center and my co-workers in Health
Information Services.

Sincerely

JoAnn Carr, ART, CCS

Figure 4-9. Resignation Letter

Table 4-2.   Log for Employment Correspondence

Date Sent	Company/Contact	Reply P/L*	Outcome
3/14	Henderson Coding Assoc. Mary Jones, President 312/999-8888	3/31P 4/2L	Interview scheduled for April 19 in Atlanta at 9 A.M. (see letter from Jones for details)
3/17	St. Mary's Hospital Martha Allison, Director of Health Information Services. 314/888-9999	4/3L	Plans to telephone me on 4/14 to discuss my qualifications
4/14	St. Mary's Hospital (see 3/17)	4/14P	Allison scheduled me for an interview on 4/29 (confirmation letter sent).

*P = phone; L = letter.

changing a few words, a paragraph or two, you can use and reuse the letters on file.

Employment Application

Most hospitals and corporations use preprinted applications. Some organizations require both a personal resume and a completed application. When you know an application form is a requirement, try to request one ahead of time so that you can complete it neatly and thoroughly without having to rush. Data will be more readily available at home and accuracy is easier to achieve.

Important sections of an application for employment are:

- Recruiting source (how you learned of the job).
- Personal information (name, address, and telephone and social security numbers).

- Education and training history.
- Employment history (dates, job title, and supervisor's name).
- Reason for leaving previous position.
- Starting salary and leaving salary by position.
- Citizenship status. (Do you have a legal right to work in the United States?)

Other items that may be included are:

- Date of availability.
- Long-range professional goals.
- Special qualifications and credentials.
- Criminal record. (Have you ever been convicted of a criminal action?)

In Figures 4-10 and 4-11 sample applications are shown. When completing an employment application, be neat, accurate, complete, and accommodating. Whenever possible follow the instructions provided, meet deadlines set by the employer, and adjust to inconveniences that can occur. To illustrate, an ART applying for a position was asked to return the next day for a coding examination because the Encoder would be available on that day. She graciously accommodated, even though it meant taking a vacation day from work. The result was she was hired for a position with increased salary and greater opportunities.

Reason for Leaving

The reason for leaving provides a prospective employer with insights into your values, goals, and career progression. When completing this section on the employment application, give reasons that are positive, directed to the future, and advance your career. Examples of reasons for leaving are:

- To advance HIM knowledge and skills.
- To seek supervisory responsibilities.
- To pursue interest in systems and computer technology.

Remember to accentuate the positive and eliminate negatives. "No supervisory responsibilities" is a negative that is better phrased "objective is to obtain supervisory experience" or to "manage a health information function."

Name: _____

Address: _____

_____

Phone: _____ Answering machine _____ Y _____ N

Social security number: _____

Education:

1] _____

_____

2] _____

_____

3] _____

_____

Experience: Name, address, telephone number, supervisor

1] _____

_____

_____

Hourly rate:_____ Reason for leaving: _____

2] _____

_____

_____

Hourly rate:_____ Reason for leaving: _____

3] _____

_____

_____

Hourly rate:_____ Reason for leaving: _____

4] _____

_____

_____

Hourly rate:_____ Reason for leaving: _____

Figure 4-10. Employment Application (Courtesy of W.B. Saunders Company, A.A. Andress, (1996) "Saunders Manual of Medical Office Management," p. 23 and 24)

Do you speak any languages other than English? _____ Y _____ N

If so, what?_____

Are there any physical problems that could keep you from performing the duties of this position? _____ Y _____ N

If so, what?_____

Have you ever been convicted of a crime? _____ Y _____ N

Are there any areas in which you think you need improvement? _____ Y _____ N

If so, what are they? _____

Like most doctors' offices, occasionally there are days that employees have to work later than their usual quitting times. Is this a problem? _____ Y _____ N

What qualities do you possess, if any, that make you more qualified than others?___

_____

_____

Are you willing to be bonded? _____ Y _____ N

Do you have any previous commitments that might interfere with this position?

_____ Y _____ N

If so, how will you handle them? _____

What are your long-range plans?_____

_____

List three professional references: Name, address, telephone

1] _____

_____

_____

2] _____

_____

_____

3] _____

_____

_____

What hourly rate are you looking for in this position?

$ _____

Date of availability: _____

Date of interview: _____

Figure 4-10. *Continued*

SAINT LOUIS UNIVERSITY

Application for Employment

LOCATION

❏ Frost & Parks Campus, Human Resources, Fitzgerald Hall, 3500 Lindell, St. Louis, MO 63103

❏ Health Sciences Center, Human Resources, 3635 Vista at Grand, PO Box 15250, St. Louis, MO 63110-0250

Note: This application remains current for 90 days. Re-application required thereafter.

Thank you for your interest in employment at Saint Louis University.

RECRUITING SOURCE (learned of job from)

❏ Classified Advertisement (which newspaper) _____

❏ Community Agency (which one) _____

❏ College or Trade School (which one) _____

❏ State Employment Service (❏ Missouri ❏ Illinois)

❏ Current Saint Louis University Employee (name) _____

❏ Came in on own accord

❏ Job Fair (which one) _____

❏ Job Information Hotline

❏ Other_____

SAINT LOUIS UNIVERSITY IS AN EQUAL OPPORTUNITY EMPLOYER

All qualified applicants will receive consideration for employment without regard to race, color, sex, religion, national origin, age, sexual orientation, disability or veteran status. All policies are administered in a manner consistent with our Jesuit Catholic identity.

If you are a disabled veteran, a Vietnam era veteran or have a physical or mental disability, you are invited to volunteer this information. This information will be used to consider identified individuals for opportunities under Saint Louis University's affirmative action programs and to comply with federal regulations. This information will be treated as confidential. Failure to provide this information will not jeopardize or affect your consideration for employment.

Individuals with disabilities who require reasonable accommodations in order to take our employment tests must inform the Employment Office at least three(3) days before the test is given.

If you wish to be identified, please check the appropriate category.
❏ Handicapped Individual   ❏ Disabled Veteran   ❏ Vietnam Era Veteran

Job hotline phone numbers: Frost and Parks Campus 977-2265
Health Sciences Center 577-8595

Figure 4-11.   Employment Application (Courtesy of Saint Louis University)

SAINT LOUIS UNIVERSITY

An Equal Opportunity/Affirmative Action Employer
Application for Employment (Please print or type)

Date _____

PERSONAL INFORMATION

Name _____ Social Security # _____
 Last   First   M.I.

Telephone _____ _____ _____
 (Home)   (Work)   (Alternate)

Address _____
 Number and Street

City _____ State _____ Zip Code _____

- Do you have the legal right to work in the U.S.? ❏ Yes ❏ No

- Are you, or have you ever been employed by Saint Louis University (including the Frost and Parks Campus, Academic/Research Division, Hospital or SLUCare)? ❏ Yes ❏ No
 Dates Employed _____ Division _____

- Have you ever been convicted of a criminal action? A conviction or court-martial is not necessarily a bar to employment. (Include court-martial convictions, but exclude minor traffic violations.)
 ❏ Yes ❏ No   If yes, list date, charge, place, court, and action taken:
 _____

- Do you have relatives who are currently employed by Saint Louis University? ❏ Yes ❏ No
 Relative's Name _____ Division _____

EDUCATION/TRAINING

Elementary and/or High School (circle Highest Grade Completed) 1 2 3 4 5 6 7 8 9 10 11 12 ❏ GED

Name and Location of Training Program College and/or University	# of yrs attended	Graduated Yes/No	Degree (Type)	Major

List Additional Coursework and Training: _____

Special Skills and Equipment: _____

Job related registrations, licenses and accreditations (for example, Chauffeur, Nursing, Security)		
Type and Number	Exp. Date	State

Military Experience (U.S. Military Only)		
Date Entered	Date Separated	Special Training Received
Present or Last Rank	Types of Duties Performed	

Figure 4-11. *Continued*

SAINT LOUIS UNIVERSITY

EMPLOYMENT HISTORY

Prefer: ❑ Full-time ❑ Part-Time ❑ Days ❑ Evenings ❑ Nights ❑ Weekends ❑ PRN pools ❑ TEMP pool ❑ Summer
Will accept: ❑ Full-time ❑ Part-Time ❑ Temporary

Please answer all questions. Resumes are no substitute but may be enclosed.
Please account for all jobs. Begin with most recent employer.

Min. Salary Desired	Date Available
$ per	

Name employed under if different than in Personal Information section: _____

Company Name		Telephone *	
Address	City	State	Zip Code
Your Job Title	Supervisor's Name		
Job Duties	Supervisor's Title	May We Contact? ❑ Yes ❑ No	
	Employment Dates From To	❑ Full-time ❑ Part-time	
	Starting Salary $ per	Salary at Leaving $ per	

Reason for leaving (resigned, laidoff, discharged) Please explain:

Company Name		Telephone *	
Address	City	State	Zip Code
Your Job Title	Supervisor's Name		
Job Duties	Supervisor's Title	May We Contact? ❑ Yes ❑ No	
	Employment Dates From To	❑ Full-time ❑ Part-time	
	Starting Salary $ per	Salary at Leaving $ per	

Reason for leaving (resigned, laidoff, discharged) Please explain:

Company Name		Telephone *	
Address	City	State	Zip Code
Your Job Title	Supervisor's Name		
Job Duties	Supervisor's Title	May We Contact? ❑ Yes ❑ No	
	Employment Dates From To	❑ Full-time ❑ Part-time	
	Starting Salary $ per	Salary at Leaving $ per	

Reason for leaving (resigned, laidoff, discharged) Please explain:

Company Name		Telephone *	
Address	City	State	Zip Code
Your Job Title	Supervisor's Name		
Job Duties	Supervisor's Title	May We Contact? ❑ Yes ❑ No	
	Employment Dates From To	❑ Full-time ❑ Part-time	
	Starting Salary $ per	Salary at Leaving $ per	

Reason for leaving (resigned, laidoff, discharged) Please explain:

FOR OFFICE USE ONLY

Typing Exercise: _____ Date: _____ Gross: _____ Errors: _____ Net: _____

(Right margin vertical text: Name Last First M.I. / Phone 1 2 3 4 5 6 7 8 9 10 11 12 / Position(s) Desired Title 1) 2) 3) 4) / Vacancy #)

Figure 4-11.   *Continued*

Applicant Read Carefully

"I hereby certify that my answers to the above are true and further that I understand that any information withheld or falsely provided by me in connection with the foregoing application will subject me to immediate termination of employment. I also recognize that my employment is based on receipt of satisfactory information from former employers or references. I hereby authorize Saint Louis University without liability to contact prior employers (present employers if authorized) or references given by me and authorize said employers or references to make full response to any inquiries by Saint Louis University in connection with this application for employment. I also authorize Saint Louis University to give any information concerning me or my employment in response to inquiries from subsequent potential employers or other inquiries concerning me without liability. In as much as said information concerning my performance as an employee, conduct and deportment is furnished at my specific request and for my benefit, I hereby agree to hold harmless Saint Louis University and all former employers or references listed on this application from any liability or claims of whatsoever nature. I agree to conform to the rules and regulations of Saint Louis University, and understand that my employment can be terminated for any reason, and with or without notice, at any time at the option of either Saint Louis University or myself. I further understand that the Staff Handbook is not to be construed as creating any form of employment agreement and that it does not serve as an independent basis of contract for employment. I also agree that upon my termination of employment (should I be hired) I will return all University property. I further certify that I have read the foregoing paragraph and herewith knowingly make this authorization by setting forth my signature below."

I have been advised that it is the policy of Saint Louis University to oppose smoking inasmuch as smoking poses a demonstrable risk of harm both to the smoker, as well as to those who are exposed to smoking. The University has implemented extremely restrictive policies against smoking and intends to abolish smoking altogether within the facilities of the Center. Should I be hired, in consideration for being hired, I will abide by all policies, including, but not limited to, any policy prohibiting smoking.

Saint Louis University is dedicated to creating a campus environment that is as safe and secure as reasonably possible. A campus security report is published every year entitled "In Your Best Interest." It covers the policies and procedures of Saint Louis University on the Frost, Parks and Health Sciences Center campuses to deter, report and respond to on-campus emergencies and crime, even minor incidents. It also summarizes campus crime statistics. Finally, it highlights programs to educate the University community about safe living habits and how to take precautions for personal security. If you would like a copy of the report, please contact the Department of Public Safety, DuBourg Hall, 221 North Grand, St. Louis, MO 63103-2097.

Signature _____   Date _____

CONDITIONS OF EMPLOYMENT (to be completed by department head)

Department _____ P.C. # _____

Date to start work (contingent upon pre-employment physical) _____

Job Title _____

Rate of Pay _____
80/8 Option ☐ Yes ☐ No   40 hr Option ☐ Yes ☐ No   Exempt status (monthly payroll) ☐ Yes ☐ No

Hours of Employment per pay period _____ Days of week to be worked S M T W Th F Sat _____

Hours of Work (from)am/pm _____ (to)am/pm _____ Shift Rotation Req. _____

Overtime Requirements _____

Availability for Any Shift or Any Department In Case of Emergency ☐ Yes ☐ No

Date _____   Department Head Signature _____

Date _____   Employee Signature _____

Department Interviewer's Comments: _____   Date Interviewed: _____

These conditions of employment are not to be construed as creating any form of employment agreement and do not serve as an independent basis of contract for employment.   REV. 6/96-appl

Figure 4-11.   *Continued*

Starting Salary and Salary at Leaving

There are several factors that determine a new employee's starting salary. However, ending salary on your last position is generally the major factor in determining how much the company will offer you. Be especially accurate in providing salary figures because these can be validated by the prospective employer.

AHIMA and other organizations periodically conduct salary surveys. These data can provide valuable information on the market demand for a position, title, and particular skill. Such surveys generally provide average salaries by region for positions. From such surveys and other data, employers set salary ranges for various positions.

When possible, try to obtain the salary range for all positions you are considering from external resources such as AHIMA surveys and from internal resources, for example, the company itself. Knowing how much the company values a particular skill may influence your decision in applying. If the salary is not in the range you have identified in your career goal, you can consider other companies.

If the application requests "minimum salary desired," you can be honest. However, if minimum salary is too low or too high, you may not be contacted for an interview. In the former, when you set the salary too low, you are not marketing your skills appropriately and the prospective employer could suppose you are not competent for the position. In the latter, when you set the minimum salary too high, you put yourself outside the range of the other employees. Rather than restructure salary ranges, the prospective employer may seek another candidate. And, again, it may be time for the company to restructure the salary scales and you have alerted them to this fact.

Using the answer "negotiable" instead of specifying a minimum salary can facilitate your being considered for an interview. When the company offers you the position at a certain salary, you can decide, based on the total benefit package, if you will accept or not. Vacation time or tuition reimbursement may be more important to you than salary.

As mentioned, if you can learn of the salary range through the library, instructors, or other resources, this will keep you from wasting your time and the company's if you are sure the compensation will be inadequate for your needs and career goals. The best scenario is when you have identified the salary and benefits you want and the prospective employer matches or even exceeds your expectations.

Summary

- The techniques for good letter writing can assist in achieving a positive impression.
- Six important considerations that improve letter writing are subject, audience, purpose, organization, style, and appearance.
- Subject, audience, and purpose respectively address the what, who, and why of a business letter.
- Organization relates to the contents of a letter. Paragraph content for most letters can be summarized as follows: (1) purpose, (2) explanation, (3) supporting evidence, and (4) positive closure.
- Style is the way words are structured. Words are powerful when active voice is used.
- Ten major sections of a business letter are letterhead, date, inside address, attention line, salutation, body of the letter, complimentary close, signature, typed name, and enclosure.
- Request letters should have a tone that will make the reader responsive.
- The purpose of the cover letter is to secure an interview.
- The interview confirmation letter has a dual purpose: to avoid confusion and to keep your name before a prospective employer.
- Thanks for the interview letter is an indication of professional behavior.
- The job rejection letter should state your reason for refusal simply, honestly, and tactfully.
- The job acceptance letter should confirm the important details of the position.
- The job resignation letter should be short, honest, and positive even when you leave under unpleasant circumstances.
- A log of letters sent and a file of letters composed can be beneficial for the present and future.
- Keep a copy of every letter you send and make notes about actions taken.
- Information frequently requested on a job application includes recruiting source, personal information, educational and employment history, citizenship status, credentials, and date of availability.
- Applications that are neat, accurate, complete, and accommodating are those that an employer will consider.

Review Activities

1. Select a business letter either from mail you receive or from another resource. Compare the paragraphs in your letter with the organizational arrangement of a business letter as covered in this chapter. Do they differ? If so, describe.

2. Consult another reference to obtain at least two other style guidelines that are not included in this chapter.

3. Write a request for an informational interview applying the ten major sections of a business letter.

4. Describe the sections that should be included in a resume cover letter.

5. Obtain and complete an application from a healthcare facility. Compare it with the one provided in Figure 4-10. List the items that are similar and those that are different.

References

American Management Association (1966). *The AMA style guide for business writing.* New York: AMACOM.

Andress, A.A. (1996). *Saunders manual of medical office management.* Philadelphia: W.B. Saunders Company.

Clark, G. (1997). Monday memo. *St. Louis Post–Dispatch,* January 13, p. 5BP.

Cook, M. (1985). *Personnel manager's portfolio of model letters.* Englewood Cliffs, NJ: Prentice-Hall.

Cross, M. (1987). *Persuasive business writing: Creating better letters, memos, reports, and more.* New York: AMACOM.

Crowther, K. (1993). *Researching your way to a good job.* New York: John Wiley & Sons, Inc.

DeVries, M. (1993). *The complete office handbook.* New York: Wings Books.

Dugger, J. (1993). *Business letters for busy people.* Hawthorne, NJ: Career Press.

Falcone, P. (1995). *The complete job-finding guide for secretaries and administrative support staff.* New York: AMACOM.

Hart, S. (1991). *How to find your first job out of college.* Los Angeles.: Burning Gate Press.

McKeown, T. (1992). *Powerful business writing: Say what you mean, get what you want.* Cincinnati, OH: Writer's Digest.

Miller, C., and Swift, K. (1980). *The handbook of nonsexist writing for writers, editors and speakers*. New York: Lippincott & Crowell.

Nauheim, F. (1982). *Letter perfect: How to write business letters that work*. New York: Van Nostrand Reinhold Company.

O'Brien, J. (1996). *The complete job search organizer*. Washington, DC: The Kiplinger Washington Editors, Inc.

Parker, Y. (1988). *The resume catalog: 200 damn good examples*. Berkeley, CA: Ten Speed Press.

Poe, R. (1983). *The McGraw-Hill handbook of business letters*. New York: McGraw-Hill Book Company.

Chapter **5**

Resume
Development

Goals

After reading this chapter, you should be able to:

1. Identify at least six uses for a resume.
2. Describe resume formats, stating which one is most widely used.
3. Apply the elements of a good resume.
4. Employ appropriate buzzwords when developing a resume.
5. Avoid at least five blunders associated with resume development.
6. Apply the principles for the development of a winning resume.
7. Discuss the advantages of a home page resume.

Introduction

Developing a resume has been compared to creating a work of art. The sketching of career objective, history, and personal qualification should be a gratifying experience. This chapter can assist you in writing or improving your resume. Your goal is to create a winning resume that will secure job interviews for the position that will start or advance your career.

The word *resume*, derived from the French, means a summary. The resume should be designed as a summary outlining the highlights of your education, experience, skills, and other relevant information.

Resume Uses

The primary purpose of the resume is to sell yourself. Your resume should advertise you in such a way that an employer is convinced that you are worth considering for a specific job. In addition to being an employment marketing tool, there are other purposes for a resume.

Discussion Tool

As you prepare your resume, your focus will be to open doors. When you have secured an interview, the resume becomes a resource to use during your discussion with the interviewer. Usually, the interviewer is a total stranger and the resume facilitates communication. Your task during the interview is to make a good impression. A resume has importance after the interview as a reminder to the prospective employer of your qualifications. Information on the postinterview process is discussed in Chapter 7.

Advanced Education

Graduates of independent study programs, propriety programs, community colleges, or undergraduate college and university programs may be required to submit a resume as part of the application process. The resume provides the admission and selection committees with a summary of accomplishments. Committee members use the resume as one of the resources to determine if the candidate is the type of person who would succeed in the program of studies. Graduate programs, such as a master's-degree program in public health, hospital and healthcare administration, informatics/information systems, or business administration, provide advanced education to health information graduates. A professional law degree is another goal pursued by some health information baccalaureate graduates. As part of the admission process to such programs the resume may be required or voluntarily included to support qualifications.

The resume can also be a useful document to include when applying for scholarships, loans, or grants.

Other Uses

When applying for promotion, the resume is generally a component of the promotion portfolio. An updated resume of accomplishments can be an important part of the documentation needed to show you deserve consideration for advancement.

To regularly update your resume and keep a copy in your portfolio is a good practice. Although you may never use it to secure another job, if an opportunity occurs, you will be ready. Also, if you are ever in a rightsizing or downsizing situation, you can avoid any delay in moving on to the next employment opportunity.

During your career, there will be times when you will be asked to make a speech or in-service presentation to groups. The resume provides information for an introduction and for validating your qualifications to address a particular topic or audience.

The resume can also be a self-motivator. By reviewing your resume prior to the interview, you can bolster your confidence. Completing a program in health information technology, management systems, or related areas is a feat in itself. The program accreditation process necessitates meeting rigorous academic standards. Courses include general education, biological and clinical sciences, business administration, computers, and information management. As you review the courses you have completed and the knowledge and skills acquired, you should feel confident about your professional capabilities.

Formats

There are several formats used for resumes. Those that will be covered are (1) chronological or historical order; (2) reverse chronological; (3) functional or skill based; (4) combination of chronological and functional; and (5) creative. Curriculum vitae and personal statements are briefly covered for informational purposes.

The format that should be used for your resume is the one that best presents your qualifications. Knowledge of the different formats can assist you in deciding which would enhance the written presentation of your strengths and versatility. Regardless of the format used, the work experience section will consist of job title, organization name, city, state, and country (if not U.S.), dates of position held, and position description that highlights skills and relevant accomplishments. A recruiter may request that if the place of employment was a hospital, the number of beds and other details be included, such as:

Regional Medical Center, Kansas City, MO (1,200 beds, teaching hospital), 1996–Present

- Managed annual employee performance evaluation program
- Designed and implemented a quality review of department database

Chronological/Reverse Chronological

Arranging your education and experience in the order of occurrence is a chronological format. If your employment history shows steady career progression as related to health information technology and/or management, the chronological format may be best. Start each work experience statement with a verb that conveys the skill you want to present. For example: Maintained a three-year summer position with a copying service, releasing information for several area hospitals and achieving high client satisfaction ratings. The statement should be explicit about what you have done.

Most widely used is the reverse chronological format. Since employers are accustomed to this style, many college career counselors will recommend this format. Starting with the most recent events and working backward brings to the forefront your current achievements. Resume readers usually look for a logical, thoughtful structure. When this is present, they may spend additional time reviewing how your accomplishments meet the organization's needs. For some reviewers, even the spacing used can serve as an indication of how you think.

The reverse chronological format is usually not recommended if you have an inconsistent work record or a history of job jumping.

Functional/Skill Based

Generally, the functional format is recommended when your education and experience do not directly support your career objective. In this type of resume, the emphasis is on the skills you have developed, not the order of accomplishment. For example, if as a graduate in health information you are seeking a position in pharmaceutical sales, you would emphasize the abilities applicable to a sales position, such as excellent communication skills, oral and written; strong organizational abilities; extensive experience with spreadsheets and other computer software; marketing experience with products for college organizations.

The skill-based format is excellent for those who have no work history, have been self-employed, or have worked as a consultant. The emphasis is placed on what you can do rather than where and when it was accomplished. Skills and experience can be acquired in a variety of ways. Some of the common ones outside of a work situation are practicums, internships, volunteering, extracurricular activities, traveling, and class/team projects.

Knowing the specific job requirements is important when developing a skill-based resume. If you have an accurate job description for the vacant position, the resume preparation process can be a more structured process. You merely tailor your qualifications precisely to the employer's needs.

One of the disadvantages of the skill-based format is that generally it is more difficult and time-consuming to read. Additional words are provided in the skill-based format. For example, in the reverse chronological format the statement would be: Ordered and inventoried departmental supplies. In the functional skill-based format the statement may expand to: Reduced cost of supplies by 15% through design and implementation of computerized ordering system.

Combination

A combination of formats can be used effectively to present education, experience, skills, and accomplishments. By borrowing elements from one format, you can integrate them into the other. For example, by using the reverse chronological format, you can add certain abilities. Thus, both employment history and skills are incorporated. Another approach is to use the skill-based approach and to indicate the name of the employer next to each accomplishment. To illustrate:

Washington University Hospital

• Designed and produced a 30-page procedures manual for Outpatient Surgery Admitting Office.

The format you select will depend largely on your career objective, education, and experience. In Appendix C, sample resumes in various formats are included.

Creative

Using originality in designing your resume can have positive as well as negative results. There are always people who are intrigued when creativity is shown. The negative aspect occurs when creativity is in an area that is different than desired for the position. For example, if the employer is looking for someone who is conservative and your resume indicates free thinking, you may never secure the interview. Even a perception of being poorly suited for the corporate culture may keep you from being asked to interview.

Curriculum Vitae

Curriculum vitae is often referred to as a c.v. or as a vita. Literally, this Latin expression means "the course of life." Professionals in law, medicine, science, and persons in academic fields use curriculum vitae to refer to the document that blends chronological and functional resumes. An individual's c.v. will generally include universities attended, degrees earned, professional achievements, credentials/licenses, published works, organizational memberships, presentations, foreign travel, consulting, a listing of positions held in the area of specialization, community and professional service, grants applied for and amounts secured, research funding, honors, awards, and other information that documents scholarly background and achievements.

Personal Statement

A personal statement is used to introduce you to selection committees for grants, awards, and scholarships; admission offices for law school, residencies, and medical school; and program directors. At times, potential employers will request the personal statement along with the resume. A personal statement will describe the experiences and events that shaped your personality, values, and goals. With this document, the reader is better able to visualize you as an individual. Items generally included in a personal statement are listed in Figure 5-1.

Elements of a Good Resume

Having a winning resume is important. The primary purpose for the resume is to obtain a personal interview for the position that will start and/or advance your career. Corporations like IBM have received more than a million resumes in one year alone. Except for the name of the applicant and

Describe experiences and events that shaped your personality, values, and goals. These can include some or all of the following:

- Secondary/postsecondary and other school experiences.
- Personal experiences that influenced your life, developed important personality characteristics, and improved your skills.
- Work experiences that are significant for graduate school or other.
- Volunteer experiences that contributed to your development.
- Travel that broadened your background and developed skills.
- Languages other than English for which you have special skills in reading, speaking, or writing.
- Research experiences and the contribution of these to the development of knowledge, skills, and abilities in science, computers, or other.
- Honors and accomplishments.
- Hobbies, sports, or other interests that shaped your personality.
- Any significant events that shaped and molded you into a unique and motivated individual with specific goals.

Figure 5-1.   Experiences and Events for Personal Statement

schools attended, resumes generally look alike. Your task is to create a resume that makes an employer want to interview you. Your resume must convince others that you are the suitable person, and usually that means having the qualifications needed for the position. If you do not have them or you do not enjoy doing the skills required for the position, you probably should not apply for the job.

Elements of a good resume that will be covered here include content, order, accuracy, consistency, and appearance.

Content

Relate the content of the resume to the career objective. Delete and synthesize until the information is concise, focused, and easy to read. The information provided should be honest and should indicate your accomplishments without exaggeration. Basic headings should include objective, education, and experience.

Depending on your qualifications, one or more of the following additional headings with appropriate information may be incorporated into your resume: credentials, licensure, awards, achievements, professional affiliations or organizational memberships, honors, interests, volunteer experience, internships/practicums, computer proficiency, extracurricular activities, community service, special qualifications or training, military experience, civic activities, language skills, and other, such as seminars attended, presentations, and publications.

The heading listed last is "References" followed by the statement: "Available upon request" or "Portfolio and references available at interview or available upon request." Using this heading is optional. If you need space, exclude it. Later the employer can request this information.

Identifying Information

Most resumes will have five to seven headings. The first heading consists of your name, complete address (permanent and/or current), and telephone number or numbers if both home and office are included. These should be in bold or large font and pleasingly presented. Using your e-mail address is optional.

Being reachable by telephone is of utmost importance in obtaining a job and advancing your career. Be sure that the telephone number you provide will result in quick access to you. You should have an answering machine with a professional message on it that is monitored daily. When you are not answering the phone, be sure your messages can be accessed daily so that your rapid response can be made. A speedy response could be just what is needed to secure an interview.

Throughout your career, providing former instructors and professional contacts with your business card or telephone number can be extremely important. Frequently, recruiters telephone university and college instructors and others to inform them of exciting job opportunities. If your current telephone number is readily available to them, you could be informed of an opportunity without even conducting a job search.

Objective

A variety of headings can be used for the objective such as professional goal, career focus, career objective, job objective, career statement, skill summary, and position desired. You should decide which one best fits you and the position you are seeking.

There are three major components for the objective section:

1. A general or specific job title such as cancer registry abstractor, correspondence supervisor, quality improvement specialist, or office manager.
2. An occupational field, industry, or organization preference, for example, healthcare, marketing, education, human resource management, ambulatory care, or home health care.
3. Specification of competencies, skills, or the like.

Examples of objectives are provided in Figure 5-2.

---

1. Entry-level position in health information technology analyzing and managing clinical information.
2. An administration position in home health that incorporates knowledge of clinical medicine and computer software.
3. Health information administration position in a well-established ambulatory-care center.
4. Position with a healthcare agency that will enhance problem-solving and teamwork skills.
5. Reimbursement specialist position using knowledge of ICD-9-CM, CPT, and encoders.
6. Director of health information services.
7. Participation in facilitywide quality improvement activities.
8. Health information management position that applies skills in cost control, leadership, and quality improvement.
9. Coordinator of health information management for rehabilitation services.
10. Entry-level position using coding and reimbursement management skills.

Remember to make your objective statement focused on the company's needs and unique so that it captures a prospective employer's attention. The contents of the resume should support the objective.

Figure 5-2.   Objective Statement Examples for Resume

A recruiter (Ellie, 1997) has stated that, "Objective statements are usually written in such general terms that they are useless." Including a targeted professional objective near the top of your resume avoids generality and defines for the reader your career goal and/or expressed interest in a specific job or vacancy. One of the review questions, at the end of this chapter, provides an opportunity to develop a resume in two formats: one with the objective included and the other with it excluded.

Educational Information

This section should include degrees (spelled out in full) and majors, months and years of graduation, and names of your degree-granting colleges and universities. Overall grade-point average should be included if it is 3.3 or better on a 4.0 scale. The grade-point average for major courses can be included if 3.5 or above. Special graduation status, such as "summa cum laude" or "honors degree" may be indicated.

If related coursework is listed, limit this to no more than eight courses and never include course numbers.

Experience

Using "Professional Experience" or "Experience" as the header for this section carries a broader career perspective than "Work History" or "Employment History." The content of this section includes job title, employer, city and state of employer, from month and year to month and year of employment, and a brief description of the work using action verb phrases. This section is an important component of your resume and generally should include specific accomplishments that make your work special.

For those who have had no work experience, this section would include internships, volunteer service, and extracurricular activities. When listing the latter, prioritize the items beginning with those of greatest relevance to the position.

Additional Information

As specified earlier, this information will vary depending on your accomplishments and the status of your career. Having a special category called "Computer Skills" can be important to include for certain positions. Subheadings as needed could be Hardware, Peripherals, Software, and Programming Languages. Under each, be as specific as possible. To illustrate, under Software, one or all of the following could be included depending on your skills: WordPerfect, Microsoft Excel, Encoder, PCSDOS, Lotus 1-2-3, dBase IV, MS-DOS, LEVEL 5, Harvard Graphics, SoftMed, Microsoft Works, FlowCharting, Microsoft Word, and MedTech. When circulating your resume prior to writing the ART or RRA examination, you may include a statement in the education section or separately under the Credentials heading: "Eligible to apply to write ART/RRA examination."

Since foreign languages are increasingly important in today's global economy, if you have reading, writing, or speaking knowledge of other languages, in most cases it is good to list these and your level of proficiency: beginner, intermediate, or fluent.

References

Do not include details regarding references on your resume. At the bottom of your resume, if space permits, you can include a statement that references will be "available upon request." You should list your references on a separate page, which would be provided to the employer when requested. Be sure to include the following for each reference: name, title, organization, complete address, and telephone number. Permission to use the person as a reference should be attained prior to inclusion on your listing. Nonfamily members who have knowledge of your skills and abilities and who would give positive remarks regarding your accomplishments make the best references.

Order

When deciding the order for presenting information on your resume, follow these four simple rules:

1. Heading first.
2. Objective second.
3. Other headings prioritized and listed as related to the objective. For example, if your professional experience is limited, list education before work experience. If your major does not support your career objective, list experience before education.
4. Generally, the most recent information should be listed first, that is, follow the reverse chronological order. A master's in business administration (MBA) earned after the bachelor's in health information admin-

istration would be listed first. If you obtained a bachelor's in nursing, followed by an MBA, and then a bachelor's in health information administration, even though you are following the reverse chronological order, list the highest degree first, that is, the MBA, and then the two baccalaureates. This order will ensure notice of the master's degree.

Accuracy

On the resume you should strive to present your qualifications and accomplishments in the best possible light. However, falsifying any part of the information can be destructive. Employment dates and college degrees can be readily verified by employers. Overstating your qualifications and claiming proficiency in areas where you have little or no background can be detected by a capable interviewer. Deception should never be used.

Being correct also involves several technical areas. Those briefly covered here are spelling, incorrect words, acronyms, hyphenation, and abbreviations.

1. British spelling for words such as *towards, judgement,* and *centre* should be avoided.
2. A spelling checker may not detect use of the wrong word, for example, *their* for *there.* Be sure to read and reread the contents.
3. BASIC, COBOL, and FORTRAN are examples of acronyms that should be written in uppercase letters. Unfamiliar acronyms should be spelled out.
4. Words with prefixes such as co-, micro-, mid-, mini-, multi-, non-, pre-, re-, and sub- should not be hyphenated. Instead write: microcomputer, minicomputer, multicultural, etc.
5. Some abbreviations may need a period, others, such as DRG and CPT, are a set of uppercase letters without periods that you can pronounce as letters. Generally, abbreviations should be avoided.

In summary, use a dictionary, refer to a style manual, such as The AMA Style Guide for Business Writing (1996) mentioned in Chapter 4. After you have thoroughly reviewed your resume, have someone who is a good speller or proofreader critique the document. Taking these steps can help ensure accuracy and clarity.

Consistency

A mistake that occurs most frequently in the development of an entry-level resume is lack of consistency. Always check to make sure that words at the beginning of lists are parallel. If you start with a verb, continue with a verb:

- Developed and implemented a proposal . . .
- Designed a questionnaire . . .
- Researched the contents for a handbook . . .

An example of inconsistency is:

- Conducted conversations with customers regarding their degree of satisfaction with various products and services, while transcribing responses into computer terminal.
- Offering information to customers when necessary.

To be consistent, the last sentence should be changed to: Offered information to customers when necessary.

Consistency should also be followed for numbers, spacing, and punctuation, including the serial comma.

Appearance

A one-page resume is preferred; if you must, two pages in length is the maximum. If you use a two-page resume, avoid using a staple. However, be sure to include on the second page your name in the upper right corner. One page is advisable unless you have ten years or more of experience or are seeking a position in academia.

Content should be organized so that the page looks balanced and centered. Margins should be no less than an inch on all four sides. Quality paper should be used. If it is watermarked, make sure to use the right side, that is, as it faces you, the mark is readable. If it is the job you have always wanted, take the extra time needed to obtain a quality resume.

To achieve sharpness, use a laser printer. When selecting the font size, avoid Courier and Gothic. Helvetica and Roman contribute to readability. Allow adequate white space to avoid a cluttered, unfriendly look. Too little or too much white space can create wrong impressions. Be consistent in line spacing and avoid right-margin justification, which hinders readability.

Buzzwords

Action words can greatly enhance your resume. Avoid passive voice. For example, instead of "Had responsibility for training and controlling eighteen file clerks," write "Supervised and trained eighteen file clerks."

Keep a thesaurus by your side as you compose your resume to assist in locating the correct action verb to use. Haft (1995) lists power verbs by categories, that is, those that demonstrate:

- Leadership, decision making, or management skills.
- Administrative, organization, and follow-through skills.
- Communication skills.
- Analytical or research skills.
- Ability to create or innovate.
- Counseling, helping, or mediating skills.
- Ability to convince or sell.
- Some more useful power verbs.

Figure 5-3 contains an abbreviated list of action verbs that can add power to your resume and cover letters.

Blunders

To enhance your resume, avoid making blunders such as:

1. Neglecting to include a career objective. Your objective should be focused, unique, and interesting enough to capture the reader's attention.
2. Using redundant and flowery words, for example, "in the competitive healthcare jungle of survival of the fittest . . ." Summarize your qualifications and work experiences without repeating and exaggerating.
3. Including personal pronouns: I, me, my, mine. A rule of thumb is to eliminate these.
4. Presenting information poorly arranged, worded, or printed. Avoid using a dot matrix printer or photocopies for your resume or cover letter.
5. Including unnecessary information such as height, weight, names of references, marital status, age, religion, and number of children. Never incorporate a personal photograph.

These action verbs powerfully convey to prospective employers your achievements. The list is not inclusive, and as your career progresses, you will find other descriptive terms to enhance your resume and cover letter.

Accelerated	Decreased	Improved	Ordered	Reviewed
Accomplished	Defined	Improvised	Organized	Revised
Achieved	Delegated	Incorporated	Originated	Revitalized
Acquired	Demonstrated	Increased	Participated	Saved
Activated	Differentiated	Influenced	Performed	Scheduled
Adapted	Designated	Informed	Persuaded	Screened
Adjusted	Designed	Initiated	Pinpointed	Secured
Administered	Determined	Innovated	Planned	Selected
Allocated	Developed	Inspected	Prepared	Served
Analyzed	Devised	Installed	Presented	Set up
Appraised	Directed	Instituted	Processed	Simplified
Approved	Disseminated	Instructed	Produced	Solved
Arranged	Documented	Insured	Proficient in	Streamlined
Assembled	Edited	Integrated	Promoted	Structured
Assessed	Eliminated	Interpreted	Proposed	Suggested
Audited	Engineered	Interviewed	Proved	Supervised
Augmented	Enhanced	Introduced	Provided	Supported
Automated	Enlarged	Inventoried	Publicized	Synthesized
Budgeted	Encouraged	Launched	Purchased	Systemized
Calculated	Established	Led	Recommended	Taught
Collaborated	Estimated	Maintained	Reconciled	Trained
Compiled	Evaluated	Managed	Recruited	Transcribed
Completed	Examined	Maximized	Reduced	Transferred
Composed	Expanded	Measured	Regulated	Translated
Conceived	Expedited	Mediated	Reinforced	United
Conceptualized	Explained	Merged	Rejected	Updated
Conducted	Facilitated	Moderated	Reorganized	Upgraded
Consolidated	Forecasted	Modified	Reported	Utilized
Constructed	Formatted	Monitored	Repositioned	Validated
Contacted	Formulated	Motivated	Represented	Verified
Controlled	Generated	Moved	Researched	Volunteered
Coordinated	Hired	Negotiated	Restored	Won
Counseled	Identified	Observed	Restructured	Wrote
Created	Illustrated	Obtained	Retrieved	
Debugged	Implemented	Operated	Revamped	

Figure 5-3.   Action Verbs for Resume and Cover Letter

Development of a Winning Resume

Principles learned in English composition may not always be applicable to resume writing. The goal of resume writing is to make the resume readily understandable. Sentences should be short and concise. Power verbs such as those in Figure 5-3 project results, which is the key to a winning resume.

Begin the writing process by compiling your personal history inventory. Education is generally a good starting point because the details are easy to secure. High school education can be included when the institution has a reputation in the geographic location you are considering or when your class ranking, honors, or other achievements indicate special abilities even at this stage in your education.

The Independent Study Program of the American Health Information Management Association, a proprietary program, would be listed in the education section.

A worksheet, such as the one shown in Figure 5-4, can be used for each college and university attended. List information such as name of institution, location (city and state), dates of attendance, degree attained or number of hours completed, major, certificates, overall GPA and GPA for your major, honors, projects, papers, scholarships, and courses significant in relation to your career objective. The worksheets in Figure 5-4 will be of assistance as you compile your resume.

Next compile your experiences. By not using the heading "Work Experience," this section could include practicums, internships, and volunteer positions. If you prefer, you can have separate headings such as "Internships" and "Volunteer Experience." In developing the worksheet, include the following information:

- Name of employer.
- Address of employer (city and state is sufficient).
- Your job title.
- Dates of employment (month and year).
- Major accomplishments. If you were promoted, include a statement regarding this. Make note of any special recognition such as "Employee of the Month" or "Two-Year Service Award."
- Major responsibilities. Recall all functions. Review the action verb, asking yourself for each: What did I coordinate, revise, teach, and so forth? Record every task that comes to mind.
- Skills acquired and areas of growth and special achievement.

(Duplicate this worksheet to use for different positions.)

1. IDENTIFYING INFORMATION

Name (Include credentials such as RRA for Registered Record Administrator. Include degrees only if beyond bachelor's degree, that is, MBA, Ph.D., J.D.)

_____

Address (Use the one best for the prospective employer to reach you; be sure to include zip code.)

_____

Telephone Number _____

(Phone with answering machine that is monitored daily)

e-mail address _____

2. CAREER OBJECTIVE

OBJECTIVE (Broad) covering a variety of positions in a specific industry: _____

_____

_____

OBJECTIVE (Specific) for a particular position such as
Reimbursement Coordinator or Ambulatory-Care Information Officer.

Position _____

Objective _____

_____

Checklist:

– Is this worded to interest the employer in reading further?

– Does this indicate that I can contribute to the organization?

– Does my resume indicate that I have the skills needed?

3. EDUCATION

High School (Do not include this if you are more than five years out of high school, or if it will take too much space on the resume without adding significant accomplishments.)

Name of high school _____

City and state_____

Attended from Month _____ Year _____ to Month _____ Year _____

Graduated Month _____ Year _____ Grade-point average _____

Rank in class (if known) _____

Honors _____

Figure 5-4.   Resume Preparation Worksheet

Awards _____

Extracurricular achievements _____

Special accomplishments_____

If you attended more than one high school, usually the one from which you graduated is sufficient.

Name of college _____

City and state_____

Attended from Month _____ Year _____ to Month ____ Year _____

Graduated Month ____ Year ____ Grade-point average _____

(Include this on your resume only if 3.3 or higher on 4.0 scale.)

Special status, such as *cum laude* _____

Grade-point average for major courses _____ (Include this if 3.5 or above.)

Degree received (Write out completely, for example: Bachelor of Science in Health Information Administration.)

_____

Minor or Certificate _____

Honors, awards, scholarships _____

_____

_____

Course work related to position (List no more than eight courses and do not include course numbers.)

_____

_____

_____

_____

List additional colleges attended, providing the same information, especially if a degree was awarded or other achievements attained.

4. EXPERIENCE

4A. WORK

Position/job title _____

Name of employer _____

Dates employed   from Month _____ Year ____

                  to Month _____ Year ____

Figure 5-4.   *Continued*

Responsibilities (Use action words as provided in Figure 5-3.)

_____

_____

_____

(List first the responsibility that most relates to the job you are seeking.)

Repeat this information for each employer

4B. INTERNSHIPS/PRACTICUMS

Name of facility _____

Dates of experience from Month _____ Year _____ to Month _____ Year _____

Major activities _____

_____

_____

_____

(Repeat this for each site for which you were scheduled for at least forty hours or more.)

5. SKILLS

Skill acquired _____

_____

Way in which acquired (activity, project, hobby, organization, etc.)_____

(Although the way the skill was acquired may not be included on your resume, this informa-tion will be of assistance during the interview process as you provide evidence of the skill.)

Skill acquired _____

Way in which acquired_____

(Continue with this until you have identified five to ten of your major skills.)

6. ACCOMPLISHMENTS

(List five to ten of your major accomplishments using the action verbs provided in Figure 5-3.)

_____

_____

_____

_____

_____

Figure 5-4.   *Continued*

7. PROJECTS, PRESENTATIONS, PUBLICATIONS

(List major ones completed during college, in the work setting, as a volunteer, or other.)

_____

_____

_____

_____

8. ORGANIZATIONS

(List those for which you hold membership that relate to the job for which you are applying.)

_____

_____

_____

_____

9. EXTRACURRICULAR EXPERIENCES

_____

_____

_____

10. OTHER

(Depending on your background or qualifications, additional sections may be added such as: credentials, licensure, awards, interests, volunteer experience, community service, military experience, civic activities, or other.)

Make your own worksheets for references and include:

Name _____

Title _____

Organization _____

Phone Number (Use bold type) _____

Best time to reach_____

Employment address _____

_____

_____

Relationship to you_____

(Be sure to contact references before providing name to prospective employer.)

After you have compiled this information, decide on the resume format best for you.

Figure 5-4.   *Continued*

For those who have had teaching, military, or other specialized experiences, a worksheet that will collect dates, locations, and other related facts can be designed.

Other listings that will assist in preparing a winning resume are:

- Certifications and licenses.
- Awards and honors.
- Extracurricular activities.
- Memberships in organizations: student, professional, and other groups.
- Presentations.
- Publications in school or other newspapers; local, state, and national journals.
- Languages—spoken, read, or written.
- Special abilities and skills.

During your college years and subsequently as a professional, you should maintain on an ongoing basis a list of accomplishments. The listing can be helpful when you are seeking a change or advancement. Activities that may be overlooked are accomplishments such as the following:

- Allocated funds for Mu Rho Sigma Fraternity inner-city project.
- Coordinated seating arrangements for precommencement.
- Directed a team of five classmates in evaluating release of information practice for ambulatory-care facilities in the Chicago area.
- Managed a college logo business during junior year of college.
- Mediated conflicts for dormitory residents.
- Organized the distribution of refreshments to more than 5,000 cyclists.
- Responded to telephone inquiries regarding a career in health information management.
- Tutored fellow students in statistics.

Using worksheets and compiling information as mentioned will assist you in the development of a winning resume. Reviewing other resumes, consulting with instructors and career development specialists, and continually striving to improve your resume can result in a quality document. Your resume will be one that makes you proud. More importantly, it will secure an interview for you.

Software

Software is available as a guide in writing your resume and cover letter. Two programs are listed in "Additional Resources" at the end of this chapter. Resume software can assist you in finding the right words. Formats provided are both chronological and functional. You will need to adapt the program to fit the situation and position for which you are applying.

Home Page Resume

Creating a home page resume is a way of using more than the printed page to relay a message of your qualifications. By combining voice, video, text, and pictures, an employer can see and hear about your education and experience. A multimedia resume can be interactive by allowing the employer to manipulate the data available. Kennedy (1996) had reviewers evaluate software programs for developing home pages on the World Wide Web. They are listed at the end of this chapter. The reviewers' first choice was a Windows-based program, InContext Spider, which proved to be great for beginners and powerful for the price.

Multimedia for the resume has at least three disadvantages: (1) Employers are hesitant to know, prior to a hiring offer, too many details related to discrimination issues such as age, sex, race, and ethnic background. (2) Not every employer has the time or the necessary equipment for previewing multimedia. (3) Appearing before a camera is difficult for some people.

Applications

Some companies, hospitals, and healthcare agencies prefer that you apply in person and complete an application. When possible, have the application mailed ahead, type in the required information, add a cover letter, and attach your resume. You can then bring this to the human resource office in compliance with the "apply in person" requirement. Be sure to make a copy of the application in case you need the information in the future. Most applications request similar information.

Applications should be filled out completely and accurately. Persons listed as references should be former employers, instructors, practicum and internship supervisors, or others who are familiar with your knowledge, skills, and abilities. Do not use relatives as references. Be sure to list, as references, only those who have given you permission to do so. Obviously, you want to select persons who will provide you with a good reference.

When an organization requests an application, do not send just a resume if you want to be considered. Take the time needed to complete the application and to append a cover letter. Whenever possible, obtain the name of the person to whom you will report if hired for the position. At times, it is a good strategy to telephone the prospective supervisor and mention that you have completed an application and that it is on file in the human resource office. This helps to ensure that your file is not delayed on someone's desk. Applications and the cover letter were covered in detail in the previous chapter on professional correspondence.

Cover Letter

A well-written cover letter is brief yet focused, indicates you researched the organization, highlights your strengths, and secures the reader's attention enough for an interview. An unsolicited resume will most likely be discarded if not supplemented by a cover letter. Whenever you send a resume, a cover letter should accompany it. Cover letter preparation and samples are included in Chapter 4.

At times, the cover letter accompanying your resume is as important as the resume itself. Be sure to incorporate the same techniques for accuracy, consistency, and appearance as you did for your resume.

To make sure your letter and resume reach your prospective employer in a timely manner, you can decide if mail, fax, or hand delivery would be best. Make sure you use the same font for the letter as you have for your resume. Proofread for spelling and grammatical errors. Reread the letter; make sure you have addressed it correctly. Are the contents of the letter and resume related to the job you are seeking?

Having a matching envelope is not essential. Your envelope should be typed, not handwritten. A larger envelope makes your resume stand out from other letters. More importantly, the contents will remain flat and in better condition for photocopying.

Once your letters and resumes are mailed, it is time to prepare for follow-up calls. Allow at least five working days and up to fourteen before contacting the prospective employer. If you have not yet heard from the organization, then telephone. Ask if the company received your letter and resume.

Follow-Up Phone Call

Practice your telephone skills on a cassette recorder or your answering machine to hear how you sound and to assist in gaining confidence. Role-playing with a family member or classmate can be helpful also. Attach a mirror to the telephone to avoid negative expression and poor posture (Allen, 1992). By looking your business best, you will convey a confident, polished, professional image. Be careful in selecting the time you call. Avoid Mondays and lunch hours.

The script you follow might be similar to the following:

Secretary:	Good morning, Nancy Haynes' office.
You:	This is Linda Clark calling. May I speak to Ms. Haynes, please?
Secretary:	I am sorry, Ms. Haynes is in a meeting. May I take a message?
You:	Yes, please. Last week I forwarded to Ms. Haynes and the medical center's human resource recruiter a copy of my resume for the medical transcription supervisor position. I would like to check on the status of this position.
Secretary:	I will convey your message to Ms. Haynes. What is your telephone number and when is a good time to reach you?

After providing the information to the secretary, thank her and wait for the return call. If it does not come after an additional three to five days, repeat the process. In the next example, you have reached Ms. Haynes:

Ms. Haynes:	Good morning, Nancy Haynes speaking.
You:	Hello, Ms. Haynes. This is Linda Clark. Recently I mailed to you and to the medical center's recruiter a copy of my resume for the medical transcription supervisor position. Have you received it?
Ms. Haynes:	Yes, I have. Next week I plan to start scheduling interviews. However, since you are on the phone, would you like to schedule one now?
You:	I would be delighted. When is it convenient for you?

In another scenario, Ms. Haynes may delay you. If so, ask if it would be convenient for her if you telephone next week, or when would be a good time. Be sure to end the conversation with a "thank you."

If the employer calls you directly with an invitation for an interview, be prepared with a response by having practiced for this situation. For example:

You: Yes, Ms. Haynes, I would be delighted to interview for the position of transcription supervisor. What day and time is convenient for you?

Summary

- Start early in your college experience to develop a winning resume.
- The goal of resume writing is to secure a job interview. Your resume can be the means of opening the door to a personal interview.
- Uses for a resume are as a resource for:
    - Discussion during the interview.
    - The prospective employer to assess your qualifications for a specific position.
    - Enhancement of your self-confidence.
    - Self-marketing.
    - Admission to colleges and universities.
    - Promotion and salary increases.
    - An introduction to groups.
- The reverse chronological format is most widely used.
- Resume contents should relate to career objective. Be concise, focused, accurate, and easy to understand. Headings range from five to seven and include identifying information, objective, education, experience, and any special categories such as computer skills.
- The appearance of a resume is an important detail that can contribute to successful marketing of your skills and abilities.
- Weigh your choice of words. Select strong action verbs, also referred to as power verbs.
- Multimedia resumes have disadvantages. However, in some situations, they can be essential to achieve an interview.
- When completion of an application is requested, comply by typing the information accurately and neatly.

- The cover letter should emphasize why you are convinced you are qualified and why the prospective employer should consider you for the job.

Review Activities

1. Identify five uses for a resume.
2. Discuss which resume format is best for you and why.
3. Obtain a resume from a recent program graduate or a family member. Using the elements of a good resume discussed in this chapter, evaluate that resume, identifying major strengths and weaknesses.
4. Review the buzzwords provided in this chapter. Identify ten others that you think should be included.
5. Select an advertisement for a position vacancy from a current newspaper or professional journal. Develop your resume with a professional goal tailored to the position. Develop the same resume without a professional goal. Have your instructor or the career placement specialist evaluate these for you.

References

Allen, J. (1992). *The perfect follow-up method to get the job.* New York: John Wiley & Sons.

Asher, D. (1991). *The overnight resume.* Berkeley, CA: Ten Speed Press.

Biegeleisen, J. (1994). *Make your job interview a success: A guide for the career-minded job seeker*, 4th ed. New York: Prentice Hall.

Boy, B. (1987). *Women's job search strategy or how to keep the wolf away from the door.* Denver, CO: Arrowstar Publishing.

Breidenbach, M. (1989). *Career development/taking charge of your career.* Englewood Cliffs, NJ: Prentice Hall.

Chapman, E. (1988). *I got the job! Win a job your way.* Los Altos, CA: Crisp Publications.

Diggs, R. (1988). *Finding your ideal job.* Homosassa Springs, FL: Progressive Publications.

Ellie, P. (1997). Your Resume: A Checklist for Today's Trends. *Journal of AHIMA*, 68 (1), 24–28.

Ellison, L. (1995). *Saint Louis University employment guide: A placement manual series publication*. Evanston, IL: Cass Recruitment Publications.

Greenwood, R. (1994). *How to land your first job and make a success of it*. Pine Bluff, AR: Common Sense Publishing.

Haft, T. (1995). *Trashproof resumes: Your guide to cracking the job market*. New York: Random House.

Jackson, T., and Buckingham, B. (1994). *Power letter express*. New York: Random House.

Kennedy, J. (1996). Creating a Home Page Resume Without the Hassle. *St. Louis Post Dispatch*, 14 April, 21G.

Kennedy, J. (1995). *Hook up, get hired! The internet job search revolution*. New York: John Wiley & Sons.

Ludmer, A. (1997). Truth, Consequences and Your Resume: Falsifying Info Can Be Career Ending. *St. Louis Post Dispatch*, 22 January, 5E.

Ludmer, A. (1995). Cover Letter Helps to Cover Your Job Hunting Bets. *St. Louis Post Dispatch*, 25 October, 5F.

Noble, D.F. (1994). *Gallery of best resumes: A collection of quality resumes by professional resume writers*. Indianapolis: IN JIST Works.

Parker, Y. (1988). *The resume catalog: 200 damn good examples*. Berkeley, CA: Ten Speed Press.

Reed, J. (1995). *Resumes that get jobs*. New York: Macmillan.

Tyfsinger, J.W. (1994). *Resumes and personal statements for health professionals*. Tucson, AZ: Galen Press.

Weddle, P.D. (1995). *Electronic resumes for the new job market: Resumes that work for you 24 hours a day*. Manassas Park, VA: Impact Publications.

Weinstein, B. (1993). *Resumes don't get jobs: The realities and myths of job hunting*. New York: McGraw-Hill.

Additional Resources

Adams Resumes and Cover Letters. Adams Media Corporation: http://www.adamsonline.com.

HotMetaL by SoftQuad: 800/387-2777.

InContext Spider: 800/263-0127.

PageMill by Adobe: 800/833-6687.

WebAuthor by Quarterdeck: 310/309-3700 or http://www.quarterdeck.com/.

WinWay Resume. Available in disk or CD ROM: 800/494-6929.

Chapter 6

The Interview

Goals

After reading this chapter, you should be able to:

1. Describe the different types of interviews.
2. Explain the various settings used for interviews.
3. Identify the preparation prior to an interview.
4. Distinguish among at least five formats commonly used by interviewers.
5. Outline the sequence followed for an interview.
6. Discuss various strategies for an interview.
7. Explain techniques for achieving self-confidence on the interview day.
8. Categorize interview questions.
9. Discuss questions that apply to discrimination issues.
10. Formulate techniques for making a lasting impression.
11. Examine ways to negotiate to maximize benefits.
12. Relate important considerations for accepting the job offer.

Introduction

The interview is an opportunity to market yourself to a potential employer. After years of attending classes, participating in internships, and maybe working in part-time or full-time positions, you now have the opportunity to highlight your knowledge, skills, and accomplishments. Securing the right job can be an aggressive challenge. The first full-time position is crucial in setting the foundation for future positions and in determining earning potential.

Your prospective employer will, in most cases, receive several resumes. For some positions, as many as a hundred persons may be in the group of applicants. That you have been selected for an interview is an indication the employer liked what you had to offer as presented on your resume. Your resume indicated that you could be qualified for the position.

Most employers, in selecting candidates to interview, match the individual applicant's abilities with the employer's needs. The interview will be designed by the prospective employer to ascertain if you are competent for the position.

To ensure that your interview is exceptional and leaves a lasting impression, learn as much as possible about interviewing techniques, the employer, and the position. Developing your interviewing skills can result in an efficient and effective marketing of yourself.

Types of Interviews

Each interview is unique because of the time, circumstances, and personalities involved. *Webster's* defines interview as "a formal consultation to evaluate qualifications" (as of a prospective student or employee). Four types of interviews will be covered in this section. The *informational* interview is mainly for educational purposes. The three others are for employment purposes and are identified by their function as *screening*, *selection*, and *hiring*. These are outlined in Figure 6-1.

Informational Interview

The informational interview is mainly educational. For students and those who have been away from the job market, the informational interview is an opportunity to talk with a professional about the knowledge and skills needed for a specific position, to learn about the functions performed, and to determine if there are opportunities in this area. The informational interview is a way to assess what actually occurs on the job and to obtain background knowledge regarding a specific position.

When a professional agrees to meet with you to discuss the details of a position, do not abuse the opportunity by asking for a job. Your purpose

---

Informational: to network; educational exchange of information

Screening: to obtain facts; determine qualifications

Selection: to weed out undesirable candidates; pick the best candidates

Hiring: to finalize responsibilities; discuss benefits.

Figure 6-1. Types of Interviews and Purposes

during the informational interview is to secure information. If mention is made about anticipated vacancies, this may be an indication that you are considered a possible candidate for an existing or future opening. Appropriate follow-up can be pursued after you leave the interview. Generally, the informational interview is to enrich your background knowledge regarding a specific position and should be valued as such.

This type of interview is frequently incorporated into the final internship of your academic program of studies. You should prepare for this in the same manner as for an actual job interview.

To schedule an informational interview outside of the internship, you may write a letter or call an organization to determine if and when the person can see you. Frequently, student organizations will invite professionals to speak to an entire class on a particular facet of health information management, such as home health, ambulatory care, and managed care. Questions that are useful in gathering information are: What are the employment prospects? In what professional organizations do you hold membership? What does your typical day involve? What do you like best about your job?

A thank-you letter after the informational interview is essential. The informational interview can be important in preparing you for the screening, selection, and hiring interviews.

Screening Interview

Depending on the position for which you are applying, you may have several interviews before receiving a job offer. The screening interview is generally conducted by a trained interviewer and can take place on the telephone, in person, or by videotaping your responses to a recruiter's questions. The purpose of the screening interview is to ascertain that the information on the resume is accurate and to determine if the applicant has the qualifications for the position. The focus of this interview will be on your work history and motivation.

The screener generally does not have the power to hire; this is left to the selection interview process. However, the report made by the screener after the initial session could end aspirations for a second interview.

In talking with the screener, remember the following:

1. *Do not attempt to control the interview.* One of the reasons for allowing the interviewer to be in charge is time. The screening interview is relatively short—usually no more than thirty minutes. The recruiter/interviewer must use the time effectively to obtain answers to specific questions. The questions are structured to determine if you have the technical qualifications needed for the position. Your task has two aspects: proving that you have the qualifications while building rapport with the interviewer. When the recruiter has a special interest in marketing your skills, this can be a plus.

2. *Avoid volunteering facts.* This is the time to allow the recruiter to do most of the talking. You can indicate your interest in the position by asking a few questions of your own such as: What challenges would occur in this position? What three skills are most important for this position? By showing that you can handle the challenges and that you have the skills for the position, you are well on your way to securing an interview and subsequently the position.

3. *Respond in a straightforward and natural manner to each question asked.* Yes/no answers give no real information, so avoid such responses. Provide facts about your qualifications and abilities. Be brief, thorough, direct, and provide specific examples.

Selection Interview

In the selection interview your background, work experience, projects during internships, previous responsibilities, personality, leadership in organizations, and achievements are probed. Your ability to do the job and to fit into the organization are being evaluated.

Hiring Interview

The purpose of the hiring interview is to finalize the major responsibilities of the position. Also, the salary and other benefits that the employer will provide to you as an employee are specified. Salary, promotion, continuing education, insurance coverage, pensions, tuition remission/reimbursement, and the types of fringe benefits are among the topics covered. These details are discussed in the negotiations section of this chapter.

A specialist from human resources and the administrator or manager who has the authority to hire can both be involved in this type of interview.

Interview Settings

Among the different settings used for all or part of the interview are:

- One-on-one
- Panel/board/committee
- Meal
- All-day on-site

Equipment that may be use for all or part of the interview includes:

- Telephone
- Videoconferencing
- Computer-assisted videoconferencing

Before or sometime during the interview, you may be asked to take a test. Test taking and each of the above are described in more detail as follows.

One-on-One

Frequently, for entry-level positions, the one-on-one interview is used. Having identified on the resume your career objective and other pertinent information, both you and the interviewer already have insights on how your knowledge, skills, and abilities will fit the position. The interviewer will seek to expand on these to determine if you can contribute to the mission of the organization.

Among the persons you could meet with for the one-on-one interview would be the person to whom you would directly report, that person's supervisor, and possibly others with whom you would be associated. After the interview, comments will be compared and you may be asked to return for a second interview.

Panel/Board/Committee

Being interviewed by several individuals at one time is given various titles such as panel, board, or committee interview. This type of experience gives one a feel for the group dynamics and team spirit present in an organization. Prior to a panel interview, you may be given a problem-solving situation. For example, in interviewing for a position as information systems manager, you may be asked by the search committee to respond to the following scenario:

Our group practice is seeking to computerize the medical office management functions. Identify for us the basic elements and criteria that should be included in any software system that is purchased.

In another situation, you may be asked to respond to a management problem, such as what steps would you take for an employee who does not meet productivity standards or does not observe the confidentiality policies for patient information.

Meal

The meal interview can be combined with the one-on-one and/or panel interviews. A prospective employer may include a meal merely to facilitate scheduling an all-day interview. Or, the purpose of the meal may be to evaluate social skills. For positions that require solicitations of contracts, recruitment of physicians, or meetings with physicians and other committee members, the meal interview aids in assessing the applicant's qualifications. Even though the atmosphere is relaxed, the candidate should be professional in behavior, words, and eating habits. Among the caveats are:

Don't spend an inordinate amount of time deciding what to eat or drink.
Never smoke even if others do so.
Avoid being too personal in conversation.
Abstain from alcoholic beverages.
Don't introduce politics or religion.
Order something that is easy to eat and take your cues for ordering from the interviewer, that is, do not overorder or select the most expensive item.

Behavior during the meal can be an indicator of decision-making skills, assertiveness, and other characteristics.

All-Day on-Site

To allow ample time for you to ask questions and for the employer to determine how you would contribute to the various teams and goals of the organization, an all-day or possibly two-day on-site interview can be scheduled. Time is allowed so that the interviewee can meet various persons and monitor a variety of functions. Candidates for positions such as director of health information services, case manager, quality assessment coordinator, or oncology research specialist can expect to encounter this type of arrangement.

Telephone

The first oral contact with a potential employer may occur over the telephone. This may be a screening interview by the potential employer or by a recruiter, referred to by some as a "headhunter." For positions that require travel expenses, the employer may use a telephone interview to determine if an on-site interview should be scheduled. Preparation for a telephone contact is essential. Create an environment free from disturbances such as a dog barking or the television playing. Once you have sent a resume, the potential employer could telephone at any time. If and when the prospective employer calls, use the caller's surname, such as Ms. Jones or Mr. Harrington, unless instructed to do otherwise. Provide factual answers to the caller's questions. Ask questions that you have regarding the position, avoiding any that relate to salary and benefits. Make sure there is closure to the conversation, such as a job offer or an appointment for a face-to-face interview. As soon as feasible, document the conversation including notes on the person with whom you spoke; the date, time, and contents of the conversation; and how you can improve, as needed, for future similar encounters.

Videoconferencing

The videoconference adds another dimension to the telephone interview. This arrangement may be used for screening or selection. For busy managers, the video is convenient in that it can be viewed at unstructured times.

Some colleges are connecting graduates with employers through videoconferencing. A few tips to improve your performance include:

1. Project the best image through appropriate hairstyle, professional dress, and positive body language.
2. Avoid broad gestures and other mannerisms.

3. Prepare strategies for difficult questions. Several questions are listed later in this chapter for which answers could be prepared prior to the interview.

Computer-Assisted Videoconferences

This type of arrangement is not intended to replace the human encounter, but it can be used to screen out candidates. A series of multiple-choice questions or open-ended questions relating to employment history, background, and qualifications are asked. This type of arrangement assists the employer in developing probing questions for a subsequent face-to-face interview. There is a growing trend for employers to use PC-based videoconferences.

Test Taking

For positions such as coder, transcriptionist, reimbursement specialist, or coder/abstractor, a test may be administered to determine skills, knowledge of medical terminology and clinical medicine, and ability to use software and computer equipment. A one-on-one interview generally is scheduled when the results of the test taking are available.

Psychological tests that are administered for managerial positions are generally used for positions beyond entry level.

Preparation for an Interview

When the resume results in an employment interview, your preparation for this event will be an important step for your career. The interview affords an opportunity to highlight your many talents and abilities. Also, you need to show that you are interested enough in the organization to have done your homework. Prior to the interview, you should seek as much information as possible about the facility: its past history, current mission, products, management structure, and future plans.

Research

To obtain information on the employer, consult with previous instructors, clinical mentors, employees who work in the facility who are known to you or your friends, college placement employees, and contacts made at professional meetings that you attended as a student or graduate.

Articles in journals, newspapers, and magazines such as *For the Record* and *Advance* are valuable resources. The latest *American Hospital Association Guide* is a major source of information about hospitals, healthcare systems, healthcare organizations, agencies, and providers. The local public library may have on file documents such as chamber of commerce publications and annual reports. The latter may be requested from organizations as shown in the sample letter in Figure 4-1 (see Chapter 4).

If the interview has been arranged by a search firm, probing the recruiter for information on the organization is appropriate. The recruiter should be eager to supply details since the search firm's reputation is on the line in recommending you. Also, if this position is in a city or other location unfamiliar to you, seek to learn as much as you can about the people and community resources. This information could be helpful in determining if you want to interview and in deciding if the location is one where you would like to live and work.

Among the information that would be of assistance to you prior to the interview are facts about the organization (Figure 6-2) and those relating to the position (Figure 6-3).

When interviewing for a position, information important to know about an organization includes the following:

- Size: number of beds for a hospital, number of encounters for ambulatory care, and similar statistics for other facilities
- History
- Mission
- Services provided
- Competition
- Geographic locations of facilities
- Structure: viewing the organization chart
- Number of employees
- Accreditation status
- Culture: esprit de corps and management philosophy/style
- Promotional path
- Recent developments
- Future plans

Figure 6-2.   Organizational Data for Interview

When interviewing for a position, information important to know includes the following:

- Job title
- Reporting relationship
- Functional responsibilities
- Number of people you would supervise or who would be performing the same function
- Reason the position is available
- Length of time the position has been available
- Problems, challenges, objectives to be addressed
- Alumni from your college/university who are employed by the organization
- Turnover rate in the department or work area
- Advancement opportunities
- Continuing education policy

Figure 6-3.   Position Data

Research will assist in giving focus to your interview strategy, in making a professional presentation, and in conveying your readiness for the position. When a job offer is made, you will be able to make an informed decision.

Strengths and Job Functions

Prior to the interview, it is helpful to list your strengths and compare them with the position that you are seeking. Identifying your own competencies will increase your confidence and give focus to how you will fit into the organization and the job. Figure 6-4 will assist you in brainstorming a list of your personal knowledge, skills, and abilities and in applying these for a job comparison. Many of your competencies have already been identified through college courses, practicums/internships and, for some, through either part-time or full-time work experiences. After an interview, the worksheet in Figure 6-4 could be updated to include additional information learned about the job functions. To save time, the Personal Strengths column could be completed only once, and the Job Requirements column could be shingled (arranged in a series of overlapping columns) as completed for each potential job to provide an overview for comparisons.

By completing the worksheet in Figure 6-4, you are already thinking about how your knowledge, skills, and abilities fit into the job you are seeking. The worksheet is a tool to assist you in preparing for a successful interview and, ultimately, in making an informed job choice. When the prospective employer asks you, "How have your education and experiences prepared you for the responsibilities of the position?" you will have done your homework and can answer completely and confidently.

Role-Playing

There are several ways of seeing yourself as others will see you at the interview. A dry run can be accomplished by rehearsing for the interview once or several times with one or more of the following:

- A classmate, parent, or friend
- An employed graduate
- An instructor or a human resources professional

Role-playing can be doubly beneficial if you take the role of the interviewee and later of interviewer. In that way, you can experience asking and answering questions. By adding the dimension of videotaping to a session or two, you can later review your behavior for body language, enthusiasm, eye contact, presentation style, nervous gestures, and appropriateness of comments. A good posture will indicate that you are alert and poised. Eye contact conveys a sense of self-confidence and honesty. Stroking hair or other nervous gestures are a distraction and keep the listener from hearing what you are saying. Work at avoiding these gestures. Later in this chapter, questions are provided. Use these for practice to facilitate a successful interview.

Through role-playing, you can refine your listening skills, eliminate unwanted gestures, practice speaking concisely with enthusiasm, and determine if your responses to questions are complete and accurate.

Logistics

You may have heard the song "Get Me to the Church on Time." Logistics involve all the actions you need to take to make sure you arrive at the interview on time, in good condition, and as relaxed as possible.

The Personal Strengths (PS) column contains specified knowledge, skills, and abilities (KSAs). This column should be completed each time your qualifications change and you acquire additional knowledge, new skills, and abilities. The Job Requirements (JR) column is to be completed for each job for which you have applied and continue to be a candidate for employment.

The procedure for completing this assessment is as follows:

1. For each knowledge/skill/ability line item, enter a checkmark if the item is one of your strengths. If not, enter "No." The "no" is merely to let you know you did not overlook the item and that it definitely is not a strength.

2. After applying for a position for which you are truly interested, complete the Job Requirements section by placing a checkmark on the line corresponding to the knowledge, skill, and ability. As you learn more about the responsibilities for the position, the Job Requirements section should be updated by adding additional checkmarks.

   This assessment can be a resource in deciding that you are qualified for the position and the extent that your knowledge, skills, and abilities are applicable to the position. If you are a candidate for several positions, you can do a comparison among the job responsibilities for various positions.

3. The total can be used in at least two ways:

   (A) As an added total. For example, if you have 10 KSAs checked in the PS column and the job requirements total 5, you can readily see that your skills are not being used. As mentioned elsewhere in the book, one of the differences between a job and a career is that in a career your knowledge, skills, and abilities are used.

   (B) By calculating a percentage. Take the total KSAs (10) and divide by the JRs (5), with a result of 2. In contrast, another job for which you are a candidate might have a JR total of 12 (10 ÷ 12), which would equal .83. In the first instance, you would be overqualified for the position. The second position would require more of you than your identified strengths. If you are looking for something that would challenge your abilities, you would go with the 10:12 ratio. On the other hand, if you are not seeking to be challenged for your first position, you may consider the 10:5 ratio.

Figure 6-4. Assessment of Personal Strengths and Job Requirements

Knowledge/Skills/Abilities (KSAs)	Personal Strengths (PS)	Job Requirements (JR)
Accounting	_____	_____
Clinical Medicine	_____	_____
Coding	_____	_____
ICD-9-CM; CPT	_____	_____
Computer Hardware	_____	_____
Computer Software	_____	_____
Word Processing	_____	_____
DBase/Excel/Other	_____	_____
Spreadsheets	_____	_____
Information Systems	_____	_____
Quality Improvement Techniques	_____	_____
Release of Information	_____	_____
Research	_____	_____
Statistics	_____	_____
Tumor/Trauma Registry	_____	_____
Managing People	_____	_____
Presentations/Speaking	_____	_____
Problem Solving	_____	_____
Team Building	_____	_____
Writing	_____	_____
Total	_____	_____

Figure 6-4. *Continued*

Arriving on time can involve knowing the exact location of the interview, having reliable transportation, allowing ample travel time, and avoiding traffic jams or other unwanted events. If you are meeting someone who will take you to your interview, be sure you have the right time and place.

Several books have been written about proper attire for an interview. Figure 6-5 lists suggestions.

For Men	
Suit	Navy blue or gray; conservative style
	For certain entry-level positions, a sport jacket may be appropriate to avoid overdressing
Shirt	White dress or solid color
Tie	Simple pattern
Shoes	Black and well shined, or in harmony with your attire
Socks	Solid colors, never white; high enough so skin is not visible when you sit
Belt	No oversized belt or buckle
Hair	Well groomed, neatly trimmed
Jewelry	Refrain from wearing earrings
For Women	
Suit or blazer with skirt, or dress with jacket	Navy, gray, or subdued colors
Blouse	Avoid low-cuts
Accessories	Avoid oversized earrings and wearing several rings or bracelets
Hose	Free from runs (take an extra pair in your attaché for an emergency)
Handbag	Use an attaché instead of a purse to add stature and show preparedness
Hair	Neatly trimmed
Makeup	Light
Shoes	Polished, low-heeled, professional

Figure 6-5. Appropriate Dress for the Interview

More relaxed dress codes are allowed in certain settings. To be on the safe side, dress neatly and conservatively. A green sport jacket will leave an impression quite different from a gray suit.

Good grooming should eliminate any unwanted body odors. If aftershave or perfume is worn, apply lightly so that the smell does not overpower the interviewer or linger in the room after you have left. Avoid garlic, onions, and alcohol to ensure your breath is not offensive.

Dressing for success can differ by geographic location, position, organization, and personalities. Impressions based on hairstyle or shoes may seem immature. However, you should be aware that personal judgments may be influenced by these things. By dressing professionally for the situation, you can eliminate being rejected for reasons other than competence (see Figure 6-6).

Figure 6-6. The Look of Success

Formats Used

There are at least five different formats commonly used by interviewers: direct, nondirect, stress, problem solving, and question–answer–question.

Direct

Human resources specialists during the screening interview will use the direct style by following a definite pattern in the questions asked. Working from an outline, specific questions are asked and a definite time frame is followed. Checklists are frequently used with notations made when needed. Since this format is structured and impersonal, it is rarely used for the selection interview.

Nondirect

The loosely structured format of the nondirect interview is the format used to bring out an interviewee's personality. Questions are general and allow the candidate to take control.

Stress

To the new graduate, every employment interview may seem like a stress interview. By being prepared, stress can be alleviated. The formal stress interview is one in which the interviewer deliberately applies stress in some way: through questioning, scheduling, seating, staring, or other techniques. Examples of each are as follows:

• *Questioning:* "Did you have any C, D, or F grades during your college experience? Comment on each and explain why such occurred." If this is asked of you, your statement may be: "This occurred once for a nonmajor course," or "The 'D' grade was repeated and raised to an 'A'." Be brief and honest.

• *Scheduling:* If you are to meet with another person, the interviewer could make your next appointment at a distance and not provide transportation or directions for the appointment. The intention would be to observe your problem-solving skills or observe how assertive you can be when faced with a perplexing situation. This type of situation can tell you a great deal about the organization. You can elect to solve the problem, or you may decide that this is not the place for you.

- *Seating:* The interviewer places you in an uncomfortable position, near a fan, in the sun, or on a crooked chair and then observes your reaction. Your first step is to recognize that you are in an awkward position. Once you realize this, it is easier to be calm and to either accept the situation or change it. Do what comes naturally, that is, follow your instincts.

- *Staring:* The interviewer does nothing but sit and stare at the interviewee. By being relaxed and composed in such a situation you indicate that you are able to deal with the unexpected.

James E. Challenger (1996), in an article relating to the stress interview, suggests that, "The job candidate should respond to all questions at the same pace throughout the interview." Fluctuations in responses can be seen as a sign of frustration or lack of confidence.

The stress format usually is combined with other styles and, though it seems insensitive, the interviewer is assessing your personality traits and your ability to deal with the unexpected. By maintaining a professional conduct, if and when deliberate stress is introduced, you will confound the situation.

Problem Solving

The interviewer may present you with a real management problem or a hypothetical situation and ask you how you would solve it. For example, the interviewer might ask: "If you were a member of our quality improvement team and learned that laboratory reports were not being posted in the ambulatory patient records in a timely manner, how would you handle this problem?" In responding to problem-solving questions remember to:

- Listen and restate the question to make sure you understand it correctly.

- Respond after considering problem identification and problem analysis.

- Discuss techniques such as cause and effect that will assist in solving this problem.

- Conclude by explaining how you would make an appropriate decision or recommendation based on the technique used.

Listening skills are enhanced when you are not preoccupied with your own ideas and complete attention is given to the interviewer. By keeping an open mind and not jumping to conclusions, a logical and analytical process can be followed. In problem-solving situations, you are provided with an opportunity to apply information acquired through college courses, readings, and practicums. This type of interview format allows you to showcase your knowledge.

Question–Answer–Question

Rather than a question–answer format, using a question–answer–question format is of value to both you and the interviewer. For example, if the interviewer says, "Tell me about a time when you experienced pressure or stress," after giving your answer, you can ask, "Would you tell me about some of the pressure that I could expect to have in the position of assistant manager?"

This type of format is good for self-esteem and for obtaining the information you will need to decide if this is the job for you. This format need not be followed throughout the interview. Certain questions after an answer can naturally elicit a related question from the interviewee.

Sequence

Although no two interviews are alike, there is a typical order that is usually followed:

1. *Greeting and introduction:* Articles have been written about the firm handshake and the importance of a smile. Both of these assist in establishing a good first impression. A professional introduction followed by some small talk can help to develop rapport between you and the interviewer. If this is the first person you are meeting, the interviewer should provide an overview of your schedule or how you can expect the interview to proceed.

2. *Describing the position:* The interviewer may briefly describe the position and how it fits into the total organizational picture.

3. *Answering the interviewer's questions:* This is the heart of the interview. During this time, you will be doing most of the talking and the interviewer will be listening. Be sure to listen to the questions asked and answer appropriately. It is your opportunity to market your skills as they relate to the position.

4. *Asking the interviewer questions:* Always ask the interviewer questions to show you have done your homework. You should have three to five good questions that will indicate your genuine interest in the position and the organization.

5. *Closing:* The final person with whom you meet should provide information such as if any testing is to occur, when you will be notified of a second interview, or your status in regard to the position. You should thank the interviewer. Be sure to end the session with another firm handshake and a friendly smile.

Strategies for an Interview

By developing a plan that is followed, chances of success are greatly increased. The strategy you take can be derived from your strengths and from the data you have on the employer's needs. For example, when an HIM graduate applied for a position with a local home health agency, the employer's need was for someone who could implement a computerized information system. Several nurses applied for the position. The health information management graduate knew that, like the nurses, she had clinical skills. Some of the nurses through work experience and college courses had mastered using the computer and various software systems. What they did not have was knowledge of Joint Commission information management standards, quality improvement techniques, and classification systems, especially ICD-9-CM. The HIM graduate emphasized throughout the interview the variety of skills and abilities that would be brought to the position. This strategy resulted in an exciting job offer: quality assessment coordinator. Now, working with a team of nurses, the HIM graduate is implementing a computerized patient record and preparing the home health agency for the on-site accreditation visit of the Joint Commission on Accreditation of Healthcare Organizations.

A variety of strategies is presented in the current literature. The perfect candidate strategy can be applied if you determine before and during the interview what factors are most important to the position. Throughout the interview you structure your comments and questions to prove that you are the perfect person the employer wants. Your questions can be as important as the answers you give to the interviewer's questions.

If the employer is searching for someone to "do better" than a previous employee, you will need to frame your skills and abilities to show that you are best for the position. Also, when the reputation of your college or program is well recognized, this should be emphasized, especially if the previous employee was from another college.

In some situations, rather than focusing on current job performance, your strategy may be to take the organization and the job into the future. In this situation, you would outline the ways you can impact on the position and advance it into the twenty-first century.

By considering various strategies and selecting one for the situation, you can put more control into the interview process. Your strategy should reinforce your strengths in relation to the employer's needs.

Self-Confidence on the Interview Day

Completion of your studies in health information technology, administration, systems management, or the like, means you have the competencies needed for an entry-level position. You are ready for the job market. The task is finding the right position for your unique talents.

Being poised and professional throughout the interview stems in part from preparation. By practicing in front of a mirror, on videotape, and with others, or by answering potential questions on a tape recorder and playing them back, you can facilitate having a successful interview (see Figure 6-7).

To relax and minimize nervousness, practice breathing techniques, walking, or other stress relievers to prepare your mind. If tennis players can succeed by saying "hit" each time the ball approaches the racket, you can succeed by focusing not on what's wrong but on accomplishments. Devise your own positive self-talk, for example: "Winner," "Great," "The brightest and the best," "They don't come any better." Or, silently applaud yourself when you have answered well. Paula Spencer, in an article on self-confidence in *Woman's Day*, discusses several techniques that people recommend or use to build self-confidence such as:

- Remind yourself it is normal to be nervous.
- Counter negative thoughts with positive ones.
- Visualize how you will handle various situations.
- Trust your credentials.
- Act confident.

Consider your successes over the years, which can include grades for certain courses, projects you have completed alone or as part of a group,

Figure 6-7. Be Prepared for the Interview

presentations you have made, or organizations where you have served as an officer or a committee chair. As you think about your accomplishments, you can gain confidence and thereby project with confidence and assurance that you are a worthwhile and valuable person.

Spend time before the interview envisioning yourself succeeding during the interview. Focus on as many details as you can: walking into the office with assurance, selecting the chair, and listening to the interviewer asking you questions. Practice answering these aloud. You can record and play them later to determine that your responses:

- Were positive.
- Indicated knowledge of the company/organization.
- Conveyed your qualifications and abilities.
- Provided concrete proof through specific examples that you have the skills the employer needs.

The four P's to improve self-confidence are preparation, practice, a positive attitude, and pondering on your past successes.

Interview Questions

Books, chapters, and articles have been written about the most common interview questions. Questions you may be asked are categorized as questions related to the organization, background questions, personal strength questions, and unique and special questions. The questions provided in this chapter are a sample to assist you in preparing for the interview. Each one of the questions could be phrased differently or other questions not included could be asked. Although education and past experience will be important for the job interview, your knowledge of the organization and the job for which you are a candidate are critical to providing successful answers.

Questions Related to the Organization

By learning as much as you can about the prospective employer, you will gain confidence in yourself and in your motivation to work for the organization. Figure 6-8 includes typical questions to determine if the interviewee is an informed candidate regarding the organization.

---

1. Why would you like to work for this hospital, agency, company?
2. What do you know about our organization?
3. What type of work environment do you find stimulating and motivating?
4. Describe what you consider the ideal work environment.
5. What do you surmise to be the major problem that would be facing this organization right now?
6. What do you consider would be the worst and the best thing about working for this organization?
7. What changes do you see occurring in this organization in the next five years?
8. How does the position you are applying for relate to what you perceive as the mission of this organization?
9. What type of person do you think will succeed with this organization?
10. Name two ways our organization will benefit by hiring you.
11. What makes working for us different (or special) from working for others?
12. If hired, where do you envision yourself in this organization in three years? In five years?

Figure 6-8. Questions Related to the Organization

Job-Related Questions

The interviewer will generally ask several questions regarding the skills needed to perform a specific job. If you are being considered for a job with a copying service, you should not expect to have questions relating to your skills with ICD-9 or CPT. However, if this is a full-service company that provides a variety of services, you can anticipate that the interviewer will ask questions relating to several job functions.

Depending on the job, you could be asked such questions as: How do you feel about working overtime? about travel? about relocating? about flextime scheduling?

The questions in Figure 6-9 are generic questions that relate to the company you would like to work for and questions that can be used for a variety of positions relating to health information systems and management.

---

1. What competencies do you think this position requires?
2. What makes you sure that you can do this job?
3. What would you consider to be the most difficult aspect of this job?
4. What would you identify as the major problems that your team leader/supervisor/manager encounters?
5. How would you describe your work/management philosophy?
6. What values would you bring to this position?
7. How do you establish work priorities?
8. What would you do to establish a good working relationship with those with whom you will associate?
9. How would you handle a conflict with a staff physician?
10. What aspect of this job do you like most? least?
11. What deficits do you bring to this job?
12. What changes do you anticipate will occur in this job in the next five years?
13. Why are you the right person for this job?
14. If you were hired for this job, how long would you plan to stay with us?
15. What makes you different from others who want this job?
16. Describe the ideal supervisor/administrator.
17. What is your strongest technical skill that you would apply to this position?

Figure 6-9. Job-Related Questions

Background Questions

Questions that relate to you, your academic and past work experiences, significant accomplishments, mistakes, interests, and hobbies are listed as background questions in Figure 6.10. A thorough review of your resume will help you see areas that could elicit background questions. If there are unaccounted periods of time, the interviewer will probably ask you to explain these. If you have had previous employment, questions can be asked such as why you left, what you liked or disliked about your supervisor, how you met deadlines, and other work-related questions.

1. Describe your educational background.
2. Did you change from another major, and if so, why?
3. Why did you choose your college (or an independent study program)?
4. What courses prepared you specifically for this job?
5. Who was your favorite teacher and why?
6. What was your most significant achievement in your program of studies?
7. Describe any past work experiences, part-time or full-time, that you may have had.
8. What mistakes have you regretted making?
9. Have you ever quit a position without giving due notice?
10. Name a book that you read in the last two months.
11. Name the organizations in which you are a member.
12. What do you like to do during vacations?
13. What foreign languages do you speak or write? Describe your degree of proficiency.
14. Describe what you did when you last volunteered for an organizational event or to head up a committee or project.
15. Give me an example or two of public speaking events in which you participated.
16. What are your hobbies?
17. Have you brought with you samples of projects or assignments that I might review? If not, tell me about the project that you enjoyed the most.

Figure 6-10.   Background Questions

Personal Strength Questions

Throughout the interview, you want to look for and create opportunities to advance your personal strengths. If your cumulative grade-point average is 2.78, you do not want to answer a question about your class ranking with a grade-point average. Instead you could inform the interviewer about courses in which you did outstanding work or about a special project at work or school that was recognized as excellent. Questions that the interviewer could ask relating to your personal strengths are in Figure 6-11.

1. What was your favorite course in college and why?

2. What do you consider to be your major strengths?

3. What is your major weakness?

4. How do you react to criticism, especially if it is undeserved?

5. What is your greatest accomplishment?

6. What is your most creative accomplishment?

7. Describe two risks that you have taken in the last year.

8. Do you prefer working as a member of a team, working alone, or being the leader of a group?

9. How would you describe success?

10. What new skills have you developed recently?

11. Describe honors and/or awards you have received.

12. What makes you unique?

13. What was the biggest challenge you ever faced and how did you handle it?

14. Have you considered advanced education and, if so, what type of studies would you prefer?

15. Discuss your career goals.

Figure 6-11. Personal Strength Questions

Unique and Special Questions

The category of unique and special questions is endless. A few typical ones are included in Figure 6-12. Each interviewer has a favorite question or two that he or she has found to be successful. The questions asked are generally determined by the type of interview, the position the candidate is seeking, the responsibilities involved, and the educational and work background of the candidate. Open-ended questions are preferred in that they allow for personal reflections. With more graduates seeking health information positions in a variety of agencies and organizations, a common

1. What are your major weaknesses?
2. Tell me about a situation in which you had considerable pressure and how you handled it.
3. What are some of the conditions you consider to be important in a job?
4. In one sentence tell me who you are.
5. How long do you plan to stay with us if you obtain this job?
6. How long do you think it will take you to become proficient at this job if it were offered to you?
7. What is the worst thing an employer or teacher has said about you?
8. What salary would you require to take this position?
9. Explain a situation in which you were criticized and how you handled it.
10. Have you ever failed?
11. Describe your management style.
12. When you are supervising people, how can you motivate them?
13. How would you handle office gossip?
14. What kind of people do you dislike the most?
15. Describe your attitude toward taking risks.
16. Describe how creativity would relate to this position.
17. What kind of decisions are most difficult for you?

Figure 6-12. Unique and Special Questions

question asked is: What is health information management? or What is health information administration? Be sure to have an answer.

Practice answering a variety of questions by using a tape recorder, role-playing with a friend or family member, or putting the answers on your computer and then reviewing them at free times prior to an interview. This will add to your confidence during an interview.

Discrimination Issues

No knowledgeable interviewer will deliberately ask questions that are discriminatory in nature. Unknowingly, however, questions that are not job related can occur. The question, "Do you own an automobile?" for most positions should not be asked because it is not job related. However, if you are seeking a position as an area manager for a company, this may be important for the job.

Some questions may not be illegal but may be inappropriate or unethical. A question like "Were you ever known by another name?" is appropriate in order for the prospective employer to check references. "What was your maiden name?" would be an unacceptable way of phrasing a question. Maiden name is not relevant to a person's ability to perform a job. Also, the maiden name could be used for a discriminatory purpose as an indication of national origin or religion. "Are you a U.S. citizen?" is legal under the Immigration Reform and Control Act of 1986, which requires evidence of citizenship.

Most antidiscrimination laws make it illegal to ask the applicant's age during the interview. After you are hired, your age may be asked for affirmative action and fringe benefit purposes. Employers that have adopted policies regarding smoking will inquire if you smoke and this is appropriate. Being asked if you have been arrested is not the same as being asked if you were convicted of a crime. The latter could be elicited but not the former.

If you are asked questions regarding marital status, age, race, religious preference, children, sexual orientation, or other that are not job related, avoid being rude, argumentative, or emotional. Be polite and professional in your response. You could tactfully end the interview or ask the interviewer how that question is job related. When questions cause you concern about their propriety, you can decide if you really want to work for this organization.

Techniques for Lasting Impressions

Your appearance can make a good first impression. Your clothing, posture, and initial greeting are important. When you first meet the interviewer, you should smile, make eye contact, offer a firm but gentle handshake, and be sure to call the interviewer by name. Do not use the first name unless directed to do so. Although nonverbal communication makes up more than half of the total message, the way we talk contributes also to the total communication. This includes tone, speed, pitch, and the volume of the voice. By role-playing, using a video camera or cassette, you can assess and improve upon your voice, your gesturing, whether you move too much or too little, and the posturing of your body.

Your actual words, that is, what you say, count for only a portion of the total message. Negative body language is any action that excludes the interviewer (see Figure 6-13). Actions that show lack of interest, such as glancing around the room, looking out the window, and crossing and uncrossing your legs, may cause the interviewer to lose interest in you.

The active listener style conveys an interest in the interviewer through actions and words. To be an active listener you will have good eye contact, proper posture, and demonstrate an understanding of the interviewer's remarks and concerns by paraphrasing them. When you paraphrase you show that you have listened, that what the person is saying is important to

Figure 6-13. Body Language Is Important

1. Can you tell me why this position is open?
2. How is successful performance rewarded?
3. What career progression do you see for someone in this position?
4. Do you encourage participation in community or professional activities?
5. Does this organization operate in a centralized or decentralized manner?
6. How does this position fit into the organization's mission?
7. What are some of the most difficult problems that I would face in this position?
8. As a department head, how many people will I supervise? How long has each one been with the organization?
9. Are other applicants being considered for this position?
10. What is the management/operating style of the company?
11. To whom will I be directly accountable?
12. Will there be opportunities for greater responsibility and broader experience?

Figure 6-14.   Questions Asked by the Job Candidate

you. Through active listening you can demonstrate the confidence you have in yourself and your interest in assisting the company to achieve its goals.

An interview should be a pleasant experience. A lasting impression can be achieved by having a positive attitude. If you think you will win, you will probably win. You can contribute to the success of the interview by asking intelligent questions confidently and resourcefully. Figure 6-14 contains questions that can be used depending on the circumstances. These questions are useful when they build a working relationship between you and the interviewer and help you assess if this is the job for you.

Answering the Interviewer's Questions

Listening to and answering questions appropriately and professionally can be persuasive. There are no answers that are guaranteed to secure the job for you. Having the right answer will depend on the culture of the organization, the management style of the interviewer, and the type of person needed to do the job.

Eliminate from your interview the following:

- Telling jokes.
- Introducing religion or political beliefs.
- Asking questions that show little interest in work, such as the length of the coffee breaks, the size of the office, the number of vacation days. The latter can be negotiated when you are offered the position.

The following five scenarios should help you in answering some common questions.

- *Scenario 1.* Not all interviewers are trained to conduct an interview. Some interviewers may confuse you by the questions they ask. When you are not sure of the question, repeat it in terms that you understand. If you have not heard correctly, this provides an opportunity for the interviewer to restate or clarify the question. For example:

Interviewer: What attributes will you bring to this position?

Interviewee: May I start by identifying the skills and personal characteristics that I would bring to this position?

Interviewer: Yes, that is exactly what I had in mind.

- *Scenario 2.* You have just finished identifying your strengths and the next question is:

Interviewer: What are your weaknesses? (variations to this basic question are: What don't you do well? or What are your vulnerable areas?)

If you answer with negative statements about yourself, or criticize a former boss, it may remove you from consideration. In answering "What are your weaknesses?" emphasize your accomplishments and do not bring up any negatives.

Interviewee: I have an inquiring mind, which my past employer (or my instructors) saw as a strength. I am eager to learn and to find solutions to problems.

If the interviewer allows time, follow up by identifying one special problem that you solved.

• *Scenario 3.* When the interviewer asks, "Why do you want to work for our company?" do not respond with: "I hear you have the highest salaries." Instead this is your opportunity to show that you have researched the company.

Your response could be: "I heard that you are implementing an electronic patient record and I would like to be involved." Another possible response might be: "Your director of health information services spoke to our class on the new optical disk system that you have. I was impressed with her and with her keen interest in technology."

• *Scenario 4.* When the interviewer asks, "Have you applied for other positions?" you want to be honest without disclosing the name of the company to which you have applied. Your response could be: "Yes, other companies are interested in me. However, your position is at the top of my list," or, "This position is of special interest to me because coding is one of my strongest skills."

• *Scenario 5.* One of the most common questions asked is, "Tell me about yourself." Be sure to have your speech ready. Focus on:

Key accomplishments.

Major strengths demonstrated by your accomplishments.

The value of your strengths and accomplishments to the prospective employer.

How you see yourself developing in the position.

When the questioning is finished, if you feel you have the qualifications and would like to work for this company, let the interviewer know that you want the job. "My qualifications indicate that I could be of assistance to your organization in promoting appropriate uses of technology to achieve the company's mission. I would like the job with this company."

Negotiations to Maximize Benefits

Generally, the higher up the ladder you climb in any organization, the more benefits you can expect. This section will cover two items: salary and the benefit package.

Salary

During your college experience you have heard from your instructors and from career planning professionals regarding the entry-level salary for graduates. Those who have had work experience that was achieved before college, during their college years, or afterward can assess the value of this information and thereby determine an acceptable salary beyond entry level. Every salary is negotiable, but the extent will depend on the range allowed for the position, your qualifications, and the supply and demand in the community. Information management is one of the most important functions needed by any organization. The breadth of skills possessed by those educated in health information technology and health information administration programs should provide leverage for most positions.

There are three important "nevers" connected with salary:

1. Never bring it up yourself. Leave the subject to the interviewer.
2. Never rush to accept the first salary offer even if it is more than you expected.
3. Never present a requirement that you are not going to observe. That is, do not say you will not work for less than $30,000 if you will take the job when offered $27,500.

In salary negotiations it is better to secure information rather than give it. Have the company's representative make the offer. This person should know what the position is worth. If you are asked how much you want, you can reply that you want the job and would like to work for the company, but you need to know what the company pays for employees in similar positions. "What is the salary range being considered for this position?" Be patient. If you hear what you want, do not prolong the negotiations to the point where the company will look for another candidate. If you truly want the job and the salary is low, but not too low, you could negotiate for a raise after you are credentialed as an accredited record technician (ART) or registered record administrator (RRA).

After the probation period, when a specified performance level is achieved, a raise could be possible. You may be able to negotiate an upgraded job title or longer annual vacation time. Information management is one of the top job market careers. A national publication identified "health career information specialist" as a "hot-track" job with "hot-track salaries" (*U.S. News & World Report*, see B. Kennedy, 1996). With the increasing demand for those with the associate's or bachelor's degree in health information management, you should be able to find a position that pays a fair salary for your abilities. The salary you achieve is a starting point for future increases. If the salary is definitely too low, do not compromise the profession or your own standards by selling yourself short. Reconcile yourself to look elsewhere. But first look the interviewer directly in the eye and ask: "Is that what you think this position is worth to be accomplished to your satisfaction?" If the salary offer remains the same, be polite and bring closure to the interview.

Two important points to remember regarding salary are:

1. When you enter into negotiations, have in mind what you want and are willing to accept for the position.
2. Remember you are negotiating a benefit package; salary is a part of it.

Benefits

The list of benefits depends on the type of job and the organization. The benefit package could include a variety of additional items that can add as much as 35 percent or even more to your salary.

Positions in education have in some institutions included the benefit of arranging time off in the summer to be with children. For some, this is as important as the salary. For a single parent, or in a situation where one spouse is self-employed, health insurance may be a priority in order to secure a family group policy. In addition to medical insurance, other types of insurance that could be included in a benefits package are accidental death, dental, disability, life, and optical. Some organizations have "cafeteria" plans in that you can pick the insurance benefits you want.

Matching programs for retirement may not seem important when a person is young with immediate needs. However, by starting early to save for retirement, with the advantages of compounded interest, a more secure future for the senior years can be attained. For pension plans, it is important to determine how many years you must work for the organization to be vested.

Paid sick leave, personal days off, and vacation time can vary for hourly or salaried positions. Vacation time can be negotiated from two to three or three to four weeks depending on the organization's personnel policies. For those whose job will involve travel, benefits could include car allowance, a car, and an expense account. The latter could be per diem, an amount allowed for each day, or could actually cover expenses incurred.

Profit sharing may be available with physician group practices and in other situations. Healthcare firms that offer profit sharing may provide the money at the end of the year, or invest the money and make it available to you when you leave the firm.

Tuition reimbursement and continuing education opportunities are important to those who are seeking advanced degrees and are eager to learn the latest developments in the profession. Continuing education is mandatory to maintain credentials as an accredited record technician and registered record administrator. When an employer allows time off from work and covers the cost of registration fees for conferences and workshops, this is a benefit for both the employer and the employee.

Determine what it is you need at this time. What compensation items are most important? Is a certain type of experience to meet your long-range career goals more important than a few thousand dollars? Consider your needs and career goals and, based on these, decide if this is the job for you.

Accepting the Job Offer

Your interview was a success. You knew it would be. Now it is time to decide if you will accept the job offer. There are good offers and there are bad ones. If the offer isn't quite what you wanted, you can say "no." Be courteous since you may want to work for the company at a future time.

You may decide, however, to take the job for the experience and future negotiating value. Developing certain skills could provide the background needed for career advancement. For example, if your goal is to start your own coding business, or to be a DRG consultant, you will probably need to have at least two years of coding experience to establish credibility and networking contacts.

One caution is that companies that provide coding services to healthcare facilities may have you sign an employment contract specifying that you cannot go to a competing organization or organize your own business within a year or two after you leave their firm. When required to sign contracts, legal advice should be sought.

Once you have completed salary negotiations and have been informed (usually by a representative from human resources) of the benefits that will be provided, you can determine the timetable for filling the position. If employed, you will need to provide your current employer with a minimum of two weeks' notice. You should not be asked by the hiring employer to begin working until sufficient notice has been given to your former employer.

At the time of acceptance, it is important to state exactly what has been agreed to: "Thank you, Mr. Nathan. I am delighted to accept the position of supervisor of transcription at a starting salary of $30,000. I will be able to start work on June 8. I understand my package will include health, life, and dental insurance. As soon as I receive your offer in writing, I will provide my present employer with a resignation."

If you have been negotiating with other companies for job offers, it is important to notify them that you have accepted a position, that you were impressed with their organization, and that in the future there may be an opportunity to work together.

Summary

An interview is the opportunity to prove to a potential employer that you are capable and competent. It is important to remember the following:

- There are four types of interviews. The informational interview is for educational purposes. The screening, selection, and hiring interviews are for employment purposes.
- Various settings can be used during any of the four types of interviews. Among the potential settings are one-on-one, the panel/board/committee, a meal, an all-day on-site, and test taking. Equipment that could be used in combination or alone includes the telephone, videoconferencing equipment, and a computer.
- Preparation for the interview includes researching the organization, assessing your strengths in relation to job functions, rehearsing through role-playing, dressing appropriately, and reaching the interview on time as relaxed and ready as possible.
- Five formats used by interviewers are direct, nondirect, stress, problem solving, and question–answer–question.
- A strategy that builds on your strengths while meeting the employer's need can facilitate success.
- Self-confidence can be improved by four P's: preparation, practice, a positive attitude, and pondering your past successes.

- Questions asked during an interview may be classified as related to the organization, job, your background, personal strengths, and the uniqueness of the interviewer or situation.

- When negotiating salary and benefits, decide what is essential for you.

- Make your decision, based on the salary offer, your career goals, your financial needs, and your personal preferences.

- Obtain the job offer in writing. If already employed, resign after agreeing with the written terms for the new position.

- Interviewing can be a pleasant experience for the person who has prepared for the event. Remember that a positive attitude and enthusiasm will increase your chances for success.

The checklist in Figure 6-15 will help you in preparing for an interview.

Review Activities

1. Discuss how the informational interview differs from the three types of employment interviews.

2. If you were in the role of the interviewer, describe the setting and format you would prefer.

3. If you were interviewing for a position, what type of setting and format would you prefer?

4. Outline what you should do to prepare for an interview.

5. Identify four techniques that could be used to build self-confidence prior to an interview.

6. Role-play an interview with a classmate, family member, or colleague. Use questions provided in the chapter and record or videotape the session. Listen to this for the purpose of having yourself or another critique the mock interview and identify strengths and weaknesses.

7. Develop five questions of your own that would be good for you to ask the interviewer.

8. Write a statement on what you would consider to be appropriate dress for an interview for the position of manager of a group practice.

Title of position_____

Organization/Corporation name_____

Contact's name _____ Phone number _____

Activities	Dates Scheduled for	Completed
Informational interview		
Researched the organization		
Researched the position		
Developed questions to ask interviewer		
Wrote answers to potential questions from interviewer		
Practiced orally answering potential questions		
Decided on professional outfit		
Participated in mock interview		
Other (Specify)		

_____

Date of interview _____

Results of interview (Include comments on strengths and weaknesses of the interview process)

_____

_____

_____

_____

Figure 6-15. Interview Checklist

References

Beatty, R. (1995). *The interview kit*. New York: John Wiley & Sons, Inc.

Biegeleisen, J. (1994). *Make your job interview a success*. New York: ARCO/Prentice Hall.

Bloch, D. (1988). *How to get ahead on your first job*. Lincolnwood, IL: National Textbook Co.

Challenger, J. (1996). Keep Cool During Stress Interview. *St. Louis Post–Dispatch*, 17 March, sec. G, 19.

Elderkin, K. (1989). *How to get interviews from job ads*. Dedham, MA: Elderkin Associates.

Hirsch, A. (1994). *Interviewing: The national business employment weekly premier guides series*. New York: John Wiley & Sons, Inc.

Jud, B. (1991). *Job search 101*. Avon, CT: Marketing Directions.

Kennedy, B. (1996). Health Care Information Specialist, *U.S. News & World Report*, 28 October, 95.

Kennedy, J. (1995). *Hook up, get hired! The Internet job search revolution*. New York: John Wiley & Sons, Inc.

Kennedy, J. (1996). Videoconferencing: Newest Trend Changes Job Interview. *St. Louis Post–Dispatch*, 17 March, sec. G, 19.

Kent, G. (1990). *How to get hired today!* Lincolnwood, IL: VGM Career Horizons, National Textbook Co.

Lamplugh, R. (1991). *Job search that works*. Los Altos, CA: Crisp Publications, Inc.

Marcus, J. (1994). *The complete job interview handbook: The fastest way to find the job you want*, 6th ed. New York: Harper Perennial.

Medley, H. (1992). *Sweaty palms: The neglected art of being interviewed*. Berkeley, CA: Ten Speed Press.

Myer, B. (1997). Interviewing Style: Key to Winning the Offer. *St. Louis Post–Dispatch*, 22 January, sec. E, 16.

Powers, S. (1996). It's in Your Hands. *U The National College Magazine*, March 20.

Spencer, P. (1995). Self-Confidence: How to Get It, How to Use It. *Woman's Day*, 25 April, 72–75.

Yate, M. (1994). *Knock 'em dead: The ultimate job seeker's handbook*. Holbrook, MA: Bob Adams, Inc.

Additional Resource

AMI American Media Incorporated. *How-to-Training Videos. More than a gut feeling I and II*. 4900 University Avenue, West Des Moines, IA 50266-6769, 800/262-2557.

Chapter 7

Postinterview Strategies

Goals

After reading this chapter, you should be able to:

1. Describe four postinterview details.
2. Outline the contents of postinterview documentation.
3. Self-assess your interviewing skills.
4. Evaluate the job offer.
5. Identify the steps for finalizing the job offer.
6. Formulate do's and don'ts for your first month on the job.
7. Prepare for your next career move.

Introduction

In the previous chapter, accepting the job offer and negotiating salary and a benefit package were introduced. In this chapter, additional details regarding postinterview strategies will be covered. Questions that will be addressed are: Should you accept the job offer that is made immediately at the end of the interview? Was there a positive or negative correlation between what interviewers said and what you thought was the culture? Did you answer all questions posed by interviewers effectively? If not, which question should you work on for improvement? How would you rate your performance?

The initial interview can be helpful for future interviews in the near and possibly distant future. Documentation after the interview is essential. A list of items for reflection are provided.

A caveat against making a hasty decision is offered in the evaluation of the job section. Involving others in your decision can be helpful. Finalizing the job offer is addressed also.

The do's and don'ts for that first month on the job will be introduced. The chapter closes with assistance in assessing your next career move. A worksheet is provided to facilitate your preparation for career progression.

Postinterview Details

Among the details to be covered following an interview are:

- Being reimbursed for expenses.
- Writing the interview thank-you letter.
- Contacting references.
- Keeping in consistent contact through networking.

Reimbursement for Expenses

Prior to the interview, you should have had an understanding of how much and which expenses will be covered by the employer. If the interview is conducted in the city in which you reside, generally there is no reimbursement. For out-of-town interviews, if the employer invites you, the airline ticket may be provided in advance; others may ask you to make the arrangements, and then reimburse you. For the latter situation, you could add a couple of sentences in your interview confirmation letter as follows: "As you suggested, I have purchased an airline ticket. If you require completion of the company's travel expense form, I will obtain this from you during my visit. In any case, receipts will be maintained and forwarded to you after the interview." This will serve as a reminder that the company has agreed to cover the expenses associated with the interview.

Do not accept an expense-paid visit if you are not interested in being employed by the organization. When two prospective employers are in the same city and you have arranged interviews during the same time period, accepting double travel expenses is a breach of ethics. You should not profit from these visits. Only necessary travel expenses are to be covered for an interview.

If an interview is arranged at your request, the expenses are usually your own. At times, new graduates have relatives or friends in various cities where they are seeking to be employed. They will travel and stay with acquaintances at their own expense during the interview process.

Interview Thank-You Letter

An example of the interview thank-you letter is included in Chapter 4. Expressing your gratitude is of the utmost importance.

The letter should sincerely state your appreciation for being considered for a position. Within three days after the interview, such a letter should be sent to all who interviewed you. There is a twofold purpose to this type of letter: (1) to express appreciation while showing you have manners, and (2) to stand out from the others who interviewed. If you want the job, a well-worded interview thank-you letter can assist in obtaining the offer.

References Informed

Generally, references are provided when the prospective employer requests them, which may occur after or during the interview. Prior to preparing a list of three to five references, you should contact them and request their permission in a telephone call or letter. The purpose is to refresh their memories as to who you are and to inform them that you are looking for a job. They may know of vacancies that they would suggest for you. After securing permission, sending a copy of your resume to each reference will help to ensure that the information provided to the prospective employer will be in accord with the information provided by your references.

For new graduates, instructors are usual references. They can validate information about the specific strengths you acquired during college courses, extracurricular activities, and clinical experiences. Clinical supervisors can provide insights into how you function in an actual work setting. For those who have had work experience, past supervisors, to whom you were directly responsible, are good references. Direct supervisors can inform others about your work ethics and about characteristics such as dependability and motivation. Your standard of conduct is especially important. Confidentiality is essential for the private and personal information that is handled routinely by health information management professionals. Prospective employers are looking to hire persons with integrity who are competent for the tasks required of the vacant position. You want to provide as references those who can speak to your integrity, competence, and reliability.

Consistent Contact

At the end of your interview, you may have been informed as to when the prospective employer will again contact you. Asking the interviewer, "About when can I expect a reply?" is appropriate. If you do not hear from the prospective employer at the anticipated time, you should initiate a timely contact to determine if a decision has been made and your status. A faxed communication is probably the best way since it allows persons to consider and respond at their convenience. You will not interrupt a meeting or a thinking session with a fax. A simple message such as:

> Dear Ms. Green:
>
> On June 15, 199X, I interviewed for the medical coder position, obtaining a perfect score on the test. My interest in the position continues. National Healthcare's mission of caring service was obvious during my visit. I am eager to contribute my reimbursement management skills to advance your mission. Please contact me at your convenience to update me on the status of this vacancy. My understanding was that the position is to be filled by the end of June. I can be reached by fax at 314/577-8877 or by telephone at 314/577-8888.
>
> Sincerely,
> Mary Jane Smith.

If the reply is that someone else has been selected, remember that just because you were not chosen for this position, does not mean your career is over. There will be future openings and you may want to apply again with the same company. Frequently, applications are maintained in human resources for six months to a year. Before placing a classified advertisement or contacting a recruiter, the applications on file may be considered and a qualified applicant contacted for an interview.

Keeping in contact with the director of health information services or human resources can facilitate the company having an active interest in you.

Telephone Contact

After the interview, if you have not heard from the prospective employer within a week, you may prefer to call instead of sending a fax. Generally, Monday is not a good day for making such calls. When you phone, be prepared. You may even want to rehearse the call in front of a mirror. Do what is necessary to sound confident and positive. Attaching a mirror to the phone has been suggested (Allen, 1992) to ensure that you are a smiling professional exuding self-assurance.

Before dialing, picture the interviewer and anticipate his or her reaction to what you have to say. When you have reached the interviewer, ask if this is a convenient time. If not, ask when would be the best time to again place your call. The person may offer to call you; in that case, leave your number.

You may be offered the position on the phone. If an offer does occur, request that the employer send a letter to you with the details: job title, salary, benefits, any special conditions, and starting date. When you receive the letter, you should follow up with a confirmation letter that again includes the details of your agreement. An example is shown in Chapter 4. Make a record in your log of the telephone call and add notes regarding the conversation.

Documentation Following the Interview

You should make every effort to do your best on each and every interview. Even if you secure the position, be sure to document the interview process for future reference. This experience is too valuable to forget; each detail can assist you in the future. Also, you may be able to assist your peers and family members.

After the interview, reflect on what happened. Written notations will contribute toward improvement of the process. Your notes should be made immediately after the interview. In Chapter 4, Table 4-1 is an example of a log for correspondence associated with a job search. The log becomes an employer file that can be useful in your career development. Documenting the interview is a key component in securing the right job offer. Information you should record includes date, contact's name, phone number, actions taken by company and you, and your comments. Electronically, an individual page could be maintained in your database for each employer interviewed and could be updated as needed.

Interview Logistics

In addition to demographics—the who, what, where, and when mentioned above—the postinterview documentation should assess the how: how the interview was conducted and how it progressed. As you reflect you will want to write descriptions for all or some of the following:

- *Receptionist:* Were you friendly? Did he or she ask you to complete an employment application? What information did you supply?
- *While waiting:* Did you read brochures on the company or other materials that showed interest in current events?
- *During interview:* Did you smile when you were greeted? Did you offer a firm handshake to each person? Was your greeting appropriate (not overly friendly)? In verbal and nonverbal communications what were your positives and what were areas for improvement? What was the behavior of the interviewer(s): friendly, cold, professional, etc.?
- *Type of interview:* Was it structured? unstructured? stress? group? one-on-one?
- *Setting:* Were there any problems with space, chairs, getting from place to place? Were you offered a tour? Did arrangements seem well organized?

Interview Recap

Make a list of the questions that you were asked. Jot down what you recall of your responses to them. Refer to the questions provided in the figures in Chapter 6, highlight, or make a mark by those that were asked. Were there others? If so, add them to the appropriate figure for future reference.

As you answered the questions, were you relaxed? How was this indicated? Which questions did you answer confidently? Which ones do you need to develop further? Could you provide good examples of your accomplishments? Did you show specific examples of your performance from your portfolio? What was said during the last few minutes of the interview? Was the next step stated by the interviewer? by you? Did you end by being clear about your interest in the position? Were there any surprises during the interview? Describe them. How did you handle them? Do you need to improve in certain areas?

Positives and Negatives

During the interview you should have learned considerably more about the position for which you have applied. Make a list of the job's positives (on one side) and negatives (on the other). The list can be a useful tool in deciding if this is the company and job for you. Your list of positives could include, for example: New Meditech software for patient accounts. Office with window view, free parking, 10% discount in cafeteria, reimbursement for an out of-town meeting annually, opportunity for growth, appropriate title and responsibilities.

Your list of negatives could include, for example: Must attend several late evening and early morning meetings; will need to travel to out-of-town satellite once a month, and/or did not meet any employees my age. If any item is especially important, it could be given a weight two or three times greater than others. Listing positives and negatives aids you in making an important decision not based on intuition alone.

Priorities

As part of career management, you have already considered your needs and values. One or more will be dominant for you. A particular lifestyle may be your major value, such as being able to participate in a particular sport, or having certain schools for your children. Lifestyle may be a higher priority than salary. For a young graduate, being of service and helping others may be the most important value. For others, the primary operative value may be job security, a managerial position, or the opportunity for on-going development of computer or technology expertise.

The job market in health information management is strong, so you have many choices. If you sense that this is not the job for you after the interview, you have at least two alternatives. You can take the offer, stay in the position for a year, gain experience, and discretely start searching for the next opportunity; or you can refuse the position and continue to interview. As you read further in this chapter, you will encounter other considerations to assist you in deciding whether to accept or reject the job offer.

Corporate Culture

The set of beliefs, traits, and values that a company practices is the corporate culture. Most healthcare institutions have a mission and claim that their culture embraces:

- A commitment to excellence.
- Total quality management and ongoing quality improvement.
- A caring, compassionate, and careful concern for patients and their rights.

One of the clinical practice sites in the St. Louis area operates on the premise that if the employers are not happy working for the institution, the patients will not be happy. As you enter the facility, the joy is felt. The corporate culture is real. The joy of students, patient-care providers, administrators, and patients is seen in elevators, the cafeteria, parking lots, and throughout the healthcare facility. Smiles, friendly looks, and gracious hospitality to visitors and even salespersons are indications of this happiness. Employees in this facility are able to counteract negative thinking with thoughts such as "I choose to have a calm and happy day" and "I can handle this." This institution provides caring and compassionate concern. The physical, emotional, spiritual, and psychological needs of patients and employees are important and it shows.

Companies that have a competency-based culture are requiring more personal accountability. Employees are required on their own to keep their skills up to date. AHIMA's Vision 2006 is designed to assist us in attaining the competencies needed for the evolution of HIM practice.

Indications of Culture

During the interview you will have had a chance to observe the corporate culture in various ways. For example, when people were introduced, were titles used such as Dr. Smith? This could be an indication of a formal work environment. On the elevator, was deference shown to certain people? Did people show helpfulness by holding the elevator open when others were approaching? What was the extent of conversation on elevators?

If incoming telephone calls occurred during your interview, how were they handled? Did you sense that the call was a bother or was it handled professionally? Considerations of corporate culture can provide insight into whether you would enjoy working for the company.

Evaluating Your Interview Skills

Your postinterview documentation is especially important for assessing your interview skills. Give yourself an overall grade or a rating. You can use: "poor, fair, or good"; "A, B, or C"; or "okay" or "needs improvement." This rating will help in determining how successful you were with the interview process. Through your documentation, you should have identified areas of weakness. Do what you can to change these weaknesses to areas of strength.

Evaluating a Job Offer

Until you have the job offer in writing, you do not have an offer. Verbal offers can be withdrawn by the employer. If the offer is made at the conclusion of the interview, do not accept immediately. Take time to reflect, to document, to consider, and to have firmly in your mind the benefit package you want. Accepting the job offer is one of the most important decisions of your life. The career for which you have invested time, money, and other resources is about to commence. Generally, the offer is discussed with others: spouse, family, parents, instructors, friends.

If other interviews are scheduled, you may wait a few days, but not too long. You should take at least a day or two to think over an offer. Once you have accepted the job, professional ethics indicates that you stop interviewing for other positions. Honor the commitment you made when you accepted the offer. A job evaluation rating form to aid you with this important decision is included in Figure 7-1.

No matter what college program you completed, you will not be completely prepared for what you will encounter in today's fast-paced work world. Be open to change, new ideas, different software, and technological developments. Enthusiasm is a quality valued by most employers. Make sure that by accepting this job offer you will have little difficulty in being enthusiastic about your work and about the mission of your employer.

The Company

During the interview, did you sense that the people working there were valued and appreciated? What were the company's strengths: team-building environment, a facility of excellence, continuous quality improvement, other? How did the company recognize the accomplishments of employees? Was mention made of any employee recognition program? Has right-sizing occurred? Has the company been involved in mergers? Does your future boss seem respected and effective? Does the organization value health information management? In what ways is this visible: through the physical space and equipment provided? the attitude of executives to the HIM director and employees? Are continuing educational opportunities encouraged? Would you feel proud to be associated with this organization?

Several positive responses can be an indication that you may want to be associated with this company.

Scale: 1 Strongly Agree; 2 Agree; 3 Neutral; 4 Disagree; 5 Strongly Disagree; NA Not Applicable

Job-Specific Questions

I would enjoy performing this work.	1	2	3	4	5	NA
This job relates to my career goals.	1	2	3	4	5	NA
I like my immediate supervisor's management style.	1	2	3	4	5	NA
The location of the job is good.	1	2	3	4	5	NA
There are opportunities for advancement.	1	2	3	4	5	NA
Continuing education will be provided.	1	2	3	4	5	NA
Salary is what was expected.	1	2	3	4	5	NA
The benefit package offered is appropriate.	1	2	3	4	5	NA
The company's mission harmonizes with my career goals.	1	2	3	4	5	NA
My lifestyle would not need to be changed.	1	2	3	4	5	NA
The company culture suits my personality.	1	2	3	4	5	NA
The office area where I will work is pleasant.	1	2	3	4	5	NA
The company maintains a smoke-free, clean, and healthy environment.	1	2	3	4	5	NA
The company rewards competence and accomplishments.	1	2	3	4	5	NA

Figure 7-1. Job Evaluation Rating

Your New Supervisor

A new graduate, Mary, mentioned that her supervisor works eighty hours a week and expects the same from her. Since Mary has two children, she finds it difficult staying longer hours at work. She is willing to take projects home, but working in the office beyond regular work hours becomes a problem. Would you want to be in this situation?

Write down everything you remember about your prospective boss. Did you feel comfortable with the person? What type of management style did you observe? Did the person seem to be a good communicator, sharing information? Did the person have trouble remembering your name? Did you sense that your opinion was valued?

Answers to these questions and others you may have will help you in deciding if you want to work with this person for an extended time period.

Career Goals

Will this job contribute to your career goals? Will there be opportunities for advancement? job enrichment? cross-training? To what extent will continuing education opportunities be available internally and externally? Will reimbursement be made for college courses? graduate courses? under what conditions? Are the HIM employees encouraged to participate in professional activities? as officers?

Your personal and career goals should be consistent with your competencies, values, and interests. Evaluate your skills, interests, and values in the context of the direction in which the company is headed. Is the company in harmony? Assess if you could accept the differences. If the company and your goals are in alignment, you have strong indications for accepting the job offer.

Finalizing the Job Offer

Never stop your job search until you have a written offer in hand that you have accepted. Your decision to accept an offer should include a letter to the employer outlining specific details of the offer. A sample is provided in Chapter 4.

By phone or a personal note, you should contact your references and any others who have been associated with your job search. This will put closure to the process. Informing them that you have accepted a job is an experience you should enjoy. Provide your references with your work phone number. You want to keep your network well informed.

If you are currently employed, you will need to submit a letter of resignation to your present employer; a sample has been provided in Chapter 4. Be sure to retain all your correspondence with employers and continue to maintain your logs and interview notes for future reference.

First-Month Do's and Don'ts

As you start a new job, listen to the comments of those with whom you will be working. As you learn more about the company, the employees, and your responsibilities, take time to offer carefully considered suggestions, preferably in writing. Spoken words can be forgotten, misunderstood, slanted, or captured by others as their own.

Be an advocate for health information management, contributing your talents. Find ways to make employees, your supervisor, and your supervisor's boss aware of your existence and of your contributions to the organization. Seize opportunities that are in keeping with organizational goals. In the next chapter, keeping a log of accomplishments is discussed.

For projects in which you are involved, give key persons a chance to be part of the project and to offer their suggestions. Obliging the boss is important to you for promotions, raises, and achieving a teamwork situation. Be competent in performing the tasks on your job description and be ready to do what is needed to grow with the organization.

Be driven by your values, which should include a strong work ethic. Being responsible, dependable, timely, accountable, and flexible are work ethic components. The book *Job Hunters: Packaging and Marketing You* (Ramos, 1991) ends with three words: smile, smile, smile. You should be happy at work and it should show in your smile, actions, and output.

The don'ts are obvious to most people and are shown in Figure 7-2. In addition to the do's already stated, additional ones are provided in Figure 7-3. As you consider these, add to the lists. Identify the do's and don'ts that are important to you.

DON'T
- Complain about the boss.
- Complain about anything; instead, offer constructive suggestions for improvement.
- Talk too much.
- Eat at your desk during lunch and breaks. This is the time to meet people.
- Humiliate or demean someone or the efforts of a co-worker.
- Spread rumors.
- Seek credit for projects—let it come when due. Document honestly your accomplishments and keep these for your supervisor at promotion and salary increase times.
- Be the first to leave when quitting time approaches.
- Talk about patients, employees, or administrators in the elevator and where others who should not hear can do so.
- Associate with negative people.

Figure 7-2. Don'ts for a Job

DO
- Encourage others.
- Give praise when praise is due.
- Eat with different people to avoid being cliquish.
- Make others feel appreciated and important to the organization.
- Perform your best at all times.
- Look for ways to turn disrespect into respect.
- Treat others as you would want to be treated.
- Find ways to be kind and thoughtful.
- Be committed to self-actualization.
- Recognize that you are unique and use your gifts in keeping with the company's mission.
- Know when to say yes.
- Take time to think.

Figure 7-3. Do's for a Job

Your Next Career Move

In *Winning People Over*, Kaplan (1996) offers sixteen ways to change your life by changing the way you dress. One of his recommendations is to "Stop dressing for the job you have. Start dressing for the one you want." Where do you see yourself in five years? Having identified your goals and priorities, start taking steps to advance your career. What is your greatest weakness? What can you do to turn this weakness into a strength? What is your greatest strength? How can you make it visible to those above you? Continue to satisfy your boss by doing things right while winning the acceptance of those around you. Develop your leadership and team-building skills. Table 7-1 can be of assistance in your search for your next position.

Table 7-1.   Next Job Worksheet

Specify the Appropriate Response in One or Both Columns to the Right	**Essential**	**Desired**
Minimum acceptable salary:		
Benefit package:		
Level of management responsibility:		
Geographic preference:		
Degree of travel:		
Lifestyle necessities:		
Computer technology:		
Corporate culture:		
Functions to be performed:		

Networking and having a mentor as discussed in Chapter 3 are important. You may want a mentor who can facilitate your development according to Vision 2006 of AHIMA. Seek every opportunity to acquire knowledge, skills, and abilities associated with one or more of the practice areas as shown in Figure 7-4.

Chusmir (1990 p. 22) states that, "A job that fulfills a person's motivation needs is likely to be a job that brings happiness." By determining a person's needs, the particular needs a job fulfills, and the extent of the match between these can help in assessing if the person will be happy in the job. Three dominant needs are explained:

- The need for achievement: to compete against some standard of excellence and to accomplish worthwhile goals.
- The need for affiliation: to have close interpersonal relationships, friendships, and social acceptance.

- Information based
- Application development
- Application support
- Data flow and reengineering
- Data item definition
- Data modeling
- Data administration
- Data auditing
- Electronic searches
- Logical data views
- Prevention and control countermeasures
- Risk assessment and analysis
- Security, audit, and control program
- Shared knowledge sources
- Statistical and modeling techniques

Figure 7-4. HIM Practice: Vision 2006 (Reprinted with permission, © the American Health Information Management Association)

- The need for power: to desire to have an impact and influence over others.

In addition to the three dominant needs, there are four other motivation need profiles, not as common, that are covered:

Balance of all three needs:

- Need for achievement and power
- Need for achievement and affiliation
- Need for affiliation and power.

When needs are not met at work, a person can change jobs, or can do things at work to help fulfill the need. For example to meet the need for achievement, one could find a mentor at work who can help with advancement. This in turn will assist in meeting the need for achievement.

If you are happy in your position, you may want to stay there, looking for opportunities within the company. Ways you can increase your visibility in the company include and are not limited to:

- Exceeding your competition by being timely, accurate, under budget, and complete.
- Volunteering for assignments that have high visibility.
- Remembering the names of key executives and using them at appropriate times.

With job changes becoming more frequent, it is important to maintain a career file. Keep your portfolio, resume, and list of accomplishments current to ensure readiness when you are contacted regarding an exciting job opportunity.

Summary

- Details to be addressed after the interview include being reimbursed for expenses, writing thank-you letters, informing references, and keeping in contact with the prospective employer.
- Documenting specifics of the interview can provide additional insights into the process.
- Self-assessing your interviewing skills will assist in identifying areas for improvement.

- Taking time to thoroughly evaluate a job offer can contribute toward your interests, values, and skills harmonizing with those of the prospective employer.
- Your job search continues until you have a written offer from an employer that you have accepted in writing.
- When you start a new job, you should be:

    A good listener

    Competent

    An advocate for the HIM profession

    Obliging to the boss

    Contributing your talents to the organization

    Responsible

    Timely

    Accountable

    Flexible

    Adaptable

    Professional

    Happy—remember smile, smile, smile

- When you start a new job, do not complain, spread rumors, or seek to be the first out the door at the end of your day.
- In career management, once you have a job, it is time to start focusing on the next goal to advance your career.

Review Activities

1. Describe at least four important details that you should take responsibility for after an interview.
2. Develop a grid, using Excel or Lotus, showing major content headings for postinterview documentation.
3. Identify at least five things you would require before you accepted a job offer.
4. Discuss the actions you would take to finalize a job offer.
5. Besides those provided in the chapter, identify at least two additional do's and don'ts for the first month on the job.

References

Allen, J.G. (1992). *The perfect follow-up method to get the job*. New York: John Wiley & Sons.

American Health Information Association (1996). *Inventing the future Vision 2006*. Chicago, IL: AHIMA.

Bernstein, J. (1990). *Resume writing, interviewing and roleplaying skills for salespeople looking for new jobs*. Manhattan Beach, CA: JB & ME Publishing.

Burke, M. (1997). *The valuable office professional*. New York: AMACOM.

Canfield, J., and Miller J. (1996). *Heart at work stories and strategies for building self-esteem and reawakening the soul at work*. New York: McGraw-Hill.

Chusmir, L. (1990). *The guide to a happier job: Thank God it's Monday*. New York: New America Library.

Deep, S., and Sussman, L. (1990). *Smart moves*. Reading, MA: Addison-Wesley Publishing Company, Inc.

Gray, J., Jr. (1993). *The winning image*. New York: AMACOM.

Green, P. (1996). *Get hired! Winning strategies to ace the interview*. Austin, TX: Bard Books, Inc.

Kaplan, B. (1996). *Winning people over: 14 days to power and confidence*. Englewood Cliffs, NJ: Prentice Hall.

O'Brien, J. (1996). *The complete job search organizer: How to get a great job—fast*. Washington, DC: The Kiplinger Washington Editors, Inc.

Quittel, F. (1994). *Fire power: Everything you need to know before and after you lose your job*. Berkeley, CA: Ten Speed Press.

Ramos, B. (1991). *Job hunters: Packaging and marketing you*. Sherman Oaks, CA: Somar Press.

Richardson, D. (1994). *Networking*. New York: John Wiley & Sons, Inc.

Shingleton, J. (1996). *Job interviewing for college students*. Lincolnwood, IL: VGM Career Horizons.

Yate, M. (1996). *Knock 'em dead: The ultimate job-seeker's handbook*. Holbrook, MA: Bob Adams, Inc.

Chapter 8

Opportunities in Health Information Management

Goals

After reading this chapter, you should be able to:

1. Discuss the term *profession*.
2. Explain how AHIMA's Code of Ethics relates to profession.
3. Clarify at least three differences between a career and a job.
4. Identify advantages associated with graduate school.
5. Interpret AHIMA's continuing education requirements for the accredited record technician (ART) and the registered record administrator (RRA).
6. Describe customs and cultures that could impact work in a foreign country.
7. Report on the history and activities of the International Federation of Health Record Organizations (IFHRO).
8. Recognize the responsibilities associated with various positions in health information management.
9. Differentiate between entrepreneurship and intrapreneurship.

Introduction

Extraordinary changes have occurred in the healthcare industry. Previously, health information managers were associated with institutions; today many are employed by systems that include a variety of healthcare services from primary to long-term care. The emphasis has shifted from the treatment of disease to the prevention of disease and wellness strategies. Quality improvement techniques are directed to the process of making healthcare better and achieving predetermined outcomes. Utilization review has been replaced with case management, which examines the patient as a whole. Figure 8-1 compares healthcare of the past with healthcare today.

A major factor necessitating change has been the transition from paper to electronic storage, from manual record keeping to electronic transmission of clinical data and claims. The result has been different roles for the HIM professional.

In this chapter, the term *profession* is defined. The distinctive characteristics that make a career different from a job are discussed. For some, lifelong learning includes graduate school. Selecting the right master's program or professional degree requires careful consideration. Guidelines are offered to assist with the process. Positions that generally require a graduate degree are discussed. The major components of AHIMA mandatory continuing education policy are identified. Career opportunities are summarized with an extensive listing of position titles and responsibilities

Past	*Present*
Inpatient setting	Outpatient setting
Treatment of illness	Maintenance of wellness
Acute episodic care	Longitudinal care
Specialist dominance	Primary-care dominance
Fee-for-service	Capitation
Utilization management (length of stay)	Case management (looking at all aspects of patient care)
Individual practice	Group practice
Individual provider of care	Teams for patient care and quality improvement
Institutions	Systems
Not-for-profit	For-profit
Paper	Electronic data transmission

Figure 8-1.   Comparison of Healthcare: Past and Present

provided in Appendix A. The international aspects of the profession are introduced. The chapter closes with mention of entrepreneurial and intrapreneurial opportunities.

Profession

Profession is an occupation requiring advanced training and involving mental rather than manual work. At one time, learned professions referred only to medicine, law, and theology. Today profession is applied to several occupations including, and not limited to, teaching, engineering, writing, and managing.

Generally, a profession is defined by a set of characteristics. These characteristics are among the attributes of the professional and include:

1. Expertise that is gained from specialized training in a body of abstract knowledge.
2. Autonomy, which is the perceived right to make choices that concern both means and ends.
3. Commitment to the work and the profession.
4. Identification with the profession and other professionals.
5. Ethics that embrace an obligation to render service without concern for self-interest and without becoming emotionally involved with clients.
6. Collegial maintenance of standards including monitoring the conduct of those in the profession (Von Glinow, 1988).

Credentialed individuals—accredited record technicians (ARTs) and registered record administrators (RRAs)—have traditionally been considered health information management professionals. In 1992, AHIMA began offering certification in coding to interested persons. Those certified in coding use the initials CCS and CCS-P after their names, that is, certified coding specialist. Some certified coding specialists also hold other credentials such as RRA, ART, or RN.

Code of Ethics

The Code of Ethics, adopted by the members of the American Health Information Management Association, defines in ten principles the standards of behavior for the HIM professional. The principles are listed in Figure 8-2.

The health information management professional:

Demonstrates behavior that reflects integrity, supports objectivity, and fosters trust in professional activities.

Respects the dignity of each human being.

Strives to improve personal competence and quality of services.

Represents truthfully and accurately professional credentials, education, and experience.

Refuses to participate in illegal or unethical acts and refuses to conceal the illegal, incompetent, or unethical acts of others.

Protects the confidentiality of primary and secondary health records as mandated by law, professional standards, and the employer's policies.

Promotes to others the tenets of confidentiality.

Adheres to pertinent laws and regulations while advocating changes that serve the best interest of the public.

Encourages appropriate use of health record information and advocates policies and systems that advance the management of health records and health information.

Recognizes and supports the association's mission.

Figure 8-2.   Capsulated Form of AHIMA Code of Ethics

The Code of Ethics is reviewed regularly by the Professional Conduct Committee of AHIMA. Copies can be obtained from the American Health Information Management Association, headquartered in Chicago, Illinois.

Career versus Job

To distinguish between career and job, the following criteria can be helpful. A career:

1. Allows you to use your education, training, skills, personal qualities, talents, and other contributions unique to you.
2. Produces an income that is commensurate with your talents and the contributions that you make.
3. Provides growth and a professional career path.
4. Gives you control, authority, and respect from management.

A job

1. Is unrelated to your strengths, or is unsatisfying to you.
2. Results in underpayment for your contributions.
3. Does not provide a career path.
4. Dictates and allows you little or no control (Siegel, 1996).

George Bernard Shaw, in his play *Mrs. Warren's Profession*, wrote: "The people who get on in this world are the people who get up and look for the circumstances they want, and, if they can't find them, make them." Those who write about careers emphasize the need to create your own opportunities. This can be accomplished by setting your goals and performing the measurable behaviors needed to achieve the goals.

You should spend at least a year in your first position impressing your supervisor and others with the effectiveness of your performance. In today's job market, the way to progress is to accomplish, accomplish, accomplish. Throughout your career, keeping an accurate record of professional accomplishments is important. Accomplishments are different from results. Results are anything that comes about as a consequence or outcome of some action or process. Accomplishments are work completed successfully. Examples of business-related accomplishments compiled from an article by West (Nov. 1996) are shown in Figure 8-3.

Education

From your job description, you know what results your employer expects from you. Are you qualified for an upward or lateral change in the organization? Do you need to remain in this position, perfecting your skills and abilities? Will you need to initiate a search for a position in another company that will challenge you by requiring additional knowledge and different skills? Will you need to relocate to find the position that will advance your career? or is it time to seek additional education?

Educational Opportunities for the Accredited Record Technician

The ART with an associate's degree can structure a career path in a variety of ways including:

Being mentioned in a professional publication or the press.

Being interviewed as an authority by a radio or television station.

Meeting or exceeding specific goals or objectives.

Establishing new methods of working, solving problems, or creating effective strategies.

Speaking to or conducting workshops for professional organizations, trade groups, a board of trustees, medical staff, or others unrelated to your field.

Being elected to the board of a professional association or organization.

Receiving awards, grants, or special recognitions.

Decreasing expenses and/or increasing profits, sales, etc.

Improving services to patients, clients, or the community.

Receiving no deficiencies following a JCAHO accreditation.

For each accomplishment, be *specific* by providing details. Examples are:

When you have made a presentation, in your memo to your immediate supervisor and again at the time of your next review, provide the name of the organization, the topic covered, and the number and type of participants.

When you have decreased expenses, provide your immediate supervisor with documentation showing how this was accomplished, for example, how much was saved by outsourcing or implementing a new system.

Figure 8-3.   Business-Related Accomplishments (Adapted from West, 1996)

Continuing education full-time for a bachelor's degree.

Working while enrolled in an external-degree program or in an academic program that is accessible and can be arranged around a work schedule. Matriculation could be full-time or part-time depending on college requirements and individual endurance.

Advancing through accomplishments, relocating as needed for advancement opportunities.

For each of these paths there are advantages and disadvantages. Factors such as finances and commitments to family and other interests will assist you in deciding the best road for you. Career paths can be altered as circumstances change.

Money's college guide (September 1996) provides detailed information on 1,115 colleges to assist in selecting the right four-year school. Tuition and fees, percentage of freshmen receiving aid, average gift aid per student, number of students per faculty member, and other details are provided.

Earning a bachelor's degree from an approved program in health information administration (HIA) can be a way of taking a direct upward educational path. Most HIA programs will accept the technical courses completed in an accredited health information technology program. The number of transfer credits varies with approximately sixty semester hours being the maximum from a community college. Each college differs on the requirements for the bachelor's degree, especially in general education courses. These could include foreign language, philosophy, additional literature, computer, mathematics, social science or humanities courses. The "Essentials and Guidelines for an Accredited Educational Program for the Health Information Technician (HIT) and the Health Information Administrator (HIA)" has a section on curriculum. Content that is appropriate for both the HIT and HIA programs is shown in Figure 8-4. The content areas that differ, with additional content areas for the HIA programs, are shown in Figure 8-5. A listing of approved programs in health information technology and health information administration are included in Appendix B. Accredited record technicians who are interested in progression can obtain specific information on program requirements by directly contacting the HIA program director at selected colleges.

External-degree programs are offered by only a few of the colleges listed in Appendix B. An advantage associated with remaining in the work world while earning a degree is that throughout the course of studies classroom assignments can be structured to improve work performance. Also, you can help your employer to become more efficient and effective. Through your accomplishments while working, you provide a foundation for advancement. This recognition could occur during your educational experience or upon completion of the degree requirements.

Everyone's career goals are different. Yours may include a move to another department or being a member of a particular team. A degree in a field other than health information administration could furnish the broadened knowledge and skills needed. A few of the degree possibilities as shown in Figure 8-6 are management information systems, computer science, accounting, healthcare administration, information science, and human resources management.

a. General education
b. Professional course content, at the appropriate level to support the entry-level competencies as identified by AHIMA, to include at least:
  (1) Medical sciences, including language of medicine, structure, and function of the human body, and disease process
  (2) Organization of the healthcare industry
  (3) Systems and processes for collecting, maintaining, and disseminating health-related information
  (4) Computer concepts and microcomputer applications
  (5) Computer applications in healthcare
  (6) Laws, regulations, ethics, and standards affecting the management of health information
  (7) HIT and HIA program differ on this content area:*
      HIT: Supervisory principles and practices
      HIA: Management theory, principles, and practices
  (8) Classifications, nomenclatures, and reimbursement systems
  (9) Data analysis and presentation
  (10) Clinical quality assessment and improvement (This is #12 for HIA)
  *Additional differences shown in Figure 8-5.

Figure 8-4.   Content Areas for HIT and HIA Programs (From Commission on Accreditation of Allied Health Education Programs, 1994)

- Systems analysis, systems design, and project management concepts (10).
- Healthcare financial management (11).
- Statistics, research and evaluation methods (13).

Figure 8-5.   Content Areas for HIA Programs (in addition to list in Figure 8-4; from Commission on Accreditation of Allied Health Education Programs, 1994)

Titles for degrees may vary, for example, in some schools the degree may be called management science. As mentioned, health information administration is most closely related to HIT. For various reasons, a health information technology graduate may prefer a degree in another field. The following suggestions do not purport to be inclusive.

Bachelor of Arts Degree (BA); Bachelor of Science Degree (BS)

Majors

- Biology
- Chemistry
- Communications
- Computer Science
- Education, especially Adult Education
- English
- Healthcare Administration
- Journalism
- Political Science (frequently a major for those considering law school)
- Psychology
- Public Policy Studies

Bachelor of Science in Business Administration Degree (BSBA)

Areas of Concentration:

- Accounting
- Decision Sciences
- Economics
- Entrepreneurship
- Finance
- International Business
- Management
- Management Information Systems
- Marketing
- Personnel and Industrial Relations
- Production/Operations Management
- Quantitative Analysis

Bachelor of Science in Nursing (BSN); Bachelor of Science in Social Work (BSSW)

Degrees in the allied health professions, such as occupational therapy, physical therapy, and physician assistant, are not a common progression path for the health information technology graduate. With these degrees, the professional is generally seeking a career involving direct patient care rather than additional responsibilities in health information management.

Figure 8-6.   Bachelor's Degrees Related to Health Information Technology

If your choice of a bachelor's degree is other than health information administration, the number of transfer credits may be significantly reduced. During the inquiry or commencement phase, you should obtain in writing from an authorized person, such as the department chairperson, the number of credits that have been accepted for transfer credit. Request also a listing of the courses you will be required to take to earn the bachelor's degree.

Educational Opportunities for the Registered Record Administrator

Graduate education is rigorous and expensive. If your company has a tuition-reimbursement program, this is a benefit that you should consider. For some, having graduate courses paid by the employer is an important part of the salary/benefit package. Other ways of financing graduate studies are through low-cost loans and direct grants. Professional organizations, fraternities, churches, and parents' employers are additional sources for funding. At times, these options may not be available to a student who is employed full-time.

There are only a few graduate programs designed specifically for registered record administrators. Generally, these programs prepare students for senior-level management positions. Courses encompass administrative information systems; planning, designing, and evaluating clinical data systems; and information engineering.

The University of Utah, through the department of medical informatics, offers both a master of science (M.S.) and a doctor of philosophy (Ph.D.) degree. Graduate programs in informatics build on knowledge and skills acquired by health information managers. There are several areas of specialization in the University of Utah's informatics program, such as expert systems, genetic epidemiology, healthcare quality, health information systems, medical imaging, and medical physics. The latter focuses on the development of noninvasive methods for obtaining physiological data.

Traditionally, registered record administrators have earned degrees from established graduate programs—that is, those that have existed for decades, for example, master's degrees in business administration (MBA), hospital administration (MHA), public health (MPH), and education (MEd). The degree in informatics is a fairly new addition to graduate schools.

Simmons College Graduate School of Management in Massachusetts was founded in 1974 and continues as the nation's only graduate business school for women. This school, which has never applied for a business school accreditation, was founded on the belief that women take a different approach toward work. The number of women earning MBAs in the nation continues to increase. Women represent an estimated 37 percent of people earning the MBA, which is a 5-percent increase from the early 1970s (Shao, 1997).

Areas of concentration are associated with some degrees. For example, the MPH, may have tracks in behavioral science, health education, biostatistics, epidemiology, and environmental and occupational health. Joint degrees are offered by some universities, for example, the MHA/MBA or the MHA/JD (law) combinations. Additional graduate programs are listed in Figure 8-7.

Master of Business Administration	(MBA)
Master of Health Administration	(MHA)
Master of Hospital Administration	(MHA)
Master of Finance	(M.Fn.)
Master of Management and Decision Sciences	(MMDS)
Master of Professional Accounting	(MPA)
Master of Public Health	(MPH)
Master in Social Work	(MSW)
Master of Laws	(LLM)
Jurisprudence Doctorate	(JD)

Master of Arts/Master of Science in:
- Communication Studies
- Computer Science
- Education
- Informatics
- Journalism
- Library Science (MLS and MSLS)
- Library and Information Science (MLIS)
- Organizational Communication
- Policy Analysis
- Public Administration

Figure 8-7.   Postbaccalaureate Degrees Related to Health Information Administration

A small percentage of students in the United States have been able to take the chemistry, biology, and other required science courses needed for admission to medical school while completing the requirements for a bachelor's degree in health information administration. This accomplishment has facilitated admission to programs in medicine, osteopathy, chiropody, and dentistry. Although the HIA degree is not often seen as a path to patient-contact professions, the bachelor of science degree in health information management provides an excellent background for future patient-care providers. The ability to use a variety of software packages and the techniques of case management and quality improvement are a few of the skills learned and valued by health information administration graduates.

Vision 2006 of AHIMA incorporates seven career scenarios. One of the positions in the scenario is for a research and decision support analyst. HIA graduates interested in such a position would benefit from an advanced degree in biostatistics, mathematics, or health services research.

Admission into graduate school is not really a difficult task, especially for the person who has achieved at least a cumulative average of 3.0 or above on a 4.0 scale. If you are seeking the MBA, there are over 700 accredited business schools available in the United States. Admission standards vary by school. Most require completion of the graduate management aptitude test (GMAT) as part of the admission process. Study guides, computer software, and courses are readily available to assist in preparing for the GMAT.

Admission to graduate school becomes difficult when seeking a college with a national reputation or one of the top-ranked programs. As previously mentioned, 700 colleges grant the MBA; of these, approximately 250 meet the standards of the American Assembly of Collegiate Schools of Business (Martinson and Waldherr, 1996). The number of institutions in the United States that grant a law degree is approximately 175. When it comes to public health, the number decreases to around 27 approved schools in the United States. Annually, *U.S. News and World Report* publishes a college ranking issue. Information is provided on the best national universities and best liberal arts colleges; rankings for engineering schools, business schools, and departments in accounting, entrepreneurship, finance, general management, and quantitative analysis; and other concerns in selecting the school best for you (September 1996).

Through career planning you save time. By envisioning your future, you can take appropriate courses in college to prepare for a specific graduate program, which will eliminate the need to take additional prerequisite courses. Most four-year colleges have minors or certificate programs that designate appropriate courses for entry into graduate programs such as the master's in business administration, computer science/informatics, law, public health, or healthcare administration.

Advantages Associated with a Graduate Degree

The advantages associated with obtaining a graduate or professional degree differ for each person. Among the benefits from an advanced degree are some or all of the following.

- Provides an opportunity for self-actualization, the ability to use your talents to the fullest.
- Prepares you for advancement. For some positions, you may be competing with other professionals who achieved a master's degree.
- Develops additional skills that enrich your current position while opening doors for advancement.
- Allows college professors and peers to further assess your accomplishments.
- Continues your professional responsibility for lifelong learning.
- Advances your status in a profession and in society.
- Facilitates your growth and development for more challenging work.
- Endows you with another accomplishment.
- Meets continuing education requirements of AHIMA.
- Increases your salary and benefits.

Selecting a Graduate Program

Since graduate programs can be expensive in terms of money, time, and effort, you want to make sure you select the one best for you. Answers to the following questions, can facilitate your choice.

1. *What is my major reason for an advanced degree?* The answer to this question can provide the basis to motivate you throughout the course of studies.

2. *What resources are available to me for this? (time, money, degree opportunities)?* The answer to this question could determine where and when you will attend school and what degree you will decide to earn. For example, you may decide to attend law school. However, you know you need to continue working to finance this education. If there is no evening program in your area, you may revise your plans and decide on a master's degree in business or another field. Or, you could work for a period of time, saving money for this, and seek scholarships or other financial assistance. After a few years, you could have the resources needed to quit work and attend a day program for your professional degree in law.

3. *Will there be jobs available in the area? Can I relocate?* If you are unable to relocate for several years because of family commitments, the types of jobs available in your area could determine your degree choice.

4. *Which courses did I like in school?* Your answer to this question might facilitate your degree choice. If your favorite course involved medicolegal issues, and you have the time, ability, and resources, you may decide on law school. If your favorite courses were those in systems, computer science, and programming, you may decide on informatics or management information systems.

5. *Who are my role models?* If there are people you admire and want to be like them, this may guide you in selecting a degree that parallels the role model's career path. If you want to be like the professors you had during your HIT or HIA program of studies, you may select the same master's degree that they did, or you may talk to them to see if they advise you to seek some other area of expertise. The health information management profession, as noted at the beginning of this chapter, has changed. Different degrees and abilities are needed to address technological advancements, managed care, and a global society.

In addition to answering the preceding questions and others you may have, developing a grid similar to the one in Table 8-1 may be of assistance in deciding on a specific program. Your individual considerations can be added to expand the table. Your final decision could be based on how you feel, what you actually prefer, or another consideration. Through a grid, such as shown in Table 8-1, you will have an opportunity to look at the information available. When you make that important final decision, you will have examined the issue carefully.

Continuing Education

The continuing education (CE) program of AHIMA requires ARTs to earn twenty clock hours in two years. RRAs are required to earn thirty CE hours in two years. Failure to complete the required CE hours can result in the person no longer being eligible to use the designated credentials. Previously, individuals could decide the subject matter that would be part of the

Table 8-1. Advanced Education Decision

Ratings you assign are from 1 to 5: 5 the best, 3 average, and 1 poor). The numbers provided here illustrate how this table can be used. A blank table is provided for your own use.

	Degree Choices			
	Law	**Informatics**	**Public Health**	**Business**
Enjoy subject matter	5	4	2	3
Ability to afford:				
X University	1	2	3	4
Y University	1	2	4	3
Financial assistance	1	2	5	2
Part-time work	1	5	4	5
Job market for this degree	3	5	3	2
Total (25)				
for X University	11	18	17	16
for Y University	11	18	18	15
Percent	44	72	68; 72	64; 60

Calculate the percentage by dividing actual points into total 25 points (derived from 5 items × 5 maximum rating), i.e., 11/25 = 44%. Percentages show that Informatics at X and Y Universities and Public Health at Y University have the highest ratings (18/25). These three would be at the top in your decision for graduate school. Other factors that could enter into your decision would be length of time to complete the program and accessibility or ability to relocate.

Table 8-1.   *Continued*

Ratings you assign are from 1 to 5: 5 the best, 3 average, and 1 poor.

| | **Degree Choices** | | | |
	Law	*Informatics*	*Public Health*	*Business*
Enjoy subject matter				
Ability to afford:				
X University				
Y University				
Financial assistance				
Part-time work				
Job market for this degree				
Total (25)				
for X University				
for Y University				
Percent				

Calculate the percentage by dividing actual points into total 25 points (derived from 5 items × 5 maximum rating).

continuing education experience. Commencing with the 1996–97 and 1997–98 credential maintenance cycles, a minimum number of CE hours must be in core educational content areas. Currently the six educational areas are technology, management development, clinical data management, performance improvement, external forces, and clinical foundations. A description of each is in Figure 8-8.

Technology (T)

Applications of existing and emerging technologies to the collection of clinical data, the transformation of clinical data to useful health information, and the communication and protection of information.

Management Development (MD)

Application of organizational management theory and practices as well as human resources management techniques to improve departmental adaptability, innovation, service quality, and/or operational efficiency.

Clinical Data Management (CDM)

Applications of data analysis techniques to clinical databases to evaluate practice patterns, assess clinical outcomes, and assure cost-effectiveness of healthcare services.

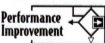

Performance Improvements (PI)

Study of fundamental organizational changes and how they are functionally organized or how they deliver patient care with special focus on the requisite changes made in medical record/health information systems and services.

External FOrces (EF)

Strategies organizations and/or health information management professionals, in particular, have been employed to effectively address emerging legislative, regulatory, or other external party action that has collection and/or use of health information.

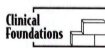

Clinical Foundations (CF)

Understanding of human anatomy and physiology, the nature of disease processes in humans, and the current methods of diagnosis and treatment of acute and chronic medical conditions and diseases.

Figure 8-8. Descriptions for AHIMA Core Educational Content Areas for Continuing Education

Health Information Opportunities

The demand for health information managers continues to exceed the supply according to AHIMA. Of all new jobs, more than three million are in healthcare. The greatest increase is for jobs in the nonacute-care setting. The American Health Information Management Association's Board of Directors has developed a strategy, Vision 2000, which continues as Vision 2006. The intent is to have the 36,000 HIM professionals work together to prepare the profession for emerging HIM roles. As shown in Figure 8-9, these include health information manager, clinical data specialist, patient information coordinator, data quality manager, document and repository manager, research and decision support analyst, and security officer.

In Appendix A, the emerging HIM roles and several traditional roles are listed with profiles of responsibilities. With the change from manual systems to computerized information systems, different skills and specialized knowledge are needed. Those who are currently obtaining their degrees are being prepared for these changes through the curriculums developed by their college or university. Those already in the profession can acquire additional knowledge and skills through graduate programs and complying with the mandatory continuing education program of AHIMA.

International Opportunities

Study abroad is an opportunity provided by most colleges.

Having graduates who are prepared to work in a global economy is a goal being sought by more and more colleges. Health information management is a career with global implications. As information systems are linked internationally, opportunities outside of the United States will increase. Graduates with a semester or an internship abroad will be attractive candidates for employers with international companies.

Health information managers have served as consultants and have been employed around the world. Their experiences over the years were documented in articles in the *Journal of the American Health Information Management Association, Advance, For the Record,* and other publications. The places in which HIM professionals have served include Korea, State of Kuwait, China, Australia, England, various countries in Latin America, several African countries, Japan, Saudi Arabia, Panama, and South Vietnam. Project HOPE, a program that provides medical training, health edu-

Health information manager: Enterprise- or facility-wide responsibility for health information management (line or staff manager). Includes working with the chief information executive and systems users to advance systems, methods, and application support; and improve data quality, access, privacy, security, and usability.

Clinical data specialist: Data management functions in a variety of application areas, including clinical coding, outcomes management, specialty registries, and research databases.

Patient information coordinator: New service roles helping consumers manage their personal health information, including personal health history management, release of information, managed-care services, and information resources.

Data quality manager: Data management functions involving formalized continuous quality improvement for data integrity throughout the enterprise beginning with data dictionary and policy development and including quality monitoring and audits.

Document and repository manager: The next generation of records and data management using media such as the CPR (computer-based patient record), data repository, and electronic warehousing for meeting current and future care needs across the continuum, providing access to the needed information, and ensuring long-term integrity and access.

Research and decision support analyst: Support senior management with information for decision making and strategy development, using a variety of analytical tools and databases. Work with product and policy organizations on high-level analysis projects such as clinical trials and outcomes research.

Security officer: Manage the security of all electronically maintained information, including promulgation of security requirements, policies and privilege systems, and the audit of performance.

Figure 8-9. Vision 2006 Career Scenarios (Reprinted with permission, © the American Health Information Management Association)

cation, and humanitarian assistance around the world, has benefitted from the expertise of health information managers. HOPE is an acronym for Health Opportunities for People Everywhere. Since it was founded in 1958, Project HOPE has worked in more than seventy countries on five continents. During the Vietnam War, the United States Agency for International Development (USAID) hired a registered record administrator to work in

Saigon training Vietnamese personnel and setting up medical record policies and procedures for the Barsky Unit of ChoRay Hospital.

An advertisement for a junior health management consultant with a firm in England, resulted in a position for an ART with six years of experience (O'Connell, 1992).

Peggy Hughes, a CMT (Certified Medical Transcriptionist) who worked as a medical transcriptionist in Saudi Arabia, offered these tips from her experience:

1. Job advertisements do not mention that the national work-week standard in Saudi Arabia is 48 hours.
2. Recruiters are paid to fill positions and they may tell you what they think you want to hear.
3. Work with the recruiter, but talk with a person who has been there or is currently on-site.
4. Secure important items regarding the position in writing and be sure to have a signed contract before you go.

International Positions

The positions available internationally have included the full spectrum of health information management. Several missionary communities have had health information managers working in their hospitals and clinics in Korea, Japan, Ghana, Hong Kong, China, and throughout Latin America. Medical centers such as Loma Linda University consider themselves global partners and have ties established throughout the world. Employees, graduates, and even students have brought health information management to various parts of the world.

In various publications there are advertisements for international health information management positions. For example, some positions in Saudi Arabia that appeared in the *Journal of AHIMA* are shown in Table 8-2. Knowledge of past positions can assist those who are planning for an international career. Benefits that have been associated with past positions in Saudi Arabia are shown in Figure 8-10.

At the annual AHIMA meeting there are at least a few Americans who are employed by hospitals in Saudi Arabia. For those who are considering an international career, talking with them can be worthwhile.

Consultant and external examiner are among the positions that have been available in various parts of the world. External examiners are used in

Table 8-2.   Examples of Saudi Arabian Positions by Hospital as Advertised in *Journal of AHIMA*

Hospital: King Faisal Specialist Hospital and Research Center in Riyadh with an international staff of over 4,000 medical and support personnel; a 500-bed specialty referral facility

Medical Record Supervisors	9/94
Supervisor, Medical Records	12/92

Hospital: King Khalid, a major university hospital in Riyadh

Coding Supervisor	5/96
Quality Assurance/In-Service Education Officer	5/96
Transcription Supervisor	5/96

Hospital: Saudi Arabian National Guard (SANG) Hospital , Riyadh, 600 beds

Coordinator	
Outpatient Services	1/92; 2/92
QA/Discharge Processing	1/92
Discharge Processing Technicians	1/92

Hospital: Riyadh Armed Forces Hospital, 800+ beds

Assistant Medical Records Director	2/92
Director Medical Records	2/92
Personal/Administrative Assistant to CEO	7/92

Hospital: Not specified

Administrative Assistant—Administration Dept.	9/93
Administrative Assistant—OB/GYN Dept.	9/93
Discharge Processing Technician	7/92
QA Director	7/92
QA Reviewer/Analyst	7/92
Supervisor—Discharge Processing	7/92
Transcriptionist	7/92

Tax-free salary

End-of-contract cash bonus

Paid leave days per year

Excellent travel opportunities

Free fully furnished housing

Free utilities

Free medical care

Free transportation

Full recreational facilities

Figure 8-10.   Benefits Package Associated with Some Positions in Saudi Arabia

the British system of education to validate that the curriculum and the students meet standards for a profession. These types of positions are usually for short periods of time and frequently are not advertised. Those selected are distinguished professionals or educators with a national reputation who have been recommended by AHIMA, colleagues, or other organizations.

Guam Memorial Hospital is another example of an international opportunity. In the past, a 192-bed acute-care and skilled nursing facility was seeking a medical health records administrator. The annual salary range offered was $31,064 to $46,596. A medical health records supervisor position vacant for the same facility had an annual salary range of $28,678 to $43,018 (11/92). The benefits included for both positions were paid vacation and sick leave; health, dental, and life insurance plan; 14 paid holidays; up to £2,500 relocation cost and one-way airfare for employee and dependents.

Global Volunteers is a nonprofit, nonsectarian organization based in St. Paul, Minnesota. Volunteers, aged 16 to 80, pay their own way to work on a community project to accomplish a goal. Overseas destinations include Russia, Poland, Tanzania, Indonesia, Tonga, and countries in Latin America. All types of healthcare background can be useful (Read, 1992).

Advantages and Disadvantages

Among the advantages that can be gleaned from an international work experience are the following:

1. Educational enrichment through the exposure to a different culture.

2. Expanded job opportunities especially in companies seeking to grow internationally.

3. Travel to different countries. Many companies require employees to take short trips to nearby countries for rest and relaxation. Part or all of the costs, including release time from work, may be covered by the employer.

4. Free housing and transportation to and from work.

5. Satisfaction in helping people in another country acquire the latest skills in health information management.

A few of the disadvantages that could be associated with even the best of international work experiences are:

1. Being treated not as a colleague but as a hired employee with few of the rights we have come to expect of employers in the United States.

2. Taking the job to save money. With a housing allowance, travel funds, and tax advantages, you think you will save lots of money, and although your international salary actually compares favorably to what you would have earned in the United States, you may not save as much as anticipated. Variations in currency exchange rates can be a significant factor.

3. Being out of the U.S. job loop. Changes generally occur more rapidly in the United States than they do in many foreign countries. You may have catching up to do upon your return.

4. Having to remain single or leave a married partner behind. Some contracts are for those with single status. Although married individuals have been accepted for positions, a spouse may need to remain in the United States during the time the other is abroad.

5. Failing to adjust. You may be unable to adjust readily to different cultures and customs. This is explained in more detail in the following section.

Cultures and Customs

Some people think that many of the conveniences readily available in the United States are present in other countries. In South Vietnam, a tropical country, air-conditioning is a luxury. Instead of supermarkets, open shops prevail in many countries with meat and poultry hanging visibly next to walkways. As you walk through the marketplace, animals are in cages waiting to be slaughtered. In China, most of the foods popular in the United States are available. However, you will also find shark fins, eel, dog, roast duck, and other foods not regularly eaten in the United States. In many countries, there is a need to boil water and to be wary when eating fresh vegetables.

Women in Saudi Arabia must be properly covered; bare arms and low-cut tops are not acceptable. There are no movie theaters and videotapes are censored.

Adapting to different food, clothing, and entertainment may not be as difficult as adjusting to the values and thinking of another culture. In our culture, people read from the top down and from left to right. This is not true for everyone. Problem solving, work ethics, and approaches to time are influenced by ancient traditions and a different focus on the issue.

In Japan, children are socialized to consider themselves members of a group, interdependent on family members, school, community, and other collectives. To be well adjusted, you must fit into groups harmoniously rather than stand out, which is quite different from Western individualism (Sai, 1995).

In Bangladesh, instead of offering thanks, a favor is returned. Countries like the Republic of Botswana practice traditional tribal customs and the population is often unfamiliar with Western ways. In Mexico, punctuality is less important than hospitality (DeVries, 1994).

Before deciding to work in a foreign country, talk to persons who have lived and worked there. By reading current literature on the people and their customs, you can learn about adapting to, and being enriched by, cultural diversity.

The International Federation of Health Record Organizations

In April 1996, the 12th Congress of the International Federation of Health Record Organizations (IFHRO) was held in Munich, Germany. Nearly 300 people from thirty-six countries from Asia, Europe, the Middle East, North America, and the Pacific Rim attended this congress, which is held every four years to bring together people dedicated to the advancement of the art and science of health records. The theme of the 1996 congress was

"The Future of Health Information Management," with 100 speakers from twenty countries speaking on hospital information technology, quality assurance, coding systems, economics and financial control, clinical and epidemiological trials, education and training, and other aspects of health record management.

The First International Congress on Medical Records was held in London in 1951 with nine countries represented. In Stockholm, on May 29, 1969, at the Fifth International Business Meeting, IFHRO was established. The aim of the organization is to improve health record practices. Specific objectives for achieving this aim are to:

- Provide a means of communication between persons working in the field of health records in the various countries of the world.
- Advance the standards of health records in hospitals, dispensaries, and other health and medical institutions.
- Promote and/or develop techniques for the efficient use of health records for patient care, statistics, research, and teaching and disseminate these techniques among member organizations.
- Provide means for exchange of information on educational requirements and training programs for health records in all countries.

You need not work in a foreign country to join IFHRO. The next congress will be held in October 2000 in Melbourne, Australia, and is open to both members and nonmembers.

National Associations in Other Countries

There are national health record associations in several countries as shown in Table 8-3. Each association usually designates a representative to IFHRO.

Barcelona, Spain, was the site for the Third World Conference on Patient Cards and Computerization of Medical Records, sponsored by the Medical Records Institute of Massachusetts. The London, England, conferences on the creation of a European electronic health record system have been so successful that plans are to continue an annual congress. Representatives from Europe and Japan have in the past been aggressive in the development of clinical information systems and are active participants in such conferences.

Table 8-3. National Health Record Associations

Country	Date Organized
Australia	1955
Canada	1942
France	1983
Germany	1972
Indonesia	1989
Ireland	1948
Israel	1977
Jamaica	1971
Japan	1974
Korea	1969
Netherlands	1963
New Zealand	1964
People's Republic of China	1988
Philippines	1982
United Kingdom	1948
United States of America	1928

Source: *Journal of AHIMA*, October 1993.

Coding and Informatic Technology Opportunities

ICD-10, published by the World Health Organization (WHO), has created opportunities for training coders worldwide. The tenth revision of the International Classification of Diseases was first implemented in Denmark in 1994 and subsequently in other countries. The year 2000 is when the system is expected to be implemented in the United States with at least two years' prior notice. WHO publishes ICD-10 in English and French only. Other countries can use these versions or translate the classification system into their own language. Since ICD is a diagnostic system, other systems must be used for procedures. South Africa, for example, has adopted the common procedure coding (CPC) system. Implementation of ICD-10 will provide opportunities for those skilled in this system both in the United States and worldwide.

India is one of the countries implementing a computer-based national health management information system. The system, which links more than 450 districts on a network, is seen as key to efficiency in India's community health centers (Indrayan, 1995). Informatics worldwide is one of the opportunities on the horizon for health information management professionals.

Entrepreneurship

Starting your own business takes energy, commitment, and a product that others want. Entrepreneurs organize, manage, and assume the risks of a business. Several HIM professionals have done this being self-employed as consultants, recruiters, and publishers. Others have started businesses specializing in a single function, such as coding or transcription, or have full-service companies to meet various needs including outsourcing and contract management services. Coding, transcription, release of information, and managing a section or department temporarily or permanently are among the outsourcing functions. Providing temporary health record employees for physician offices and healthcare facilities is another business that has been started by, for, and with HIM professionals. Manpower services can be purchased to perform tasks from filing to managing an entire department.

Most entrepreneurs start a business based on a particular skill. Expert coders, transcriptionists, or release-of-information specialists will decide to market their abilities to others. Growth may be planned for a local area, regionally, or nationwide. Some have sold their business to others. Transcription and coding businesses are examples of mergers that continue to occur.

A second way of becoming self-employed is to acquire an existing business, which usually requires more money than starting on your own. Franchising, a third way of becoming self-employed, involves purchasing the rights to sell or use a product owned by another. The payment made for a franchise generally covers the costs for training, accounting, start-up assistance, and/or goodwill.

An RRA who is president of a placement service advises that being well networked professionally and with employers is an important factor for his nontraditional route to success. Self-employment includes tax implications, legal issues, and the purchasing of office resources. Having an outgoing personality and being a risk taker can help (Detwiler, 1993).

Self-employment is not for every HIM professional. However, the challenge of being your own boss can be appealing. For those who are not ready to take the risk associated with entrepreneurship, there are home-based businesses with just one employee. This type of venture can be started without quitting your present job. As a side business, it can develop slowly, or more rapidly, depending on the time expended and the demand for the product or service. You can try new ideas and implement your dreams while your regular salary continues.

Intrapreneurship

Every HIM professional should be an intrapreneur, which is accomplished by assuming personal responsibility for marketing at your place of employment the profession and the knowledge and skills of the HIM professional. There are several ways to publicize the skills of the health information management profession to those with whom you work and associate:

1. Learn to present your ideas clearly and forcefully. There are software packages, such as PowerPoint, that are available to enhance your formal presentation skills.

2. Develop a support group consisting of mentors and peers with whom you converse on special issues and developments in the profession.

3. Keep a list of accomplishments with specific details such as the date, who was involved, and the types of issues involved. Categories for which you could include specific examples of accomplishments are ethics, safety, systems, organization, management, human resources, productivity, staff development, in-service, and confidentiality. Announce your specific accomplishments in annual reports, through newsletters, at meetings, and whenever an opportunity is available. When team effort is involved, acknowledge it.

4. Select an area that you want to make your own. Be a specialist in this area by reading everything you can find that is written on the subject. By applying your skill, you acquire a demonstrated ability.

5. Write, write, write. Submit articles to the *Journal of AHIMA* and other publications. If a rejection occurs, learn from the experience, improve, and try again.

Health information management professionals have a responsibility to continue their education and to educate others. Through writing and sharing information, the HIM profession is marketed to others.

Summary

- Changes in the healthcare industry have resulted in new and challenging roles for the HIM professional.
- *Profession* is an occupation requiring advanced training and involving mental rather than manual work.
- The AHIMA Code of Ethics defines the standards of behavior for the HIM professional.
- A career differs from a job in that the professional is able to apply education, training, skills, personal qualities, and talents to the position; is compensated appropriately; is provided with professional growth opportunities; and has control in managing his or her responsibilities.
- Throughout a career, maintenance of an accurate record of professional accomplishments can be valuable for promotion and other advancement opportunities.
- For the accredited record technician, a bachelor's degree in health information administration, management information systems, computer science, and human resources management are among the choices available.
- For the registered record administrator, advanced education could include, and not be limited to, law, public health, informatics, healthcare administration, business administration, education, and management information systems.
- Continuing education is mandatory for ARTs and RRAs consisting of twenty and thirty clock hours, respectively, within a two-year cycle.
- Health information management opportunities occur in fields from accountancy to zoology nationally and internationally.
- International jobs have advantages and disadvantages. Research a position thoroughly before signing a contract.
- To be an HIM intrapreneur, you need to be competent in the profession and market your competencies by sharing accomplishments judiciously with others.

Review Activities

1. Discuss how a career differs from a job.
2. Compare various advanced degrees and explain which one you would select and why.
3. Outline at least three advantages and disadvantages of working outside of the United States.
4. Write a paragraph stating why you would or would not like to start your own HIM business.
5. Differentiate between entrepreneurship and intrapreneurship.

References

American Health Information Management Association (1996). *Inventing the future: Vision 2006 the vision continues.* Chicago, IL: AHIMA.

Anderson, S., and Smith K. (1989). *Manpower resource guide for roles and functions of the medical record practitioner in the health care industry.* St. Louis: First Class Solutions.

Bell, A. (1990). *International careers.* Holbrook, MA: Bob Adams, Inc.

Blum, L. (1996). *Free money for graduate school*, 3rd ed. New York: Facts On File, Inc.

Commission on Accreditation of Allied Health Education Programs (1994). *Essentials and guidelines for an accredited educational program for the health information technician and the health information administrator.* Chicago, IL: AHIMA, pp. 4–5.

Day-Oliver, D. (1997). 97 Exam to Be Held Sept. 13. *Advance for Health Information Professionals,* 6 January, 22.

Dayhoff, S. (1987). *Create your own career opportunities.* Andover, MA: Brick House Publishing Co.

Detwiler, M. (1993) Designing a Life. *For the Record,* 1 November, 7, 24.

DeVries, M.A. (1994). *Internationally yours: Writing and communicating successfully in today's global marketplace.* Boston, MA: Houghton Mifflin Company.

Eichenwald, S., LaTour, K., and Watkins, S. (1992). Council on Education Report: ART Progression and Long-Range Educational Goals. *Journal of AHIMA,* 63 (7), 114–115.

Gannon, C. (1993). International Federation of Health Records Organizations (IFHRO). *Journal of AHIMA,* 64 (10), 26–27.

Gennusa, C. (1994). Higher Education Critical for HIMs in Light of Changing Environment. *Advance for Health Information Professionals*, 12 September, 12–13.

Huffman, E.K. (1994). Health information management, 10th ed. Berwyn, IL: Physicians' Record Company.

Hughes, P. (1996). MT Working in Saudi Arabia Receives Cultural Experience. *Advance for Health Information Professionals*, 2 December, 6; 34.

Indrayan, A. (1995). Informatics: The Key to Efficiency. *World Health Forum*, 16 (5), 305–311.

Jones-Burns, M. (1997). Seeing Your Way Through to AHIMA's Vision 2006. *Journal of AHIMA*, 68 (1), 30–33.

Jud, B. (1994). *Help wanted: Inquire within*. Avon, CT: Marketing Directions, Inc.

Kasky, J. (1996). Money's Guide to 1,115 Colleges. *Money*, September, 138–161.

Keefer, B. (1993). East Meets West: A Story of How to Establish a Tumor Registry in a Developing Country. *For the Record*, 22 November 1993, 6–7.

Kennedy, J. (1996). College Students Told to Consider Internships Abroad. *St. Louis Post–Dispatch*, 15 December, G15.

Kloss, L. (1997). Career Management. *Journal of AHIMA*, 68 (1), 18.

Law, J. (1996). IFHRO Holds 12th Congress, Investigates Future of Health Information. *Advance for Health Information Professionals*, 17 June, 21.

Martinson, T., and Waldherr, D. (1996). *Getting into graduate business school today*. New York: Macmillan, Simon & Schuster.

McUsic, T. (1997). Micropreneurs Climb Ladder to Success Step by Step. *St. Louis Post–Dispatch*, 6 January, 6BP.

O'Connell, J. (1992). Serving British Health Care. *For the Record*, 17 August, 4 (33), 1–6.

Read, A. (1992). Noble Be Man. *For the Record*, 21 December, 4–5.

Rocek, S. (1970). Vietnam Report: A Medical Record Librarian in Saigon. *Medical Record News*, 41 (June), 10–20.

Sai, Y. (1995). *The eight core values of the Japanese businessman*. Binghamton, NY: International Business Press.

Shao, M. (1997). Woman's MBA Program Uses the Non-traditional Approach. *St. Louis Post–Dispatch*, 22 January, 7E.

Siegel, R. (1996). Do You Have a Career or a Job? *St. Louis Post–Dispatch*, 15 December, 15G.

U.S. News & World Report (1996). Best Colleges: What School Is Right for You? *1997 Annual Guide*, 16 September, 110–122.

Von Glinow, M.A. (1988). *The new professionals managing today's high-tech employees*. Cambridge, MA: Ballinger Publishing.

Watson, Phyllis, J. (1992). International Federation of Health Records Organizations (IFHRO)—Past, Present, and Future. *Journal of AHIMA*, 63 (2), 72–74.

Weber, S. (1994). University of Utah Leader in HIM Advanced Education. *Advance for Health Information Professionals*, 10 October, 9.

West, P. (1996). What Have You Accomplished in Your Career? *St. Louis Post—Dispatch*, 17 Nov., 19G.

Zender, A. (1997). Speakers Explore ICD-10 Frontier. *Journal of AHIMA*, 68 (1), 60.

Additional Resources

All are paperbacks from Nolo Press, Berkeley, CA 94710; e-mail cs@nolo.com; fax 800/645-0895; phone 800/955-4775.

McKeever, M. (1996). *How to write a business plan*, 4th ed. ISBN 0-87337-184-4.

Steingold, F.A. (1996). *The legal guide for starting and running a small business*, 2nd ed. ISBN 0-87337-237-5.

Woodard, C. (1997). *Starting and running a successful newsletter or magazine*, 1st ed. ISBN 0-87337-357-X.

Chapter 9

Stress Management and Burnout

Goals

After reading this chapter, you should be able to:

1. Identify the signs of stress.
2. Describe how stress affects your health.
3. Recognize factors that cause burnout.
4. Illustrate methods to reduce the chances of stress and burnout.
5. Explain the importance of balancing your life.
6. Discuss how the trends in healthcare today may or may not enhance stress.
7. Understand the effects of job instability, change, and relocation.
8. Relate ways that stress can be minimized.

Introduction

Rarely does a book targeted to individuals who are early in career development address the issues of stress and burnout. However, sometime during your career it is likely that you will face these factors. Stress and burnout are often the primary causes for people to change jobs or seek other careers.

In this chapter, you will learn how to identify the signs and causes of stress; to relate physical illness and burnout to stress; to develop and implement stress management techniques; to prevent stress; and to maintain balance in your life.

Identifying Stress in Your Current Job

Imagine that you are sitting at your desk working on a project when your boss calls and informs you that an important planning session for the new information system is in progress. You are strongly encouraged to drop what you are doing and attend the meeting! Checking your calendar, you see the meeting was scheduled. Why didn't you remember? Unfortunately, it is not the first time this has happened. During the past week, you have forgotten about two other meetings. Is it because you are not feeling well? Lately you have felt on edge and impatient. Things that never bothered you before are now upsetting. It seems as though you hear the words "calm down" continually.

The healthcare industry has not been isolated from the trend in business to do more with less but maintain quality. In healthcare, this trend is evidenced by cost-containment efforts whether in the hospital, physician's office, other ambulatory setting, or long-term-care facility. Downsizing or rightsizing and the evolution of managed care are the products of cost-containment efforts. As a result, healthcare workers are seeing:

- Reductions in staffing, which necessitates longer workdays.
- Higher productivity expectations.
- Mergers of hospitals for the purpose of cost reduction by minimizing duplication of services and maximizing purchasing power.
- Efforts by the healthcare facility to gain a larger share of the market.
- Purchases of physician practices by provider organizations.
- Measures implemented to decrease the amount of time patients are allowed to remain in the hospital.

What Causes Stress?

Everything can be a source of stress: work, debt, relationships, friends, change, not achieving your goals, and so forth. If you are a recent graduate from a health information technology or health information administration program, your stress could be trying to find a job in the healthcare field that does not require three to five years of experience! One uniform cause of stress cannot be identified for everyone. For the health information management professional, sources of stress might include:

- Working with the medical staff.
- Lack of support or recognition by administration.
- Rightsizing of your department necessitated by organizational reengineering.
- Information systems that do not function the way they were intended.
- Inability to obtain qualified employees.
- Decrease in the budget.
- Insufficient release time to attend continuing education opportunities.

Whether working in the business world or the healthcare industry, there are other stresses that have been added during the 1990s. Fathers and mothers often experience guilt when work must come before their children. It is not unusual for parents working outside the home to see more of their co-workers than of their children. Another stressor may be acting as a caregiver to an ill or aging spouse, child, parent, or relative. People are beginning to address the issue of balancing their life in an attempt to have a career while having a quality life outside the workplace. Companies are becoming more and more aware of this trend because they are losing very qualified and valuable employees who are choosing to take positions involving less time rather than compromise family and friends. In response to this trend, companies are initiating policies to balance employment with time provided outside the workplace. While some companies have had these policies in place informally, now formalization of policies is occurring. The most popular initiatives being implemented include flexible schedules, working at home, compressed work weeks, and job sharing. Responses from companies and employees to these initiatives are positive. People feel that they are more in control of their lives, that they are being treated with respect, and that they are empowered to achieve results. It should be noted that although implementation of this form of decentralization of the workplace alleviates some stressors, others will surface that perhaps have yet to be identified. One thing is for certain: change is always a catalyst for stress.

Change is a significant stressor. The healthcare industry, which at one time was a relatively stable work environment, has become extremely volatile. During the 1990s, the demand for cost containment, while providing quality of care, became the primary focus for third-party reimbursers. Healthcare organizations responded by downsizing and rightsizing, forming alliances with other healthcare organizations, or merging with other healthcare facilities. The impact on health information management practitioners can be demonstrated with this scenario. Following graduation from a health information administration program, your goal was to obtain a coding position in a health information services department of an acute healthcare facility. Once this was achieved, your next goal was to obtain a management position in the health information services department. Over the years, you have progressed up the career ladder and achieved the position as assistant director, supervising the functions of inpatient and outpatient coding, chart analysis, and the incomplete record system. One day you go to work and are told the healthcare facility for which you work is merging with another facility. The department director discusses how this merger might impact your job. She outlines the following:

> You may be removed from your position.
>
> All positions may be reporting to the director of health information services for the facility with which your hospital is merging.
>
> Tasks associated with your position may change.

The undesired altering of your vertical career path could lead to frustration, job uncertainty, and an intensified feeling of insecurity, which is manifested in stress.

Learning to cope with change involves becoming a master of change, not a victim of change. Learning and comprehending the dynamics of change can assist in managing stress. In her book, *Managing Stress, Keeping Calm Under Fire*, Braham (1994) describes four progressive stages of change:

1. *Denial:* During this stage, you doubt that a change will ever transpire even though it has been announced. You may question why changes are needed. Denial will occur. This denial is an essential stage that must be experienced.

2. *Resistance to change:* This will occur once you realize that the change will take place. During this phase, the "fight or flight" reaction may occur. In this situation, you may decide not to accept the new ways and remain with the old methods, or simply remove yourself from the environment. Emotions develop, namely, tense muscles, anger, guilt, frustration, fear, and confusion, to name a few. When you make the decision to neither fight nor flee, you feel powerless and stress results. The underlying feeling of not knowing how to handle the emotions involved in the resistance phase will prevail. Often people try to incorporate old methods into the new way of doing things. Resistance occurs when you are deciding how or when to incorporate the new way into the old. Once integration has occurred, the third step follows.

3. *Exploring opportunities created by the change:* People say change is good. This is difficult to imagine while progressing through the denial and resistance phases and while you are experiencing negative feelings. However, during the third phase, feelings turn to the positive. You begin to realize that benefits can be attained through change and you begin focusing on how to maximize the benefits of the change.

4. *Acceptance:* As you move through exploring opportunities, acceptance of the change is realized. The new ways have been incorporated into the old ways. You are no longer self-absorbed into the change process, but are ready to move on to new challenges.

In any of these stages, you can get stuck and chronic stress could result. When this happens, burnout is likely to occur. Symptoms of fatigue, emotional outbursts, inability to make a decision, and irritability may be indicators of burnout. To maintain emotional stability, it is imperative to address and resolve the factors causing the stress. Causes of stress may not always be a single overt act, but rather a combination of incidents that pile up, which is referred to as "sneaking stress." For example, you wake up to find that the electricity went off during the night and you have overslept. You rush around dressing for work and then run into the kitchen to find something to eat quickly. Finding nothing, you proceed to work. Once on the highway, traffic is backed up for miles. By the time you get to work, you are an hour late and have missed a meeting. In this example, one factor has not caused the stress. If similar events keep occurring, chronic stress can result.

In the workplace, sneaking stress can occur if you feel you are being overlooked for promotion due to gender or race; your boss never says you are doing a good job; your requested budget items are never funded; your supervisor rarely communicates with you; and unrealistic expectations are set by superiors. When frustration, irritability, insomnia, and negative feelings about yourself or your job occur, sneaking stress may be the cause.

Sneaking stress and chronic stress can be detrimental to your health. Identifying the causes of stress is the first step in mastering stress by taking control over your life. To assist in the identification of causes of stress, respond to the items in Figure 9-1 as honestly and reflectively as possible. After completing Figure 9-1, highlight the factors that seem to cause the greatest stress. Those are the ones you need to master in order to regain control over your life.

1. Itemize what has taken place in your workplace for the past six months.
   Consider factors that have involved you directly or indirectly, such as a
   job layoff; continual conflicts with boss, peers, or subordinates; discon-
   tinuing employment; assumption of new duties; a change in bosses; a
   promotion; or the organization for which you work merging with another.

   _____

   _____

   _____

   _____

   _____

2. Itemize what has taken place in your personal or home life during the
   past six months. Consider a prolonged illness of a family member or
   friend, unstable relationships, relocating, financial instability, or graduating from school.

   _____

   _____

   _____

   _____

   _____

3. Itemize what you would like to do or try but for which you do not have
   the time or energy.

   Activity   Reason it cannot be accomplished

   _____   _____

   _____   _____

   _____   _____

   _____   _____

Figure 9-1.   Inventory of Stress Producers

Mastering Stress

The best method for coping with stress is to try to prevent it from happening in the first place. This can be achieved by asking yourself these questions for every task you encounter:

1. Can this work be delegated?
2. Is the deadline realistic?
3. Is the deadline imperative?
4. Can something else be substituted?
5. Should I say "no"?

To illustrate this concept, consider Jordan, who is the director of health information services for a healthcare facility. Jordan must present a departmental staffing proposal to administration by 3 P.M. Although Jordan has been working on the proposal for the past two weeks, it has been difficult to devote the time needed to finalize the document. Today, Jordan is scheduled to facilitate a departmental meeting, attend two committee meetings, and discuss an optical imaging system with a vendor. With that schedule, there is no way Jordan will be prepared for the 3:00 meeting. In trying to accomplish it all, Jordan will experience an increase in stress. What can Jordan do? Consider the following questions:

• *Can this work be delegated?* For some, delegating is not easy, because they feel that by asking for help, they are acknowledging their inability to achieve something on their own. Those individuals perceive delegating as a sign of weakness. Others want to control everything. To them, the more you have, the more powerful you are. Still there are those who feel only they can perform the function correctly. In the scenario, Jordan is overwhelmed with the tasks to be completed. Jordan recognizes the importance of the 3:00 meeting to discuss the departmental staffing proposal and should focus all attention on finalizing the proposal. To accomplish this, consideration should be given to delegating attendance at the two committee meetings to others in the department who have knowledge of the subject matter. Also, would it be possible to have an assistant director or supervisor conduct the departmental meeting? If not, the meeting could be rescheduled for another day.

• *Is the deadline realistic?* Probably when the staffing proposal was assigned to Jordan, the deadline was realistic. However, other commitments developed, compounding the inability to meet the deadline. What can be done to ease the pressure? Consider presenting a rough draft at 3:00 or try to reschedule the meeting.

• *Is the deadline imperative?* When prioritizing tasks, sort by two categories: (1) essential tasks and (2) nonessential tasks. For example, Jordan should consider if attendance at the committee meetings is essential. If not, then do not attend. Is meeting with the optical imaging vendor essential today? If not, reschedule. Is it essential that the departmental staffing proposal be completed or is a draft form for the meeting sufficient? The exercise regarding essential and nonessential is important in deciding priorities.

• *Can something else be substituted?* Again, the example already provided for substituting a draft of the departmental staffing proposal could be considered. The draft should be as complete as possible, but just not in final form.

• *Should I say "no"?* Learn to say no and really mean it! People like to feel needed and wanted. It is common for people to agree to do something just to be accepted or to gain recognition. However, it is not possible to do everything! In viewing the task from a realistic perspective, ask yourself if the task can be delegated. If, in your opinion it cannot, then reconsider saying "yes." Acceptance of the task could lead to stress.

To gain control over stress, carefully and critically analyze each task or situation you are considering. Prior to saying yes, anticipate situations such as budget preparation, employee evaluations, or departmental staffing that may occur. Learn to let go by seeking assistance in completing the task when needed. Maintain control over stress by setting limits rather than adding on to existing commitments. Take breaks during the day to relax. By doing so, you will have a healthier body and mind.

Job Burnout and Its Relationship to Stress

Job burnout is the lack of motivation to work. If going to work is a daily dredge and a horribly frustrating experience, or if you are experiencing emotional outbursts or perhaps you choose to withdraw from others, then you are exhibiting symptoms of job burnout. If these symptoms are neglected, health problems can develop. Other symptoms of job burnout include anxiety, fatigue, declining job performance, inability or difficulty to concentrate on projects, substance abuse such as alcohol, drugs, smoking, or food, and the feeling of "who cares" or "so what."

The healthcare industry lends itself to burnout because the work environment is so demanding and deals with life-and-death decisions. Healthcare requires precision and working under intense time constraints. From an organizational standpoint, increased absenteeism, job turnover, poor performance, and an overall sense of dissatisfaction among employees are signals of burnout. Every employee can experience burnout, not just those in management positions.

Burnout occurs slowly, not overnight, through the accumulation of pressures and stress encountered every day. Although burnout and stress do not follow the same patterns of intensity, there is a relationship between stress and burnout. Stressors that are unattended will enhance the chances for burnout. The primary difference is stressors can be changed, but once burnout has occurred, it is very difficult to reverse the situation.

In a survey that appeared in the February 26, 1996, edition of the *Wall Street Journal*, 46 percent of the workers surveyed reported they felt their job to be extremely stressful, 34 percent considered quitting their job due to stress, 34 percent anticipated job burnout during the next two years, and 27 percent felt their job was the single greatest cause of stress in their lives.

The Stages of Work

As stated before, burnout does not occur overnight but is the culmination of many factors. To develop an understanding of burnout, recognizing the stages of work is essential. In their book, *Take This Job and Love It: How to Change Your Work Without Changing Your Job*, Dennis Jaffe and Cynthia Scott (1988) outline the following stages:

- *Stage 1—The honeymoon period:* Your job is new, challenging, and exciting. The possibilities for growth and learning are limitless. You find you have endless energy and feel you have truly accomplished something by the end of the day.
- *Stage 2—Stagnation:* One of two feelings will be realized. Either your enthusiasm for the job wains and you feel you have mastered all the skills needed for completion of your function, so now work is boring and unchallenging, or you are overwhelmed and do not have time to complete the tasks required in your position. When stagnation occurs, it is time to make a career change.

- *Stage 3—Frustration:* At this stage, you will begin to exhibit many of the symptoms found in the burnout inventory. Anger, hostility, and irritability toward others will begin to surface. You are frustrated because you feel the more you do, the less you accomplish. No one appreciates what you are doing.

- *Stage 4—Apathy:* The "who cares" attitude develops. This is the final stage of burnout and by now the apathetic attitude is influencing everything you do.

What Can You Do to Combat Burnout?

First, watch for the signs and symptoms of burnout. When they surface, acknowledge there is a problem and take steps to rectify the situation. This may mean finding another position or confronting stressors.

Second, find another way to perform your job. Do not get into a rut. Look for new and innovative ideas. Investigate how others perform your function.

Third, become a lifelong learner. Continually renew yourself by learning new skills, taking part in professional organizations, taking a class, or participating in community service activities. Growing as an individual will maintain a balance in your life, which will assist in controlling the feelings of stress and burnout.

Fourth, think positively. Pat yourself on the back for all you have accomplished. Reflect on accomplishments instead of negatives.

Remember, you are in charge of your career. Survival in today's work environment involves the readiness to make ongoing improvements in your work. Whether improvement involves changing careers or just focusing on your current career, it is essential to take a critical look at your employment situation. George Lafikes, president of Executive Marketing Group in St. Louis, Missouri, suggests the following Career Fitness Checkup:

1. *How well are you doing in your current position?* Are you meeting or exceeding the expectations outlined in the job description? What about those expectations that are unwritten?

2. *How is the work environment?* Evaluate the trends that are occurring that may or may not affect your current position. Are you attending seminars related to your expertise? Are you maintaining your network of contacts?

3. *What is your growth rating?* Review your answers to questions 1 and 2. Were you able to give positive answers? Are you current on trends and issues affecting your industry? On a scale of 1 to 10, with 10 being the highest, rate your career knowledge and then your industry knowledge. If you score less than 5, it is time to take steps to increase your marketability. Take charge of your career to attain the satisfaction you desire. If you do not, no one else will.

Finding a Balance between Life and Work

In this chapter, we have discussed stress, job burnout, and career fitness. A stress inventory and burnout inventory have been provided to assist you in learning about yourself. Now it is time to look at how to balance work and personal time to enhance the possibility of attaining a happy, healthy, and fulfilled life.

In an article that appeared in the June 16, 1996, *St. Louis Post–Dispatch*, Joanne Waldman, a senior consultant at the IMPACT Group in St. Louis, Missouri, stated that IMPACT's clients are seeking assistance in obtaining careers that allow for more time with family, friends, and leisure. Polls conducted by a variety of organizations support this statement by revealing that over 85 percent of women surveyed felt that they did not have enough of a personal life. Ms. Waldman refers to this trend as downshifting. In downshifting, people are looking for fulfillment other than careers. Men as well as women are feeling the strain caused by the pressures of work including uncertainty about job security, more demands for productivity, which necessitates working longer hours, less flexibility in the workplace, and the instability of the work environment itself. If you are not currently able to seek another position or career, stress reduction techniques may assist you through the stressful moments and stages in your life.

Stress Reduction Techniques

These stress reduction techniques have been researched and found helpful:

- Breathe correctly. Take slow, deep breaths to relieve tension.
- Shut your office door. For a few minutes, think about where you would rather be in the mountains, skiing, on a beach, or perhaps lying in a hammock under the trees. Focus on whatever makes you relax.

- Close your eyes and concentrate on relaxing each muscle that is tense. To enhance muscle relaxation, try the following:

    Face and neck: Squint your eyes, wrinkle your nose, or move your neck from side to side.

    Arms and hands: Dangle your arms next to your body, then gently shake your hands, clasp your hands above your head, and squeeze your hands gently.

    Upper body: Roll your shoulders slowly to the front and then to the back, push your shoulder blades together, and stick out your chest.

    Lower body: Sit in your chair, extend your legs, and point your toes up and then down.

- Build a support system in the workplace by showing interest in others. Go to lunch with your co-workers, be helpful, complimentary, and ask for advice when needed.
- Pursue a job that meets your needs. Study your stress and burnout inventories and seek a job or career that minimizes those.
- Learn how to meditate to obtain mental relaxation.
- Make an effort to find something positive in what you do. Feel good about yourself and reward yourself.
- Develop outside interests so work does not dominate your life.
- Commit to not taking work home routinely. Spending time with family and friends will assist in balancing your life. Remember, the demands of work will encompass your life only if you allow it to happen.

Stress Associated with Job Change

Up to now, this chapter has focused on stress in your current position, and how it affects you both physically and mentally. After analyzing your stress and burnout factors, you may have decided it is time to make a career change. Once you have made the decision to change jobs, the stress related directly to your existing position will begin to decrease with the anticipation of the challenges and opportunities a new position will bring. However, a job search in itself can bring new stress to replace the old. The new stress is easy to internalize because personal assessment and evaluation by you or a prospective employer are involved. Your strengths and skills should harmonize with the expectations of potential employers. Stress can occur when matches are not present.

One of the factors of stress often not evaluated is the effect of the job change on the family unit. While the stress from your current job may have been affecting your attitudes and moods at home, the decision to change jobs can create stress on other family members. What can be done to minimize this type of stress?

1. Develop a plan that addresses a "what-if" scenario. Work through this plan with your spouse so a comfort zone can be reached.
2. Communicate with your spouse. Keep him or her informed of what is happening in the company.
3. Involve your spouse in decision making. Discuss the advantages and disadvantages of remaining with the company or seeking another position.
4. Begin to network within the community. Put out feelers to see what employment opportunities might be available.
5. Involve the children in discussions to the extent they need to know. Keep discussions with the children positive and at their level.
6. Assist your spouse in identifying potential employers when requested.
7. Participate in the actual relocation by looking at houses in the new city and selecting the new school, church, doctor, and dentist.
8. Maintain a positive attitude about the change. A positive attitude will be conveyed to all family members. This results in a sense of security.

Consider the above advice and then read this scenario.

For the past two years, you have been very unhappy and totally dissatisfied with your job. You feel the job is going nowhere, you do not receive any recognition for the work you do, your boss does not give you or your department any support, and basically you feel bored and frustrated. According to family and friends, you have had a noticeable mood change during this time period from being a happy person who laughed easily to someone no longer wanting to socialize and seemingly preoccupied with work. After much consideration and analysis of your current position, you decide the negatives outweigh the positives and it is time for a job change. Once the decision is made to find a new job, both you and your family are relieved. Stress immediately is diminished, but what new stress will you and your family encounter as you search for another position?

- *Insecurity:* The interviewing process can be stressful. You may hear that you are too experienced, inexperienced, or overqualified.
- *Anxiety:* Whether preparing for an interview or answering an advertisement for an opening, anxiety can be experienced.
- *Frustration:* A job search can be a frustrating experience as you seek out new opportunities and wait to hear from those you contacted or interviewed.
- *Instability:* Your family does not know if the new job will require relocating or readjusting their lifestyle.
- *Financial concerns:* Will you be able to find a position with a salary comparable to your current salary?

What can be done to minimize the stress that may be associated with these new feelings?

1. Develop a timeline to achieve your objective, which is to acquire another job.
2. Communicate your concerns to your spouse.
3. Maintain a steady income while searching for your new position.
4. Discuss your progress with your spouse or significant other only. Do not involve the children in the details of the job hunt. Children will read into a job search. They may feel a new job would require moving to a new city, or they may fear their family has no money because of the search for a new job. Try to minimize stress by limiting potential anxiety.

This scenario addresses issues pertaining to someone who is currently in the workplace and the impact a job change will have on the immediate family. If you are a new college graduate and have chosen to seek a job in a location not close to home, you may experience the same situation but with your parents. On the one hand, parents are excited for their child to begin their career. On the other hand, feelings of emptiness and loneliness may surface, which could become stressors for them. Keeping parents informed about the job search, soliciting their guidance, and involving them in your progress may alleviate stress.

In the book, *Management of Health Information*, Mattingly (1996) career curves are illustrated. Figure 9-2 indicates job enthusiasm at the beginning of the career. Stagnation along with the decline of interest result if the

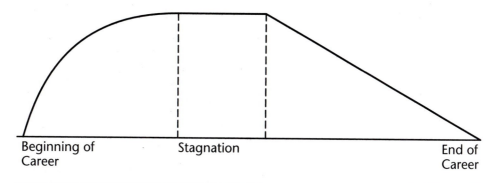

Figure 9-2.   Lack of New Vision Experience

health information professional does not take a proactive role in career development. Enthusiasm ends and so does the career.

This can be compared to Figure 9-3 which illustrates the career course when you "revitalize" your career. Accepting new challenges and pursuing additional education opportunities are two ways to achieve revitalization. Stagnation will not occur if you become visionary with your career.

Along the career path, setbacks may occur. When this happens, do not discontinue your efforts in meeting your career objectives. Pursue measures that will assist you in restoring your self-confidence. In this way the

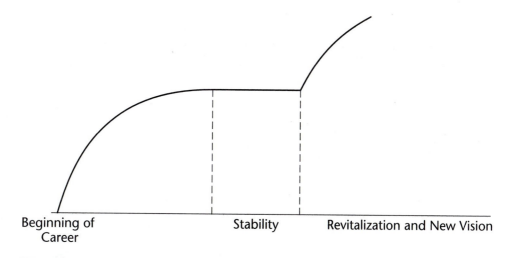

Figure 9-3.   New Vision Experience

effects of the setback will be minimized. If this is not accomplished, then stress could enter or return to your life.

A career in health information management can be exciting and rewarding for those who manage their careers. The time and effort expended is an investment in yourself.

Summary

- Stress is prevalent in our lives. Unfortunately, we do not always take the time required to thoroughly analyze the underlying etiologies of stress.
- The physical and psychological conditions manifested by stress must be addressed.
- Sneaking stress or chronic stress can be detrimental to your health. Let go of stressors that are harmful to you. Focus on those things that bring balance into your life.
- Empower yourself by developing the following skills:
  1. *Establishing personal goals:* Where do you want to be and what needs to be accomplished to get you there?
  2. *Assuming responsibility:* Learn from any setbacks and do not blame others.
  3. *Being perserverant:* Do not give up. Stay focused on your goal.
  4. *Implementing flexibility into your way of thinking:* In doing so, the effects of change will be minimized. You will not focus on what did not work, but will be open to trying something new.
  5. *Practicing proactiveness:* Feeling frustrated on the job can lead to burnout. Accepting a challenge to improve yourself or confronting a conflict will minimize the effects of frustration.
  6. *Resolving to delegate:* This will assist in time management, which is one of the biggest sources of stress.
- Remember that job instability, change, and relocation can affect family members.

Review Activities

1. Provide a short scenario illustrating how stress can develop in the workplace.

2. Explain the cause-and-effect relationship between stress and burnout.
3. Job burnout in the healthcare professions is high. In your opinion, is this assumption true or false, and why?
4. What is meant by "balancing your life"? Should you strive for this?
5. Select one element you identified as a stressor on the stress inventory and develop a plan to either eliminate or minimize the effects.

References

Barker, J. (1995). Family Ties. *Performance*, September, 18–23.

Braham, B. (1994). *Managing stress, keeping calm under fire.* New York: Irwin Professional Publishing.

Feeling Squeezed (1996). *Wall Street Journal*, 26 February, R4.

Jaffe, D., and Scott, C. (1988). *Take this job and love it: How to change your work without changing your job.* New York: Simon and Schuster.

Lafikes, G. (1996). *Time for a Career Fitness Checkup. St. Louis Post–Dispatch*, 21 January, 16H.

Leatz, C., and Stolar, M. (1993). *Career success/personal stress/how to stay healthy in a high stress environment.* New York: McGraw-Hill, Inc.

Lovelace, R. (1990). *Stress master.* New York: John Wiley and Sons.

Mattingly, R. (1996). *Management of health information: Functions and applications.* Albany: Delmar Publishers.

Potter, B. (1987). *Preventing job burnout.* Los Altos: Crisp Publications, Inc.

Tate, M. (1992). *Truth about stress.* St. George: LDI Publishing.

Waldman, J. (1996). Downshifting: Finding a Balance Between Life and Work. *St. Louis Post–Dispatch*, 16 June 19G.

Position Titles

Followed by Responsibilities Frequently Associated with the Position

Account Representative

- Demonstrates computerized health and financial information and clinical software.
- Recommends changes to improve product.
- Communicates with clients and groups to market product.
- Prepares reports to advise clients of strengths and uses for the product.

Accounts/Imaging Coordinator

- Supervises staff.
- Maintains all accounts receivable.
- Directs inpatient and outpatient chart retrieval upon discharge.
- Organizes preparation and scanning of charts into a computerized information system.
- Oversees quality review of documentation.
- Ensures integrity of patient numbering system.

Admitting and Medical Reservationist

- Directs computerized inpatient registration functions.
- Sets guideline for preregistration of patients.

- Trains employees to use guest-relations skills when admitting patients and communicating with families.
- Recommends software and systems.

Alternative Services Director

See Health Information Manager. Responsibilities would be similar; however, instead of being an acute-care hospital the facility could be:

- Long-Term Care
- Behavioral/Mental Health
- Hospice Care
- Nursing Home, or other.

The Alternative Services Director in a nonacute facility may have responsibility for facilitywide quality improvement activities.

Ambulatory-Care Administrator

- Manages facilitywide quality improvement activities.
- Directs and evaluates employees and information systems.
- Recommends purchases.
- Determines guidelines for coding.
- Assists with research studies.
- Coordinates release of patient information.

Ambulatory-Care Business Manager

- Applies financial management and cost accounting principles to ensure efficiency and effectiveness of services.
- Prepares timely reports in accordance with government regulations and administrative needs.
- Assists with marketing and public relations.

Audit Specialist

- Analyzes hospital bills for comparison with health information documentation.
- Prepares narrative and graphic reports of conclusions and recommendations.
- Applies utilization review skills and regulatory requirements.

Cancer Registry Coordinator

- Locates and registers cancer patients.
- Abstracts information and conducts follow-up studies of cancer patients.
- Coordinates cancer registry activities to meet internal and external regulatory and time requirements.
- Prepares data for presentation.
- Completes patient care evaluation studies.
- Produces special and annual reports.

Chief Information Officer

- Organizes information systems.
- Leads the strategic planning process for information systems.
- Integrates organizational information technology, e.g., data process, office systems, and telecommunications.
- Develops and coordinates policies and procedures for technology acquisition, implementation, and operation.
- Maintains information systems that are functional and ensures data integrity and security.
- Establishes techniques to ensure confidentiality of patient information and access to authorized users only.
- Develops annual budget and monitors adherence to the plan.

Clinical Data Specialist/Supervisor

- Determines codes using ICD-9-CM and CPT-4 to accurately reflect the diagnoses and procedures documented.
- Maximizes the DRG reimbursement.
- Meets regulatory coding requirements.
- Applies encoder skills and knowledge of pathophysiology, anatomy, and clinical medicine.
- Analyzes outcomes to improve efficiency and effectiveness of services.
- Maintains special registries and research databases as needed by the users.

Clinical Pertinence Analyst

- Develops and applies criteria for clinical pertinence reviews.
- Oversees database modifications.
- Enters clinical pertinence data according to criteria and within specified time frames.
- Presents results to appropriate committees for review and evaluation.
- Uses with proficiency dBase, DOS, spreadsheet software, and Windows.

Clinical Reimbursement Analyst

- Coordinates reimbursement activities for medical records and patient financial services.
- Expedites coding.

Clinical Research Associate

- Assists in the design, implementation, and monitoring of clinical research studies.
- Reviews and summarizes clinical data.
- Designs data collection instruments and forms.

- Prepares reports of study findings.
- Tests research findings for validity and reliability.
- Disseminates research findings.

Coder/Analyst; Coding Specialist

- Applies accurately current principles of ICD-9-CM and CPT-4 and DRG documentation and assignment.
- Uses computerized abstracting system and DRG Grouper System.
- Complies with PRO regulations.

Coding Auditor

- Audits patient charts.
- Maintains ICD-9-CM and CPT-4 system updates.
- Conducts on-site training classes.
- Delivers formal presentations as requested.
- Interacts professionally with physicians, nurses, administration, and personnel.

Coding Compliance Coordinator

- Provides consultation and education for physicians, staff, and personnel on documentation and coding.
- Participates in defining data elements for institution-wide data collection.
- Monitors quality of documentation, coding, abstracting, and transcription.
- Generates reports as needed for administration and medical staff.

Coding Documentation Educator

- Enhances physician documentation through education.
- Provides continuing education sessions on documentation and systems for physicians in a healthcare network.

- Applies knowledge of ICD-9-CM and CPT-4.
- Conducts educational sessions on guidelines and regulatory requirements for documentation.
- Displays excellent oral and written communication skills.
- Travels regularly to various client sites.

Consultant, Medical Records

- Leads process improvement projects to improve patient intake processes.
- Directs operational effectiveness for coding and third-party billing practices.
- Plans and implements electronic patient record systems.
- Participates in DRG optimization reviews.
- Assists with quality improvement projects.
- Prepares oral and written reports as requested or needed.
- Travels regionally and nationally.

Correspondence Coordinator

- Solves problems associated with release-of-information activities.
- Coordinates release of information in conformance with statutes, rules, and regulations.
- Monitors the release of information to ensure confidentiality of patient-related data.
- Updates policies and procedures to comply with optimal standards for appropriate release of information.
- Maintains daily work flow.
- Assists with insurance and PRO audits.
- Coordinates activities of outside copy service.
- Applies excellent written communication skills.
- Interacts professionally with internal and external professionals and public.

CPT Coder–Auditor

- Reviews medical and billing records to verify CPT codes for surgery, labs, and radiology.
- Verifies payment accuracy.
- Identifies payment methods for reimbursing claims.
- Screens and analyzes audit samples.
- Evaluates special requests for audits.
- Resolves discrepancies with internal and external personnel.
- Applies knowledge of medical terminology, diagnostic evaluations, and pathophysiology.

Credentialing Coordinator

- Performs physician and allied health credentialing.
- Applies knowledge of computer systems.
- Maintains medical staff files.
- Serves as staff to credentialing committee.
- Develops and maintains database of medical staff members.

Data Analyst; Medical Data Analyst

- Codes and abstracts for ICD-9-CM, CPT-4, HCPCS, and DRG assignments.
- Conducts utilization and resource management activities.
- Participates in medical staff credentialing and committee functions.
- Communicates with physicians and other professionals.

Data Quality Manager

- Ensures data integrity through policy development.
- Conducts training programs, quality monitors, and audits.
- Implements controls to maximize effectiveness of services.

- Supervises personnel.
- Serves as problem-solving resource for encoder system.
- Formalizes continuous quality improvement for data integrity.
- Develops data dictionary and data quality policies.

Director of Health Information Services

- Manages health information functions to achieve state-of-the-art information technology.
- Supervises and develops personnel.
- Coordinates daily operation of assigned functions.
- Ensures data integrity and accessibility to qualified users.
- Communicates fluently on global health information systems and services.
- Applies excellent physician and interpersonal relationship skills.

Director of Medical Records

- Supervises personnel in medical records department.
- Develops policies and procedures that will improve the management of information services.
- Participates in committees: medical records, quality improvement and utilization review.
- Prepares and monitors annual budget.
- Interacts with other department directors to promote cooperation and communication.
- Participates in accreditation processes.

Discharge Planning Coordinator

- Directs discharge processing and chart completion.
- Supervises area activities and personnel.
- Monitors quality and productivity.

- Conducts quality assurance audits.
- Prepares activity reports.
- Applies decision-making and communication skills.

Document and Repository Manager

- Ensures long-term data integrity and access by authorized users only.
- Establishes retention policies and procedures.
- Determines appropriate media for records and data storage.
- Maintains inventory of where and how data are maintained.
- Prepares and monitors annual budget.

DRG Coordinator/Validator

- Validates DRGs.
- Communicates professionally with physicians to optimize reimbursement.
- Codes accurately inpatient and outpatient diagnoses and procedures using ICD-9-CM and CPT-4.
- Compiles patient information to ensure completion of the diagnostic and procedural indices.

Educator/Instructor

- Demonstrates current knowledge in course content and effectiveness in teaching assigned subjects.
- Participates in departmental and institutional committees.
- Acts as a resource to the community in area of expertise.
- Conducts research and scholarly activities.
- Provides service to professional organizations.
- Serves as an advocate for the profession.

Educator HIA and HIT Program Director/Chairperson

- Provides leadership for program and profession.
- Determines mission, goals, and objectives for program in harmony with those of the institution.
- Coordinates the scheduling and assignment of courses.
- Directs activities in compliance with accreditation standards.
- Prepares and monitors program budget.
- Represents the program at university and professional functions.
- Recommends appointments to school/college/university committee in collaboration with program faculty.
- Initiates and participates in recruitment activities.
- Conducts research and scholarly activities.
- Provides service to professional organizations.

Extended-Care Facility—Medical Record Director

- Supervises personnel.
- Manages healthcare information for effective and efficient use by the facility.
- Provides systems for health data retrieval and retention, which meet the needs of the facility, consumers, providers, and external forces.
- Develops and coordinates systems to assess the quality and utilization of services.
- Assures conformance to statutes, regulations, and standards from external agencies as they apply to medical record information and related documentation.

Field Representative/Coordinator; Field Operations Manager

- Trains and meets new clients.
- Travels within assigned area.
- Applies excellent oral communication skills.

File Supervisor

- Trains and supervises employees.
- Delegates work assignments to assure smooth operation and optimal standards.
- Coordinates interactivities associated with information needs.

Film Library Supervisor

- Selects, trains, develops, and organizes support staff to perform and meet department objectives effectively.
- Supervises employees.
- Manages acquisition and inventory control.
- Maintains physician-responsive retrieval of diagnostic records.
- Assists in development and monitoring of policies and procedures.

Health Data Analyst/Health Information Analyst

- Analyzes impatient, outpatient, and ambulatory surgery records quantitatively and qualitatively.
- Assigns code using ICD-9-CM and CPT-4.
- Uses encoder effectively.
- Retrieves coded data as needed from databases.

Health Information Management Specialist

- Implements and maintains new systems.
- Coordinates quality improvement activities to ensure systems are efficient and effective.
- Assists in the development and analysis of the annual capital budget.
- Applies communication and interpersonal skills.
- Participates in redesigning the computerized information systems.
- Conducts ongoing assessment of new technology, equipment, and productivity techniques.

- Demonstrates understanding of medical record technical activities.

Health Information Manager

- Coordinates information system with application developers and users to improve functions and data quality.

Health Information Product Manager Specialist

- Manages personnel assigned to team.
- Educates users on product upgrades.
- Performs end-user training.
- Coordinates installation of the system.

Health Information Technician

- Abstracts and codes proficiently diagnoses and surgical procedures according to ICD-9-CM and CPT-4 principles and federal Medicare reimbursement regulations.
- Performs DRG assignments for inpatient, outpatient, and emergency room records.
- Applies skills in using billing, encoding system, and computer systems.

Home Health Agency, Health Information Manager

- Maintains computerized health information database.
- Manages utilization review and quality improvement functions.
- Organizes analysis of health information quantitatively and qualitatively.
- Applies principles of ICD-9-CM.
- Establishes long- and short-range goals for the agency's health information services.

- Evaluates patient information systems to achieve goals and meet standards of accrediting, licensing, and regulatory agencies.
- Participates in committee and other functions.

Hospice, Medical Record Coordinator; Clinical Information Manager

- Justifies, purchases, installs, and updates clinical information system.
- Evaluates patient record system to attain goals and meet standards of regulatory agencies.
- Maintains acceptable methods for documentation.
- Serves on forms and other committees.
- Searches for grant money to fund projects.
- Coordinates accounting software with clinical information system.
- Creates and monitors inventory tracking system for supplies.

Implementation Analyst/Consultant

- Provides initial and additional training on new computer information system to internal and external customers.
- Creates written educational/training materials for computer information system.
- Applies surveillance checks to monitor accuracy of data.
- Travels to various facilities regularly and for special requests.

Internal Auditor

- Audits physician medical records to ensure that documentation reflects the services billed.
- Monitors for compliance with federal, state, and other regulatory requirements.
- Applies proficiently coding, billing, and medical terminology skills.
- Communicates findings orally and in writing to appropriate persons.

Managed-Care Specialist

- Obtains and maintains managed care contracts.
- Reviews and reports on managed care statistics.
- Coordinates managed care activities with coding, billing, and quality assurance functions.
- Assists with filing claims and posting payments.
- Conducts surveys to determine customer needs and satisfaction.

Manager Professional Fee Support Services/Ambulatory Care

- Develops and implements programs to capture professional fee.
- Assures accurate coding for reimbursement.
- Analyzes financial data.
- Prepares reports identifying payment trends.
- Conducts medical record/financial audits.

Market Research Analyst

- Assists the director in providing support to full-service research divisions.
- Designs customer satisfaction research according to appropriate design and analytical techniques.
- Applies excellent presentation skills.
- Uses principles of continuous and total quality improvement systems.
- Measures and tracks customer satisfaction through research techniques.

Medical Office Manager

- Selects, trains, and manages office staff to perform assigned responsibilities.
- Directs the preparation, maintenance, and distribution of reports required for management purposes including performance appraisals and work evaluations.

- Enforces adherence to rules and regulations regarding proper maintenance of records, affirmative action, safety, and confidentiality of patient information.
- Ensures expeditious and appropriate billing practices.
- Maintains an office environment that is functional for physicians and staff and pleasant for patients.

Medical Record Coders

- Reviews and classifies clinical data from medical records.
- Assists with reimbursement and quality improvement activities.
- Complies with institutional procedures and external regulatory requirements relating to coding and reimbursement.

Medical Record Product Manager

- Selects, trains, develops, and organizes a support staff to perform and meet product development and marketing needs.
- Assists clients.
- Facilitates contract negotiations.
- Researches and applies latest technology.
- Achieves effectiveness in accordance with goals and mission of the organization.

Medical Staff Coordinator

See Credentialing Coordinator.

Medical Writer

- Creates manuscripts for publication.
- Solicits authors for journals, textbooks, and other publications.
- Researches photographs and graphics appropriate for figures and tables to enhance printed materials.

- Acts as a liaison between authors and publishers.

Medisgroup Data Abstractor

- Enters clinical data into abstracting system.
- Validates accuracy of data.

Occupational Health Record Supervisor

- Advises medical practitioners on proper recording of medical findings for computerized information system.
- Interfaces effectively with all levels of personnel.
- Displays organizational skills in accomplishing goals.
- Communicates with medical practitioners regarding medical data accuracy.
- Analyzes medical information.
- Assigns code numbers to physician findings.
- Generates reports for administration and medical staff.
- Supervises data-entry employees and distributes work flow to promote a team approach.
- Participates in meetings and continuing education activities.

Oncology Manager; Oncology Data Quality Coordinator

See Tumor Registrar.

Operations Manager

- Supervises the daily operations and departmental personnel.
- Assists the director of health information management in developing and implementing departmental goals and procedures.
- Communicates with professionals, personnel, and patients.
- Applies knowledge of medical terminology, computer systems, coding, and master patient index.

Paralegal, Medical

- Conducts Medline and other searches.
- Scans documents for editing and legal formatting.
- Prepares documents.
- Assists with research and documentation reviews.

Patient Information Coordinator

- Educates consumers on maintenance of personal health information.
- Assists patients in compiling personal health history and updating this as needed.
- Mediates release of information.
- Discusses managed-care services with patients and their families.
- Seeks grants to fund services as appropriate.

Patient Records Technician

- Develops statistical reports from maintenance and analyses of medical records and information.
- Codes for JCAHO and Medicaid/Medicare certified facility.

Patient Review Analyst

- Conducts preadmission and concurrent reviews.
- Reports on quality-of-care issues.
- Analyzes patient care/institutional data in relation to regulatory and accreditation standards.

Photocopy Services Manager

- Determines pricing for facilities locally or regionally.
- Coordinates and oversees the on-site team at facilities.
- Performs quality assessments and productivity studies.

- Adheres to rules and regulations established for proper disclosure of information, in accordance with state and federal laws.
- Develops and directs the orientation program for new employees.
- Maintains a work environment that promotes the retention of employees and attracts qualified prospective employees.

Physicians' Incomplete Chart Coordinator

- Assists physicians in chart completion.
- Uses strategy to enhance rapid processing.
- Prepares reports daily, monthly, and annually to indicate current status and progress.

Product Development Specialist

- Develops products for health information management systems.

Project Coordinator

- Oversees project from initiation to completion.
- Maintains time schedules for the project.
- Develops progress reports for management and others as required to facilitate progress of the project.

Prospective Payment Analyst/Coordinator

- Codes Medicare and non-Medicare records.
- Applies effectively principles, rules, and regulations for coding.
- Assists with DRG optimization and validation.

Psychiatric Center, Medical Records Director

- Selects, trains, develops, and organizes a support staff to perform and meet department responsibilities and objectives effectively.

- Provides leadership by conforming to internal and external rules and regulations of conduct.
- Maintains a work environment that promotes retention of employees.
- Facilitates completion of continuing education requirements for credentialed employees.
- Develops and monitors adherence to annual budget.
- Promotes compliance with JCAHO information management standards.

Quality Assurance/Quality Improvement/Quality Management Coordinator/Director

- Participates in setting expectations, developing plans, managing processes, and setting priorities to measure, assess, and improve the quality of clinical and patient-care services.
- Develops and presents educational in-services to staff at all levels to communicate progress in meeting goals and standards.
- Recommends performance improvement activities.
- Manages the change processes leading to quality improvement.
- Assists in assessing that processes and activities that affect patient outcomes are systematically and regularly assessed and improved.

Radiology Records Coordinator/Film Library Manager

- Develops policies and procedures for record retention.
- Selects, trains, develops, and evaluates personnel.
- Meets department responsibilities and objectives efficiently and effectively.
- Participates in quality improvement activities.
- Assists with coding issues for physician reimbursement.
- Compiles statistical reports as needed to assess progress toward goals and achievement of standards.

Record Processing Supervisor

- Trains and supervises support staff to file, retrieve, and process records.
- Manages admission record processing and record completion.
- Monitors work flow under span of control.
- Collects data on the quality of documentation in health records.
- Tracks location of medical records.
- Develops reports on the status of incomplete records and documentation.
- Evaluates compliance with policies and procedures for health records.
- Participates in committee activities as assigned.
- Calculates institutional census and other statistical data.

Registered Record Administrator

- Directs and manages activities of medical records department.
- Complies with JCAHO and other regulatory requirements.
- Recommends and implements computer systems and latest reimbursement methodologies impacting medical records.

Rehabilitation Health Information Services Director

- Selects, manages, evaluates, and develops personnel.
- Conducts educational programs for departmental and rehabilitation physician and staff.
- Provides leadership relating to health information services and systems.
- Develops departmental policies and procedures.
- Maintains standards to meet accreditation and regulatory requirements.

Reimbursement Specialist

- Audits daily inpatient and outpatient reports.
- Performs concurrent coding.

- Conducts inpatient and outpatient peer review for accuracy of coding and sequencing.
- Facilitates corrective action for coding errors.
- Plans and participates in training sessions for staff.
- Applies skills in reimbursement optimization.
- Upgrades encoder software as needed.

Release of Information Specialist

- Serves as hospital's representative in court, in response to subpoenas and depositions.
- Processes external requests for clinical information in accordance with statutes and standards to ensure confidentiality of patient-related data.
- Makes decisions in pressured situations.
- Communicates professionally with third-party payors, patients, and legal professionals.
- Applies excellent verbal and written communication skills.

Research and Decision Support Analyst

- Supports senior management with information for decision making and strategy development.
- Provides support for high-level projects such as clinical trials.
- Develops informational reports in narrative and graphic formats for decision making and strategic planning.
- Participates in projects designed to assess outcomes and patient satisfaction.

Research and Statistics Supervisor

- Coordinates all internal and external audits.
- Supervises and develops technical and clerical staff.
- Conducts quality assurance activities relating to medical record documentation.

- Prepares reports of study findings.
- Confers with peers, providers, and users of services.

Risk Manager

- Performs conflict resolution activities.
- Provides consultation, education, and training.
- Acts as the liaison between the healthcare enterprise and legal counsel.

Sales Representative

- Applies excellent presentation and communication skills.
- Demonstrates knowledge of health information functions and systems.
- Solves problems with the ability to move others into action.

Security Officer

- Manages the security of all electronically maintained information.
- Develops and promulgates security requirements.
- Designs and enforces policies for data integrity and retention.
- Audits compliance with policies and procedures for electronically maintained information.
- Conducts training and educational sessions for physicians, health professionals, and users of information systems.

Service Consultants in Clinical Information

- Thrives in a fast-paced environment.
- Applies powerful analytical problem-solving skills.
- Communicates proficiently verbally and in writing.
- Provides consultation on information systems, claims processing, case management, managed care, and other areas as needed.

Software Representative

- Installs and provides educational support for software.
- Trains users.
- Consults with professionals on operational issues.
- Applies communication skills, computer experience, and knowledge of DOS, networking, and health information systems.

State Association Executive Coordinator

- Organizes strategic planning process.
- Participates in budget process and monitors compliance with the plan.
- Maintains updated computerized roster of members by category of membership, including business and home addresses and telephone numbers.
- Directs issues to appropriate persons for response and resolution.
- Assists with meeting planning, scheduling, organizing, and smooth functioning.

Statistician/Epidemiologist

- Supports decision making.
- Promotes quality improvement efforts.
- Provides consultation in research design, data retrieval, database design, statistical analysis, and reporting findings.
- Applies skills in statistical analysis, research design, epidemiology, and survey design.
- Uses proficiently SAS or SPSS, spreadsheets, database and graphics software.

Supervisor Medical Records

- Demonstrates supervisory skills.
- Provides performance assessments to employees formatively and annually.

- Implements corrective action in a timely manner.
- Displays strong analytical and problem-solving skills.
- Compiles, interprets, and evaluates statistical data.
- Develops and monitors staffing schedules.
- Performs job analysis.
- Updates job descriptions.
- Assigns projects and duties to appropriate personnel.
- Prioritizes functions, services, and assignments.

System Manager, Medical Records

- Monitors systems outcomes in relation to costs, benefits, and accuracy.
- Recommends changes and improvements in systems.
- Determines variations from established goals and objectives.
- Designs and applies surveillance of accuracy techniques.
- Develops policies and procedures to ensure confidentiality of computer data and access to authorized users only.

Team Leader—Health Information Services

- Assists the HIS manager with daily operations.
- Monitors quality of department coding, abstracting, and transcription.
- Participates in defining data elements for institutionwide data collection.
- Defines documentation requirements to meet external and internal requirements.
- Encourages employee compliance with policies and procedures.

Third-Party Physician Reimbursement Specialist

- Develops and implements programs to ensure utilization of proper CPT-4 and ICD-9-CM coding for optimal reimbursement of physician billing.

- Ensures compliance with third-party regulations and documentation requirements.
- Compares claims submitted to third-party payers with reimbursement received.
- Collects data on the quality of documentation.
- Monitors status of incomplete records and amount of outstanding accounts.

Transcriptionist

- Applies knowledge of medical terminology, anatomy, pathophysiology, and English language.
- Uses designated equipment effectively, meeting the standards required for quality and productivity.
- Refers to resources to facilitate the accuracy, clarity, and completeness of reports.
- Participates in in-service and continuing education activities.
- Formats reports according to guidelines.
- Verifies information for accuracy, completeness, consistency, and appropriateness.

Transcription Supervisor

- Implements and maintains transcription system to achieve optional quality and quantity standards.
- Applies digital dictation techniques and coordinates activities with professional staff.
- Supervises employees.
- Monitors work flow.

Tumor Registrar

- Maintains tumor registry.
- Abstracts required information on cancer and other reportable tumors.

- Participates in conferences and committees.
- Prepares narrative and graphical reports.
- Presents to medical staff and committees.
- Applies knowledge of ICDO coding.
- Abstracts information from records of patients diagnosed with malignancy.
- Assists in cancer-related studies and research.
- Develops quality improvement and control measures.

Utilization Review Coordinator

- Reviews medical information concurrently with the medical staff and outside agencies.
- Prepares narrative and graphical reports for quality improvement and utilization management functions.
- Communicates clinical data to a variety of audiences.
- Participates in institutional quality improvement activities.
- Confers with peers, providers, and users of departmental and institutional services.

Vendor of Hospital Software

- Designs software for computerized medical record applications to meet users' requirements.
- Applies knowledge of the healthcare industry and data collection requirements for health record documentation, quality improvement, and utilization review.
- Demonstrates in-depth understanding of prospective payment system, coding, billing, and regulatory requirements.
- Communicates effectively vis-à-vis or in a group.
- Advises on long-term product direction.

Veterinary Medicine, Medical Records Administrator

- Plans and implements computerized systems.

- Participates in defining data elements for data collection.
- Compiles statistical reports monthly and annually.
- Develops policies and procedures for data collection, storage, and retention.
- Manages current systems to ensure accuracy, completeness, consistency, and timeliness of information.

Review Activities

1. Name at least three additional position titles that you have seen in journals or the newspaper that could be added to the list provided.
2. Of the position titles listed, name two that you think will be discontinued in the next ten years. State your reasons.
3. Select one position and identify at least one additional responsibility that should be added to the list.
4. Identify three positions that you would like to have after you complete your studies.
5. On every position listed, "Meets standards of professional and ethical conduct" could be added. Name another responsibility that would be universal in that it would apply to almost every position in health information management.

Accredited Education Programs

Health Information Technology (HIT)

All of the following programs for health information technicians have been accredited by the Commission on Accreditation of Allied Health Education Programs (CAAHEP), 515 North State Street, Chicago, Illinois 60610, in cooperation with the Council on Accreditation (COA) of the American Health Information Management Association (AHIMA), 919 North Michigan Avenue, Suite 1400, Chicago, Illinois 60611.

For detailed information about a program, contact the college or university. Programs listed may offer one or more of the following and are indicated as such:

CS   **Coding specialist** program/track. Although coding programs are not accredited by AHIMA, the association does acknowledge coding programs offered by accredited educational programs.

⊕   **Multiple campuses/sites**

(Revised October 1996)

State	Institution	Address Line 1	Address Line 2	Program Director	Office #
1. AK	University of Alaska Southeast	1332 Seward Avenue	Sitka-99835	Carol Liberty MS RRA	907.747.7718
2. AL	Bishop State Community College	351 North Broad Street	Mobile-36603	Annalesia Sharp RRA	205.690.6413
3. AL	Wallace State College	PO Box 2000	Hanceville-35077	Donna Stanley EdS RRA	205.352.2090
4. AR	Garland County Community College [CS]	PO Box 3470	Hot Springs Nat'l Park-71914	Susan Wallace MEd RRA	501.767.9371
5. AZ	Phoenix College	1202 West Thomas Road	Phoenix-85013	Deborah Dennis RRA	602.285.7148
6. CA	Chabot College	25555 Hesperian Blvd	Hayward-94545	Diane Premeau RRA	510.786.6904
7. CA	City College of San Francisco	1860 Hayes Street John Adams Campus	San Francisco-94117	Marie Conde BS ART	415.561.1818
8. CA	Charles R. Drew University	1621 East 120th Street	Los Angeles-90059	Barbara Penn RRA	213.563.5888
9. CA	Cosumnes River College	8401 Center Parkway	Sacramento-95823	Sharon Stith MA RRA	916.688.7244
10. CA	Cypress College	9200 Valley View	Cypress-90630	Rosalie Majid RRA	714.826.2220
11. CA	East Los Angeles College	1301 Avenida Cesar Chavez	Monterey Park-91754	Lea Davidson MPH RRA	213.265.8884
12. CA	Fresno City College	1101 East University Avenue	Fresno-93741	Christine Sherrill RRA	209.442.8217
13. CA	San Diego Mesa College	7250 Mesa College Drive	San Diego-92111	Teddy Scribner MS RRA	619.560.2606
14. CO	Arapahoe Community College	5900 South Santa Fe Drive	Littleton-80120	Annette Bigalk RRA	303.797.5888
15. CO	Pueblo Community College	900 West Orman Avenue	Pueblo-81004	Jill Sell-Kruse RRA	719.549.3143
16. CT	Briarwood College	2279 Mount Vernon Road	Southington-06489	A.H.Lenne Klopfer MS RRA	203.628.4751
17. FL	Broward Community College	3501 Southwest Davie Road	Davie-33314	Mary Spivey RRA	305.475.6786

State	Institution	Address Line 1	Address Line 2	Program Director	Office #
18. FL	Daytona Beach Community College	PO Box 2811	Daytona Beach-32115	Nancy Thomas EdD, RRA	904.255.8131
19. FL	Florida Community College	601 West State Street	Jacksonville-32202	Eudelia Thomas MS RRA	904.632.5065
20. FL	Indian River Community College	3209 Virginia Avenue	Fort Pierce-34981-5599	Claudia Keating MEd, RRA	407.462.4265
21. FL	International College	2654 Tamiami Trail East	Naples-39962	Deborah Howard RRA	813.774.4700
22. FL	Miami Dade Community College	950 NW 20th Street-Rm 2241	Miami-33127	Josephine Gordon RRA	305.237.4043
23. FL	Pensacola Junior College	5555 West Highway 98	Pensacola-32507	Barbara Edwards MEd RRA	904.457.2213
24. FL	Sant Petersburg Junior College	7200 66th Street North	Pinellas Park-33733	Sheila Newberry RRA	813.341.3623
25. GA	Darton Colleges	2400 Gillionville Road	Albany-31707-3098	Ruth Shingleton MBA RRA	912.430.6894
26. GA	Medical College of Georgia	School of Allied Hlth Sciences-AL22	Augusta-30912	Charlotte Johnston PhD RRA	706.721.3436
27. IA	Indian Hills Community College	525 Grandview Avenue	Ottumwa-52501	Heidi Clayton BS RRA	515.683.5163
28. IA	Kirkwood Community College	6301 Kirkwood Boulevard SW	Cedar Rapids-52406	Joanne Becker ART	319.398.2068
29. IA	Ncrtheast Iowa Community College	Box 400	Calmar-52132	Linda Hess RN RRA	319.562.3263
30. ID	Idaho State University	Campus Box 8380	Pocatello-88209	Suzanne Griffin MEd RRA	208.236.4169
31. ID	Boise State University	1910 University Drive	Boise-83725	Patricia Ellison MA RRA	208.385.1130
32. IL	Belleville Area College	2500 Carlyle Road	Belleville-62221	Wendy Holder RRA	618.235.2700
33. IL	College of DuPage	22nd & Lambert Roads-IC1028	Glen Ellyn-60137	Kim Pack MS RRA	708.858.2800
34. IL	Co lege of Lake County	19351 West Washington Street	Grayslake-60030	Denise Anastatio MPA RRA	708.223.6601
35. IL	Mcraine Valley Community College	10900 South 88th Avenue	Palos Hills-60465	Charlotte Razor MHA RRA	708.974.5315
36. IL	Oaxton Community College	1600 East Golf Road	Des Plaines-60016	Cynthia DeBerg MA RRA	708.635.1957
37. IL	Robert Morris College	43 Orland Square	Orland Park-60452	Marie Giacomelli, Interim	312.349.5140
38. IL	Southern Illinois Collegiate Common Mkt	106 Airway Drive	Marion-62959	Mary Sullivan MS RRA	618.993.5282
39. IL	Truman College	1145 West Wilson Avenue	Chicago-60640	Daphine Leton RRA	312.907.4781
40. IN	Indiana-Purdue University	2101 Coliseum Boulevard East	Fort Wayne-46805	Barbara Ellison BS RRA	219.481.6966

267

State	Institution	Address Line 1	Address Line 2	Program Director	Office #
41. IN	Indiana University Northwest	3400 Broadway	Gary-46408	Margaret Skurka MS RRA	219.980.6654
42. IN	Vincennes University [CS]	1002 North First Street	Vincennes-47591	Darrel King MS RRA	812.885.4243
43. KS	Dodge City Community College	2501 North 14th Street	Dodge City-67801	Barbara Reulian RRA	316.225.1321
44. KS	Hutchinson Community College	815 North Walnut Street	Hutchinson-67501	Loretta Horton RRA	316.665.4955
45. KS	Washburn University of Topeka	1700 Southwest College Ave	Topeka-66621	Michelle Shipley RRA CCS	913.231.1010
46. KY	Eastern Kentucky University	Dizney 117	Richmond-40475	Frances Hindsman MBA RRA	606.622.1915
47. KY	Western Kentucky University	Academic Complex 207	Bowling Green-42101	Karen Samsom MS RRA	502.745.2427
48. LA	Delgado Community College	615 City Park Avenue	New Orleans-70119	Melissa LaCour RRA	504.483.4435
49. LA	Louisiana Tech University	PO Box 3171	Ruston-71272	Helen Baxter MA RRA	318.257.2854
50. LA	Southern University-Shreveport	610 Texas Street 328A	Shreveport-71101	Ann Marohn MS RRA	318.674.5058
51. MA	Bristol Community College	777 Elsbree Street	Fall River-02720	Edward Dobbs RRA	508.678.2811
52. MA	Fisher College	118 Beacon Street	Boston-02116	Nancy Allen-Tuch MBA RRA	617.236.8800
53. MA	Holyoke Community College	303 Homestead Avenue	Holyoke-01040	Marylou Theilman BA MEd	413.538.7000
54. MA	Laboure College	2120 Dorchester Avenue	Boston-02124	Eileen Perry MBA RRA	617.296.8300
55. MA	Northern Essex Community College	Elliott Way	Haverhill-01830	Patricia Taglianetti MBA RRA	508.374.5827
56. MD	Baltimore Community College	2901 Liberty Heights Avenue	Baltimore-21215	Betty Neely Mitchell RRA	410.333.5928
57. MD	Hagerstown Business College	18618 Crestwood Avenue	Hagerstown-21742	Beth Shanholtzer RRA	301.739.2670
58. MD	Montgomery College	Takoma and Fenton Streets	Takoma Park-20912	Sue Meiskey MSA RRA	301.650.1337
59. MD	Prince George's Community College	301 Largo Road	Largo-20772	Muriel Adams RRA CCS	301.322.0744
60. ME	Kennebec Valley Technical College	92 Western Avenue	Fairfield-04937	Joan Frisina RRA	207.453.5157
61. ME	University of Maine-University College	128 Texas Avenue	Bangor-04401	Susan Benson MPA RRA	207.581.6144
62. MI	Baker College System [⊕]	128 Apple Avenue	Muskegon-49442	Cheryl Foster RRA	616.726.4904
63. MI	Davenport College	4123 West Main Street	Kalamazoo-49006	Cecilia McDermott RRA	616.382.2835
64. MI	Ferris State University	200 Ferris Drive VFS 402	Big Rapids-49307	Ellen Haneline MEd RRA	616.592.2313
65. MI	Gogebic Community College	E4946 Jackson Road	Ironwood-49938	Carla Pogliano MA RRA	906.932.4231
66. MI	Henry Ford Community College	22586 Ann Arbor Trail	Dearborn Heights-48127	Marsha Steele MA RRA	313.730.5975

State	Institution	Address Line 1	Address Line 2	Program Director	Office #
67. MI	Schoolcraft College	1751 Radcliff Street	Garden City-48135	Patricia Rubio MSA RRA	313.462.4770
68. MN	Anoka-Hennepin Technical College	1355 West Highway 10	Anoka-55303	Gwen Enzler RRA	612.427.1880
69. MN	College of Saint Catherine [CS]	601 25th Avenue South	Minneapolis-55454	Joanne Valerius MPH RRA	612.690.7756
70. MN	Northwest Technical College	1900 28th Avenue South	Moorhead-56560	Carolyn Linnell RRA	218.236.6277
71. MN	Rasmussen Business College	245 37th Avenue North	St. Cloud-56301	Margaret Johnson	612.687.9000
72. MN	Wilmar-Hutchinson Technical College	PO Box 1097	Wilmar-56201-1097	Pete Fisk RRA	612.231.2949
73. MO	Heart of the Ozarks Technical College	PO Box 5958	Springfield-65801	Beth Climer RRA	417.895.7078
74. MO	Missouri Western State College	4525 Downs Drive	St. Joseph-65407	David Heizer RRA	816.271.5913
75. MO	Penn Valley Community College	3201 Southwest Trafficway	Kansas City-64111	Suzanne Brown MS RRA	816.759.4245
76. MO	Saint Charles County Community College	4601 Mid Rivers Mall Drive	St. Peters-63376	Candace Neu RRA CCS	314.922.8000
77. MS	Hinds Community College	PO Box 10428	Raymond-39154	Judith Moore RRA	601.857.5261
78. MS	Meridian Community College	910 Highway 19 North	Meridian-39307	Robin Allen-Jones RRA	601.484.8759
79. MT	Montana State Univ College of Technology	2100 16th Avenue South	Great Falls-59405	Irene Mueller MLS RRA	406.771.1310
80. MT	Salish Kootenai College	Highway 93	Pablo-59855	Roberta Yankovich RRA	406.675.4800
81. NC	Catawba Valley Community College	Route 3 Box 283	Hickory-28602	Debra Cook MAEd RRA	704.327.7000
82. NC	Central Peidmont Community College	PO Box 35009	Charlotte-28235	Susan McDermott RRA	704.342.6452
83. NC	Davidson County Community College	PO Box 1287 Highway 29-70	Lexington-27293	Mary Daniel RRA	704.249.8186
84. NC	Edgecombe Community College	225 Tarboro Street	Rocky Mount-27801	Christy McBride RRA CPHQ	919.446.0436
85. NC	Pitt Community College	PO Drawer 7007 Hgwy 11 South	Greenville-27835	Kay Gooding MPH RRA	919.321.4361
86. NC	SE Regional Allied Health Consortium	PO Box 30	Supply-28462	Kathleen Howard RRA	910.754.6900
87. ND	North Dakota State College of Science	801 North 6th Street-Room 305	Wahpeton-58075	Brian Gaarder RRA	701.671.2269
88. ND	United Tribes Technical College	3315 University Drive	Bismarck-58504	James Steen BS RRA	701.255.3285
89. NE	College of Saint Mary	All Women's College 1901 South 72nd Street	Omaha-68124	Ellen Jacobs MEd RRA	402.399.2400
90. NJ	Burlington County Community College	Pemberton-Browns Mills Road	Pemberton-08068	Sue Davis RRA	609.894.9311

State	Institution	Address Line 1	Address Line 2	Program Director	Office #
91. NJ	Hudson County Community College c/o Jersey State College	25 Journal Square Pathside Building	Jersey City-07305	Jacqueline Gibbons MHA RRA	201.200.3320
92. NM	University of New Mexico-Gallup	200 College Road	Gallup-87301	Carol Fleming RRA	505.863.7659
93. NV	Community College of Southern Nevada	3200 East Cheyenne Avenue	North Las Vegas-89030	Hyla Winters MHCA RRA	702.877.1133
94. NY	Adirondack Community College	Bay Road	Queensbury-12804	Lisa Potocar RRA	518.743.2286
95. NY	Borough of Manhattan Community Coll	199 Chambers Street	New York-10007	Camille Layne RRA	212.346.8739
96. NY	Broome Community College	PO Box 1017	Binghampton-13902	Mary Rosato MA RRA	607.778.5000
97. NY	Erie Community College	6205 Main Street	Williamsville-14221	Gail Lauritsen EdM RRA	716.851.1513
98. NY	Mohawk Valley Community College	1101 Sherman Drive	Utica-13501	Sue Ellen Bice MS RRA	315.792.5513
99. NY	Molloy Community College	1000 Hempstead Avenue	Rockville Center-11571	Ellen Spector-Haigney MPA RRA	516.678.5000
100.NY	Monroe Community College	1000 East Henrietta Road	Rochester-14623	Sharon Insero BS RRA	716.424.5200
101.NY	Onondaga Community College	Health Info Tech Program	Syracuse-13215	Judy Chrissman RRA	315.469.7741
102.NY	Rockland Community College	145 College Road	Suffern-10901	Isabelle Janzen RRA	914.352.0411
103.NY	State University of New York-Alfred	Allied Health Building	Alfred-14802	Janette Thomas MPS RRA	607.587.3661
104.NY	Trocaire College	110 Red Jacket Parkway	Buffalo-14220	Deborah Shelvay BA ART	716.826.1200
105.OH	Bowling Green State Univ-Firelands	901 Rye Beach Road	Huron-44839	Mona Jackson MA RRA	419.433.5560
106.OH	Cincinnati State Technical Comm Coll	3520 Central Parkway	Cincinnati-45223	Gail Smith RRA	513.569.1678
107.OH	Columbus State Community College	550 East Spring Street Box 1609	Columbus-43216	Lisa Cerrato BS RRA	614.227.2541
108.OH	Cuyahoga Community College	2900 Community College Avenue	Cleveland-44115	Nancy Donahue RRA	216.987.4456
109.OH	Hocking College	3301 Hocking Parkway	Nelsonville-45764	Karen Lewis RRA	614.753.3591
110.OH	Sinclair Community College	44 West Third Street	Dayton-45402	Catherine Huber RRA	513.226.2973
111.OH	Stark Technical College	6200 Frank Avenue NW	Canton-44720	Eilleen Dunlap RRA	216.494.6170
112.OK	Rose State College	6420 Southeast 15th Street	Midwest City-73110	Cecil Brooks RRA	405.733.7578
113.OK	Tulsa Junior College	909 South Boston Avenue	Tulsa-74119-2095	Sandra Smith RRA	918.595.7201

State	Institution	Address Line 1	Address Line 2	Program Director	Office #
114.OR	Central Oregon Community College	2600 Northwest College Way	Bend-97701	Gloria Ahem RRA	503.383.7736
115.OR	Portland Community College	PO Box 19000	Portland-97280	Susan Williams RRA	503.244.6111
116.PA	Community College of Allegheny County	808 Ridge Avenue	Pittsburgh-15212	JoAnn Avoli MEd RRA	412.237.2614
117.PA	Community College of Philadelphia	1700 Spring Garden Street	Philadelphia-19130	Joyce Garozzo MS RRA	215.751.8425
118.PA	Gwynedd Mercy College	Sumneytown Pike	Gwynedd Valley-19437	Kathleen Lynch MS RRA	215.646.7300
119.PA	Lehigh County Community College	2370 Main Street	Schnecksville-18078	George Peters MS RRA	215.799.1596
120.PA	Sawyer School	717 Liberty Avenue	Pittsburgh-15222	Susan Niebert RRA	800.321.1993
121.PA	South Hills Business School [CS]	480 Waupelanie Drive	State College-16801	Dan Christopher MBA RRA	814.234.7755
122.PR	Colegio Universitario Del Este	Dept of Sciences/ Technology Apartado 2010	Carolina-00983	Ada Lily Torres-Tirado RRA	809.758.7171
123.PR	Huertas Junior College	PO Box 8429	Caguas-00726	Nelida Anderson RRA	809.743.1242
124.PR	Inter American Univ of Puerto Rico	Call Box 5100	San German-00683	Magda Lopez MS RRA	809.264.1912
125.PR	Universidad Adventista de las Antillas	Box 118	Mayaguez-00681	Zilma Santiago RRA	809.834.9595
126.SC	Florence-Darlington Tech College	PO Box 10058	Florence-29501	Lucreia McCormick RRA	803.661.8146
127.SC	Midlands Technical College	Airport Campus PO Box 2408	Columbia-29202	Lynn Hudson RRA	803.822.3590
128.SD	Dakota State University	CB Kennedy Center 151	Madison-57042	Sheila Carlon RRA	605.256.5170
129.SD	National College	Box 1780	Rapid City-57709	Marilyn Holmgren MS RRA	605.394.4839
130.TN	Chattanooga State Tech College	4501 Amnicola Highway	Chattanooga-37406	Kathryn McMillan RRA	615.697.4772
131.TN	Roane State Community College	Patton Lane	Harriman-37748	Alice Moore RRA	615.882.4624
132.TN	Volunteer State Community College	Nashville Pike	Gallatin-37066	Lois Knobeloch MS RRA	615.452.8600
133.TX	El Paso Community College	PO Box 20500	El Paso-79998	Jean Garrison RRA	915.534.4074
134.TX	Houston Comm College System [⊕]	3100 Shenandoah	Houston-77021	Carla Tyson MHA RRA	713.746.5337
135.TX	Howard College	3197 Executive Drive	San Angelo-76904	Martina Ruble RRA	915.944.9585
136.TX	Lee College	511 South Whiting Street	Baytown-77520	Marice Ivey MS RRA	713.425.6569

State	Institution	Address Line 1	Address Line 2	Program Director	Office #
137.TX	North Central Texas College	1525 West California Street	Gainesville-76240-4699	Annette Gonzalez RRA	214.420.0089
138.TX	St. Phillips College	2111 Nevada Street	San Antonio-78205	Elizabeth Bernasconi RRA	512.531.3416
139.TX	South Plains College	1302 Main Street	Lubbock-79401	Bette Green RRA	806.747.0576
140.TX	Tarrant County Junior College NE	828 Harwood Road	Hurst-76054	Delores McDonald RRA CCS	817.788.6544
141.TX	Texas State Technical College	2424 Boxwood	Harlingen-78550	Gayla Holmes MS RRA	512.425.0763
142.TX	Tyler Junior College	PO Box 9020	Tyler-75711	Charlotte Creason BS RRA	903.510.2669
143.TX	Wharton County Junior College	911 Boling Highway	Wharton-77488	Mary King MS RRA	409.532.6363
144.UT	Weber State University [CS]	3911 University Circle	Ogden-84408	Chris Elliott RRA	801.626.7298
145.VA	College of Health Sciences	Comm Hospital of Roanoke PO Box 13186	Roanoke-24031	Mildred St. Leger BA RRA	703.985.4020
146.VA	Northern Virginia Comm College	8333 Little River Turnpike	Annadale-22003	Sandra Bailey RRA	703.323.3414
147.VA	Tidewater Community College	1700 College Crescent	Virginia Beach-23456	Gussie Hammond MS RRA	804.427.7262
148.WA	Shoreline Community College [CS]	16101 Greenwood Ave North	Seattle-98133	Donna Wilde MPA RRA	206.546.4757
149.WA	Spokane Community College	N 1810 Greene Street-MS 2090	Spokane-99207	Shirley Higgin MEd RRA	509.533.8032
150.WA	Tacoma Community College	5900 South 12th Street	Tacoma-98465	Ingrid Bentzen MEd RRA	206.566.5163
151.WI	Chippewa Valley Technical College	620 West Clairemont Avenue	Eau Claire-54701	Carol Ryan RRA	715.833.6423
152.WI	Gateway Technical College	101 South Main Street	Racine-53403	Cynthia Fickenscher RRA	414.631.7308
153.WI	Moraine Park Technical College	2151 North Main Street	West Bend-53095	Lucia Francis BS RRA	414.335.5730
154.WI	Northeast Wisconsin Tech College	2740 West Mason Street	Green Bay-54307	Marilyn Toninato RRA	414.498.5577
155.WI	Western Wisconsin Tech College	304 North 6th Street	LaCrosse-54601	Tamra Brown MEd RRA	608.785.9549
156.WV	Fairmont State College	Locust Avenue	Fairmont-26554	Sr. Marie Horvath RSM RRA	304.367.4764
157.WV	Marshall Univ Comm and Tech Coll	400 Hal Greer Boulevard	Huntington-25755	Jane Barker RRA	304.696.6796

Convenient independent study options are also available: You may choose to study at home through AHIMA's independent study program. Students find that independent study is a flexible method of acquiring job knowledge and skills often while maintaining full-time jobs. Successful completion of the independent study program allows you to earn the ART credential after passing the credentialing exam. To learn more about the program, contact AHIMA at 312/787-2672 and ask to speak to someone in our Independent Study Division.

Health Information Administration (HIA)

All of the following programs for health information administrators have been accredited by the Commission on Accreditation of Allied Health Education Programs (CAAHEP), 515 North State Street, Chicago, Illinois 60610, in cooperation with the Council on Accreditation (COA) of the American Health Information Management Association (AHIMA), 919 North Michigan Avenue, Suite 1400, Chicago, Illinois 60611.

For detailed information about a program contact the college or university. Programs listed may offer one or more of the following and are indicated as such:

PG **Progression** opportunities for accredited record technicians desiring to become registered record administrators.

PB **Postbaccalaureate** and/or certificate program in health information administration. Such programs allow students already possessing a baccalaureate degree and specific prerequisites to enter a postbaccalaureate and/or certificate program. Upon satisfactory completion the student may be awarded a certificate and/or a bachelor's degree in health information administration with eligibility to apply to take the National Certification Examination.

M **Master's-degree** program with an emphasis in health information.

CS **Coding specialist** program track. Although coding programs are not accredited by AHIMA, the association does acknowledge coding programs offered by accredited educational programs.

⊕ **Multiple campuses/sites**

Revised October 1996

State	Institution	Address Line 1	Address Line 2	Program Director	Office #
1. AL	University of Alabama [PG,M,CS]	1675 University Boulevard Webb Building-Room 644	Birmingham-35294	Sara Grostick MA RRA	205.934.3509
2. AR	Arkansas Tech University [PB,CS]	105 Wilson Hall	Russellville-72801	Melinda Heaton MEd RRA	501.968.0441
3. CA	Loma Linda University [PG,PB]	1905 Nichol Hall	Loma Linda-92350	Marilyn Davidian RRA	909.824.4976
4. CO	Regis University	3333 Regis Boulevard	Denver-80221	Deb Bennett-Woods RRA	303.458.4157
5. FL	Florida A&M University	Ware-Rhaney Bldg-Rm 223D	Tallahassee-32307	Barbara Mosley PhD RRA	904.599.3822
6. FL	Florida International University	ACI-394C North Campus	N. Miami-33181	Maha Yunis RRA	305.919.5631
7. FL	University of Central Florida	Box 25000	Orlando-32816	Carol Barr MA RRA	407.823.2359
8. GA	Clark Atlanta University [PB]	James Brawley Dr. at Fair St. SW	Atlanta-30314	Barbara Brice PhD RRA	404.880.8115
9. GA	Medical College of Georgia [CS]	School of Allied Hlth Sciences-AL22	Augusta-30912	Charlotte Johnston PhD RRA	706.721.3436
10. IL	Chicago State University [PG]	9501 South King Dr.-BHS 610	Chicago-60628	Leona Thomas RRA	312.995.2552

State	Institution	Address Line 1	Address Line 2	Program Director	Office #
11. IL	Illinois State University [PG]	103 Moulton Hall	Normal-61761	Frank Waterstraat MBA, RRA	309.438.8329
12. IL	Univ. of Illinois at Chicago [PG]	1919 West Taylor-Room 811	Chicago-60612	Karen Patena RRA	312.996.3530
13. IN	Indiana University Northwest [CS]	3400 Broadway	Gary-46408	Margaret Skurka MS RRA	219.980.6654
14. IN	Indiana Univ. School of Medicine	1140 West Michigan St.-CF 326	Indianapolis-46202	Mary McKenzie MS RRA	317.274.7317
15. KS	Univ. of KS Medical Center [PG]	39th and Rainbow Boulevard KU Hospital G124	Kansas City-66160	Sue Malone MPA RRA	913.588.2423
16. KY	Eastern Kentucky University	Dizney 117	Richmond-40475	Frances Hindsman MBA RRA	606.622.1915
17. LA	Louisiana Tech University [PG]	PO Box 3171	Ruston-71272	Lou Stebbins MBA RRA	318.257.2854
18. LA	Univ. of SW Louisiana [PG,CS]	PO Box 41007 USL Station	Lafayette-70504	Carol Venable MPH RRA	318.482.6629
19. MA	Northeastern University [PG,PB,CS]	266 Ryder Hall 360 Huntington Avenue	Boston-02115	Annalee Collins RRA	617.373.2525
20. MI	Baker College System	123 Apple Avenue	Muskegon-49442	Cheryl Foster RRA	616.726.4904
21. MI	Ferris State University [PG]	200 Ferris Drive VFS 402	Big Rapids-49307	Ellen Haneline MEd RRA	616.592.2313
22. MN	Coll. of St. Scholastica [PG,PB,CS]	1200 Kenwood Avenue	Duluth-55811	Kathy LaTour MA RRA	218.723.6011
23. MS	Univ. of Mississippi Med Center	2500 North State Street	Jackson-39216	Rebecca Yates MEd RRA	601.984.6305
24. MO	Saint Louis University [PG,PB]	3525 Caroline-Room 510	St. Louis-63104	K. Jody Smith MSM RRA	314.577.8516
25. MO	Stephens College [PG,PB]	Campus Box 2083 1200 East Broadway	Columbia-65215	Joan Rines PhD RRA	314.876.7283
26. MT	Carroll College [CS]	Faculty Box 90	Helena-59625	David Westlake RRA	406.442.3450
27. NE	College of St. Mary [PG,PB]	All Women's College 1901 South 72nd Street	Omaha-68124	Ellen Jacobs MEd RRA	402.399.2400
28. NJ	Kean College of New Jersey [PG,PB]	Morris Avenue T206	Union-07083	Natalie Sartori MEd RRA	908.527.3010
29. NY	Ithaca College [PG]	953 Danby Road	Ithaca-14850	Christine Pogorzala MS RRA	607.274.3355
30. NY	Long Island University	CW Post Campus Life Science Bldg-Room 257	Brookville-11548	Nancy Katz-Johnson RRA	516.299.2485
31. NY	State Univ. of New York [PG,PB,CS]	450 Clarkson Avenue Box 105	Brooklyn-11203	Isaac Topor EdD	718.270.7770
32. NY	State University of New York [PG,CS]	PO Box 3050	Utica-13504	Donna Silsbee MS RRA	315.792.7391

State	Institution	Address Line 1	Address Line 2	Program Director	Office #
33. NC	East Carolina University	School of Allied Health Sciences Belk Building	Greenville-27858	Elizabeth Layman PhD RRA	919.328.4444
34. NC	Western Carolina University	139 Moore Hall	Cullowhee-28723	Walter Floreani RRA	704.227.7113
35. OH	Ohio State University [PG,PB,M,CS]	1583 Perry Street	Columbus-43210	Melanie Brodnick PhD RRA	614.292.0567
36. OK	East Central University [PG]	Dept of Health Info Management	Ada-74820	Sandra Dixon MEd RRA	405.332.8000
37. OK	Southwestern Oklahoma State Univ	100 Campus Drive	Weatherford-73096	Marion Prichard MEd RRA	405.774.3287
38. PA	Duquesne University	School of Hlth Sciences-Rm 323 600 Forbes Avenue	Pittsburgh-15282	Joan Kiel PhD Interim	412.396.4772
39. PA	Gwynedd Mercy College [PB,CS]	Sumneytown Pike	Gwynedd Valley-19437	Kathleen Lynch MS RRA	215.646.7300
40. PA	Temple University [PG]	3307 North Broad Street	Philadelphia-19140	Laurinda Harmon PhD, RRA	215.707.4811
41. PA	University of Pittsburgh [PG,PB,M]	308 Pennsylvania Hall	Pittsburgh-15261	Mervat Abdelhak PhD RRA	412.647.1190
42. PA	York College of Pennsylvania [PG]	Country Club Road	York-17403	Jean Fultz MS RRA	717.846.7788
43. PR	University of Puerto Rico [PG]	Medical Science Campus GPO Box 5067	San Juan-00936	Ana Garcia-Hestres, MPH RRA	809.758.2525
44. SC	Medical Univ of South Carolina [CS]	171 Ashley Avenue	Charleston-29425	Karen Wager MHS RRA	803.792.4491
45. SD	Dakota State University [PG,CS]	CB Kennedy Center 151	Madison-57042	Sheila Carlon RRA	605.256.5170
46. TN	Tennessee State University [PG]	3500 John Merritt Blvd Box 654	Nashville-37209	Elizabeth Kunnu MEd RRA	615.320.3702
47. TN	University of Tennessee [CS]	822 Beale Street 300	Memphis-38163	Mary McCain MPA RRA	901.448.6486
48. TX	Southwest Texas State University	Health Info Mgmt Program	San Marcos-78666	Sue Biedermann MSHP RRA	512.245.8242
49. TX	Texas Southern University	Nabritt Science Building 3100 Cleburne	Houston-77004	Debora Butts MA RRA	713.527.7265
50. TX	Univ. of Texas Med. Branch [PG,PB]	School of Allied Hlth Sciences	Galveston-77555	Tella Williams BA RRA	409.772.3051
51. VA	Norfolk State University	2401 Corprew Avenue	Norfolk-23504	Joyce Harvey PhD RRA	804.683.8209
52. WA	University of Washington [PG,PB]	1107 NE 45th-Suite 335 Mail Stop JD-02	Seattle-98105	Mary Alice Hanken PhD RRA	206.543.8810
53. WI	University of Wisconsin [PG,CS]	Box 413	Milwaukee-53201	John Lynch PhD	414.229.5615

275

Appendix **C**

Sample Resumes

Sample Resume
Mary Kline
303 South Main #104
St. Louis, MO 63104
(H)314-977-4444 (W) 314-577-1111
email: klinem@slu.edu

Objective: **To seek an entry-level position as a coding specialist using my academic background and knowledge of ICD-9 and CPT.**

Education 8/93-5/97
Saint Louis University
St. Louis, MO
Bachelor of Science in Health Information Management
Cumulative GPA 3.45/4.0 - GPA for major courses 3.90/4.0
> **Honors/Awards/Scholarship:** Dean's List, Dean's Scholarship recipient
> **Coursework:** Classification Systems I and II, Health Care Statistics, Quality Improvement, Medico-Legal Aspects, Management Information Systems, Research Methodology, Anatomy, Physiology

Credentials
Eligible to apply to write Registered Record Administrator National Exam in October 1997

Work Experience 7/96-present
St. Louis University Health Sciences Center
St. Louis, MO
Admitting Registrar
> •Interview and register patients
> •Explain policies and procedures associates with admission process
> •Conduct follow-up activities for incomplete admissions

Clinical Experience
Saint Joseph's Hospital, Kirkwood, MO April 1997
Department of Health Information Management

> **Responsibilities:** Audited incomplete records, retrieved records, coded in patient records, flow charted record processing; recommended improvements in information systems

Washington University, St. Louis, MO May 1996
Department of Otolaryngology

> **Responsibilities:** Processed record requests, assisted physicians with research studies

St. Louis Zoological Hospital, St. Louis, MO May 1995
Medical Records

> **Responsibilities:** Assisted in completion of animal record database, evaluated database accuracy

Organizations
American Health Information Management Association
Illinois Health Information Management Association

References
Available upon request

Sample Resume
Teresa Conte
729 High Street
St. Louis, Missouri 63132
(314) 993-4444
conte@slu.edu

EDUCATION

Saint Louis University, St. Louis Missouri
Bachelor of Science in Health Information Management, May 1997
Major GPA: 3.69/4.00

RELEVANT COURSE WORK

- Quality Improvement
- Health Information Systems
- Health Care Statistics
- Finance
- Health Care Management
- Research Methodology

WORK EXPERIENCE

Washington University, Department of Otolaryngology, St. Louis, Missouri
(December 1995 -January 1997)
- Generated flow diagrams
- Performed reimbursement analysis
- Audited Medicare/Medicaid records
- Developed a disaster plan for medical records
- Created a new correspondence and billing form
- Assisted with correspondence and data entry

Cardinal Glennon Children's Hospital, St. Louis, Missouri
(March 1994 - December 1994) Phlebotomist
- Capillary sticks on newborns up to the age of 18

Dr. Jones' Office, Highland, Illinois (February 1991 - March 1994)
Office Clerk
- Data Entry
- Filing charts
- Filled out insurance claims

COMPUTER SKILLS

- Windows 95
- Microsoft Office
- Lotus 1-2-3

HONORS & ORGANIZATIONS

Dean's List, Fall 1996
American Health Information Management Association

REFERENCES

Available upon request

Sample Resume
REVERSE CHRONOLOGICAL ORDER
Experience Listed Before Education

Natalie J. Perkins
775 Tailgate
Tulsa, Oklahoma 74127
(916)342-1898
alt@aol.com

OBJECTIVE

To obtain a sales representative position in the healthcare industry applying communication, persuasion, and time management skills.

CAREER-RELATED

Sales Coordinator, Irvine Realtors, Tulsa, (January 1994 to May 1996)

EXPERIENCE

•Organized mass mailings to specific farm areas.
•Researched tax information using Stellar Software.
•Coordinated inspection times to coincide with property closing dates.

Telebusiness Representative for Merit
Customer Information Center, Tulsa, (Summer 1993)

•Conducted conversations with customers regarding degree of satisfaction with products and services; simultaneously transcribed responses into computer terminal.

**ADDITIONAL
EXPERIENCE**

Camp Counselor, (Summer 1991 and 1992)
Camp Running River, Bear Creek, CO

EDUCATION

Bachelor of Science in Health Information Management
Magna cum laude (August 1996)
East Central University, Ada, OK

Associate of Arts Degee in Social Sciences (May 1994)
Rose State College, Midwest City, OK

**COMMUNITY
AND CAMPUS
INVOLVEMENT**

Marketing Club:	Vice- President
Sociology Club:	Program Committee Chair
Habit for Humanity:	May, 1993

**PORTFOLIO
& REFERENCES**

Provided upon request

Sample Resume

Carrie Korb

9572 Trailtop Court	314-855-6222
St. Louis, Missouri 63127	314-855-4300

Education

Saint Louis University
Saint Louis, Missouri 63103

Bachelor of Science in Health Information Management, May 1997 (3.8/4.0)

Eligible to apply to write the RRA certifying exam   10-97

Internship Experience

Cancer Registry, Coding ICD-9 and CPT manually and with encoder, Admission Procedures, Daily Census, Monthly Statistics, Health Information Analysis, Computer Entry, Interaction with Management.

Work Experience

Johnson Electronics
Richmond Heights, Missouri 36117
1987-Current

•Ten years experience in fast-paced environment. •Exceptional communication, interpersonal and organizational skills. •Poised and competent as a business representative. •Record of accomplishments in communicating with professionals and non-professionals. •Responsibilities have included Telecommunicator, Administrative Assistant, Data Processing and Problem Solver. •Well organized with an eye for detail. •Skilled in setting priorities. •Able to transcend cultural and language differences. •Effective as team member. •Application of reasoning skills when confronted with discretionary decisions. •Ability to formulate appropriate courses of action for nonprocedural situations.

Professional and Campus Involvement

American Health Information Management Association	1996-present
Missouri Health Information Management Association	1996-present
Allied Health Alumni Board	1996-present
Mu Rho Sigma (HIM Organization)	1995 - present
Student Government Association	1996 - present
Saint Louis University Food Drive	1996

Awards Received

Alpha Eta Society, Allied Health Honors	1996
Alpha Sigma Nu, Jesuit Honor Society	1996
Golden Key National Honor Society	1996
Who's Who Among American Universities	1996
Saint Louis University Dean's List	1995 - 1996

Sample Resume
FUNCTIONAL
Skills Based

DONALD COLE
1721 Washington Street
Ann Arbor, Michigan
(313) 521-7080

POSITION DESIRED

To obtain a management position in the healthcare industry using skills in cost control, leadership, and quality improvement.

COST CONTROL SKILLS

- Decreased personnel costs by 15% without eliminating personnel by increasing output through computerization.
- Recommended revised employees' benefit package to decrease sick days by 20%, with over $100,000 savings to organization.
- Provided data summarization and analytical support to various process redesign and cost improvements teams.

LEADERSHIP SKILLS

- Named Leader of the Month for system affiliated organization.
- Trained and coordinated Facilitation Teams for six-months during which a system-wide computerized clinical patient record was implemented.

QUALITY IMPROVEMENT SKILLS

- Implemented effective clinical quality control systems for standards of the Joint Commission on Accreditation of Healthcare Organizations.
- Edited monthly quality improvement newsletter.
- Maintained high level of effectiveness by evaluating performance and controlling.

EMPLOYMENT HISTORY

- Vice President for Quality (March 1991 to present)
  Health Network, Ann Arbor, Michigan
- Director of Quality Management (July 1989 to March 1991)
- Coordinator of Quality Improvement (June 1988 to July 1989)
  Southern Health System, Atlanta, Georgia

EDUCATION

- Stephens College, Columbia, Missouri
  Bachelor of Science in Health Information Management (May 1996)
- Wallace State College, Hanceville, Alabama
  Associate in Applied Science (May 1988)

CREDENTIALS

- Registered Record Administrator (October 1996)
- Accredited Record Technician (October 1988)

REFERENCES

Provided upon request

Sample Resume
ANDREA SMITH
739 Dallwood Drive
Boise, ID 83725

OBJECTIVE
To obtain an administrative position where experience and commitment will be valued and advanced.

QUALIFICATIONS
    *Computer skills: WordPerfect; Lotus.
    *Knowledge of medical records and health information management.
    *Detail-oriented, organized, efficient, goal directed.
    *Self motivated with outstanding communication skills.

EDUCATION
Boise State University
Bachelor of Science, Health Information Management, January 1997
Dean's List; Summa Cum Laude

CLINICAL MANAGEMENT EXPERIENCE, Boise, ID; September to December 1996
Life Care Center: Chart auditing
Medical Associates, Inc.: Group practice functions
Lansdowne Orthopedic: ICD-9 coding and CPT-4
Healthcare West: Problem solving management activities

EMPLOYMENT
University Hospital
September 95-present, Medical Record Clerk

Houlihans Restaurant
May 94-September 95, Service Coordinator

Island Tan
October 90-April 94, Supervisor

PERSONAL BACKGROUND
Member of Golden Key National Honor Society
Volunteer at Health South Hospital; assisted Occupational Therapists
Member of American Health Information Management Association

REFERENCES
Provided upon request.

Sample Resume
DAWN SMITH

Current Address   Permanent Address
908 South Grand   200 West Street
Redlands, CA 92373   Hayward, CA
(909)977-5108   (510) 786-6666

GOAL

To obtain a challenging position that incorporates computerized medical
information systems.

EDUCATION

Loma Linda University, Loma Linda CA
Bachelor of Science in Health Information Management
May 19_ _   GPA: 3.3/4.0

EXPERIENCE

Correspondence Clerk, Record Masters of Los Angeles, August 1996 - present

Office Assistant, Loma Linda University, Residence Life, January - August 1996

Sales Associate, Limited, Express, Redlands, September 1994 - January 1996

Customer Service Associate/Cashier, Target, October 1992 - September 1994

Program Assistant, San Bernardino Local Health Department, Summer Arts and Athletics
        Tulsa, Oklahoma, June - August 1992

VOLUNTEER EXPERIENCE

Veterans Administration Hospital, Loma Linda, CA, September 1993 - 1994

AFFILIATIONS

Loma Linda University Black Student Alliance, September 1994 - present
Loma Linda University Student Volunteer Programs, September 1994 - present

AWARDS

Helen Hayes Scholarship   University Scholarship

Sample Resume
Reverse Chronological Order
Relevant Courses Listed

Markeisha Rivers

544 Hill Street
Chicago, Illinois 60628
(312)212-6755 home
(312)494-0093 work

PROFESSIONAL OBJECTIVE

To obtain an entry-level position in the healthcare industry applying clinical medicine, coding, research, and systems skills. Interested in opportunities for advancement.

EDUCATION

UNIVERSITY OF ILLINOIS, Chicago, IL
Master of Science in Health Information Management, December 1996
EASTERN MICHIGAN UNIVERSITY, Ypsilanti, MI
Bachelor of Science in Therapeutic Recreation, May, 1994

RELEVANT COURSE WORK

- Systems Design & Analysis
- Research Methods
- Parametric and Nonparametric Statistics
- Health Information Systems
- Classification Systems

INTERNSHIP

Anderson Accounting International, Chicago, IL (Summer 1996).
- Designed flexible labor reporting system for system affiliated hospitals.
- Provided data and analytical support to cost improvement teams.
- Conducted inservice programs on encoder computer system.

ADDITIONAL EXPERIENCE

Foster G. McGaw Hospital of Loyola University, Chicago, (May 1994 to June 1996)
Blind Rehabilitation Assistant

ACTIVITIES AND HONORS

- Dean's List, 8 semesters
- National Dean's List, 3 years
- Active in intramural sports
- Recipient of 5 academic scholarships

Sample Resume
MARY C. CLARK

College Address:	Home Address:
123 East Main	Oak Street
Charleston, SC	Columbia, SC
(803)123-4567	(803)123-7777

Professional Goal: To obtain a career oriented position in health information management.

Education: Southern University, Charleston, SC
Bachelor of Science in Health Information Management
Anticipated date of graduation- June 19_ _

Relevant Courses/   Classification Systems I & II   Accounting
Special Skills: Medico-Legal Aspects, Business Law   Lotus, Word Processing
Management (Human Resource, Records)   Medical Terminology
Customer Services, Sales   Leadership

Work Experience: Southern University, Charleston, CS
Residence Life, Office Assistant, May 1995 - December 1996

Famous Department Store, Columbia SC
Sales Associate, May 1994 to April 1995

Honors/Awards: Athletic Scholarship Recipient, 1993-1996
Academic Scholarship Recipient, 1993-1996
INROADS Talent Pool Participant, 1996
Achievement Award, 1994; 1995

Extracurricular   Health Information Management Fraternity 1995-1996
Activities: American Health Information Management Association, student member
1996 to present
Student Alliance,1993-1996

Volunteer   YWCA TEEN/TOOLS Program,1995
Experience: Children's Hospital Child Life, 1993; 1994

References: Provided upon request.

	ANDY ANDERSON	
226 Ladue Road	Chesterfield, Missouri	(314) 434-0009

Objective
To obtain a challenging position in Management Information Systems.

Education
Saint Louis University, St. Louis, Missouri (May, 1997)
    Bachelor of Science in Business Administration
    Bachelor of Science in Health Information Management
    Majors: Management Information Systems - GPA: 3.53/4.00
              Health Information Management - GPA: 3.72/4.00

Computer Experience

Hardware
    IBM-Compatible PCS   Apple Computers

Software

WordPerfect	Lotus 1-2-3	Harvard Graphics	Microsoft Word
Microsoft Excel	dBASE IV	SoftMed	MedTech
Encoder	MS-DOS	Microsoft Works	Aldus PageMaker
PCSDOS	LEVEL 5	FlowCharting	

Peripherals

CD-ROM	Laser Printers	Data/Fax Modem	Internet Network

Languages
    BASIC   PRL

Employment History

Baptist Hospital, St. Louis, Missouri - November, 1995 to Present: <u>Medical Records Abstractor</u>

Leadership Background

Alpha Kappa Psi (Business Fraternity)
    <u>President</u> - 1996
    <u>Fund Raising Chairman</u>
    <u>Professional Activities Chairman</u>

Chesterfield Youth Chairman
    <u>Assistant Moderator</u>

Honors/Activities

University Scholarship
Mu Rho Sigma member (Health Information Management Fraternity)

Sample Resume

Sample Resume
Reverse Chronological Order
Education Listed Before Experience

Stephen P. Williams

3894 West Pine Place - St. Louis, MO 63104
314/577-1966

CAREER OBJECTIVE

To obtain an entry-level position in the healthcare industry using education and experience in health information technology.

EDUCATION

Associate in Applied Science, May 1996
St. Charles County Community College
St. Charles, Missouri
Major: Health Information Technology
GPA: 3.85/4.00

EXPERIENCE

Practicums

St. Luke's Hospital, Chesterfield, Missouri (April 1996)
•Compiled survey information and prepared the report on security issues.
•Assisted DRG coordinator with coding and encodes.
•Participated in quality improvement studies and Quality Assurance committee meetings.

BJC Health System, St. Louis, Missouri (May 1995)
• Abstracted inpatient medical records.
• Completed pre-registration for outpatients.
• Assisted with record completion process.
• Revised release of information policies and procedures.
• Verified addresses and other data for Tumor Registry.

Office Assistant (Summers 1994 and 1995)

Health Care Medical Group, St. Louis, Missouri
•Retrieved patient records for appointments.
•Completed requests for patient information.
•Answered multi-line phone system with paging.
•Transcribed physician dictation.
•Conducted surveys by telephone and questionnaires of patients' satisfaction with services.

EXTRA-CURRICULAR ACTIVITIES

•Raised funds for Cystic Fibrosis 1994
•Treasurer for Health Information Technology Association 1994

Sample Resume

Harry A. Black

blackha@slu.edu

4525 Watson Road   St. Louis 63104   314-233-9787

EDUCATION

Saint Louis University
St. Louis, MO
    BACHELOR OF SCIENCE   1993-1997
    IN HEALTH INFORMATION MANAGEMENT (MAY 1997)

    GRADE POINT AVERAGE IN MAJOR: 3.90/4.00

WORK EXPERIENCE

Saint Louis University Hospital   1995 - present
St. Louis, MO
    DEPARTMENT OF HEALTH INFORMATION MANAGEMENT

    MEDICAL RECORDS

    GENERAL CLERICAL, DATA ENTRY, DATA ANALYSIS, MEDICAL RECORDS ANALYSIS AND
    ABSTRACTING

COMPUTER EXPERIENCE

BASIC PROGRAMMING

<u>SOFTWARE:</u> MICROSOFT WORD, MICROSOFT EXCEL, WORDPERFECT, LOTUS, SAS, SPSS,
      MEDITECH

CLINICAL EXPERIENCE

Memorial Hospital   June 1996
Belleville, IL

   ICD-9 CODING

Life Care Center of Saint Louis   April 1997
St. Louis, MO

   UTILIZATION REVIEW, QUALITY IMPROVEMENT AND ADMITTING PROCEDURES

VOLUNTEER EXPERIENCE

CHILDREN'S MIRACLE NETWORK

BOWL FOR KID'S SAKE (BIG BROTHERS, BIG SISTERS)   March 1995

Health Education Resources

Health information management professionals have a responsibility to continue their education and to be knowledgeable regarding sources of health information for health and allied health professionals, patients, and families.

The following organizations are valuable resources to contact for health education materials:

Agency for Health Care Policy and Research
Research on health care systems and costs
General Information
Clearinghouse Tel. 800 358-9295
Web site http://www.ahcrp.gov/

American Association of Medical Assistants (AAMA)
20 N. Wacker Drive
Chicago, IL 60606-2903
Tel. 800 228-2262
Fax 312 899-1259

American Association for Medical Transcription
P.O. Box 576187
Medesto, CA 95357
Tel. 800 982-2182

American Association of Poison Centers
For regional Poison Control Center numbers
Tel. 202 362-7217

American Diabetes Association
National Center
1660 Duke Street
Alexandria, VA 22314

American Health Information Management Association
919 North Michigan Avenue
Chicago, IL 60611
Tel. 312 787-2672

American Medical Association
Order Department OP632290
P.O. Box 10946
Chicago, IL 60610

American Medical Technologists (AMT)
710 Higgins Road
Park Ridge, IL 60068-5765
Tel. 847 823-5169
Fax 847 823-0458

American Red Cross
431 18th Street NW
Washington, DC 20006

Centers for Disease Control and Prevention
1600 Clifton Road
Atlanta, GA 30333
Tel. 404 639-3311

Choice in Dying
For living wills and other free-of-charge materials and services
200 Varick Street
New York, NY 10014
Tel. 800 999-WILL
Fax 212 366-5337

Council on Health Information and Education
444 Lincoln Blvd., No 107
Venice, CA 90291

Drug Enforcement Agency
United States Department of Justice
Central Station
P.O. Box 28083
Washington, DC 20038
Tel. 800 882-9539

EEOC Office of Communications and Legislative Affairs
For information on the Americans with Disabilities Act
1801 L Street NW
Washington, DC 20507
Tel. 202 663-4398

Joint Commission on Accreditation of Health Care Organizations
P.O. Box 75751
Chicago, IL 60675
Tel. 708 916-5600

Morbidity and Mortality Weekly Report
Prepared by the Centers for Disease Control and Prevention
Web site http://www.cdc.gov/epo/ mmwr/mmwr.html

**National Clearinghouse for Alcohol and Drug Information
(Prevention Online)**
Current information about alcohol and other drugs
Web site http://www.health.org/

National Health Security Plan
Full text of the National Health Security Plan
Web site: http://sunsite.unc.edu/ nhs/NHS-T-o-C.html

National Institute of Diabetes and Digestive and Kidney Disease
Web site http://www.niddk.nih.gov/

National Institutes of Health
Web site http://www.nih.gov/

Occupational Safety and Health Administration
Tel. 800 321-6742
Web site http://www.osha.gov/

**Superintendent of Documents
United States Government Printing Office**
For U.S. mail publications
P.O. Box 371954
Pittsburgh, PA 15250-7954

For CLIA '88 and the OSHA Bloodborne Standard
Washington, DC 20402

Time-Warner Inc./Time-Life Medical
Videos on 30 healthcare issues
School or bulk orders: 800 393-2889
Individual purchases can be made at most video retail stores.

United States Department of Health and Human Services
Web site http://www.os.dhhs.gov/
Includes:

Administration for Children and Families
Tel. 202 401-9200

Administration of Aging
Tel. 202 619-0556

Agency for Health Care Policy and Research
Tel. 301 594-6662

Centers for Disease Control and Prevention
Tel. 404 639-3311

Food and Drug Administration
Tel. 301 443-1544

Health Care Financing Administration
Tel. 410 786-3000

Health Resources and Services Administration
Tel. 301 443-3376

Indian Health Services
Tel. 301 443-3593

National Institutes of Health
Tel. 301 496-5787

Substance Abuse and Mental Health Services
Tel. 301 443-8956

Sample Forms

Develop your value statements and indicate their importance to you by circling the number most reflective of your feelings (1 = not important; 4 = very important).

Value Statement	Rating
1.	1 2 3 4
2.	1 2 3 4
3.	1 2 3 4
4.	1 2 3 4
5.	1 2 3 4

Rank the following statements in order of their importance to you (1 = lowest; 5 = highest).

_____ Recognition

_____ Salary

_____ Job security

_____ Opportunity to be the best you can be

_____ Ability to work with people you enjoy

_____ Other

Your most important value is _____.

Your most important need is _____.

Use this assessment to guide you as you begin job searching and defining your career path.

Figure E-1. Values and Needs Assessment

Last Name	First	Company	Telephone	Date(s) Contacted	Outcome

Figure E-2. Networking Contacts

(Duplicate this worksheet to use for different positions.)

1. IDENTIFYING INFORMATION

Name (Include credentials such as RRA for Registered Record Administrator. Include degrees only if beyond bachelor's degree, that is, MBA, Ph.D., J.D.)

_____

Address (Use the one best for the prospective employer to reach you; be sure to include zip code.)

_____

Telephone Number _____

(Phone with answering machine that is monitored daily)

e-mail address _____

2. CAREER OBJECTIVE

OBJECTIVE (Broad) covering a variety of positions in a specific industry: _____

_____

_____

OBJECTIVE (Specific) for a particular position such as Reimbursement Coordinator or Ambulatory-Care Information Officer.

Position _____

Objective _____

_____

Checklist:

– Is this worded to interest the employer in reading further?

– Does this indicate that I can contribute to the organization?

– Does my resume indicate that I have the skills needed?

3. EDUCATION

High School (Do not include this if you are more than five years out of high school, or if it will take too much space on the resume without adding significant accomplishments.)

Name of high school _____

City and state_____

Attended from Month _____ Year _____ to Month _____ Year _____

Graduated Month ____ Year ____ Grade-point average ____

Rank in class (if known) _____

Honors _____

Figure E-3. Resume Preparation Worksheet

Awards _____

Extracurricular achievements _____

Special accomplishments_____

If you attended more than one high school, usually the one from which you graduated is sufficient.

Name of college _____

City and state_____

Attended from Month _____ Year _____ to Month _____ Year _____

Graduated Month _____ Year _____ Grade-point average _____

(Include this on your resume only if 3.3 or higher on 4.0 scale.)

Special status, such as *cum laude* _____

Grade-point average for major courses _____ (Include this if 3.5 or above.)

Degree received (Write out completely, for example: Bachelor of Science in Health Information Administration.)

_____

Minor or Certificate _____

Honors, awards, scholarships _____

_____

_____

Course work related to position (List no more than eight courses and do not include course numbers.)

_____

_____

_____

_____

List additional colleges attended, providing the same information, especially if a degree was awarded or other achievements attained.

4. EXPERIENCE

4A. WORK

Position/job title _____

Name of employer _____

Dates employed   from Month _____ Year _____

                        to Month _____ Year _____

Figure E-3.   *Continued*

Responsibilities (Use action words as provided in Figure 5-3.)

_____

_____

_____

_____

(List first the responsibility that most relates to the job you are seeking.)

Repeat this information for each employer

4B. INTERNSHIPS/PRACTICUMS

Name of facility _____

Dates of experience from Month _____ Year _____ to Month _____ Year _____

Major activities _____

_____

_____

_____

_____

(Repeat this for each site for which you were scheduled for at least forty hours or more.)

5. SKILLS

Skill acquired _____

_____

Way in which acquired (activity, project, hobby, organization, etc.)_____

(Although the way the skill was acquired may not be included on your resume, this information will be of assistance during the interview process as you provide evidence of the skill.)

Skill acquired _____

Way in which acquired_____

(Continue with this until you have identified five to ten of your major skills.)

6. ACCOMPLISHMENTS

(List five to ten of your major accomplishments using the action verbs provided in Figure 5-3.)

_____

_____

_____

_____

_____

Figure E-3.   *Continued*

7. PROJECTS, PRESENTATIONS, PUBLICATIONS

(List major ones completed during college, in the work setting, as a volunteer, or other.)

_____

_____

_____

_____

8. ORGANIZATIONS

(List those for which you hold membership that relate to the job for which you are applying.)

_____

_____

_____

_____

9. EXTRACURRICULAR EXPERIENCES

_____

_____

_____

10. OTHER

(Depending on your background or qualifications, additional sections may be added such as: credentials, licensure, awards, interests, volunteer experience, community service, military experience, civic activities, or other.)

Make your own worksheets for references and include:

Name _____

Title _____

Organization _____

Phone Number (Use bold type) _____

Best time to reach _____

Employment address _____

_____

_____

Relationship to you _____

(Be sure to contact references before providing name to prospective employer.)

After you have compiled this information, decide on the resume format best for you.

Figure E-3. *Continued*

Scale: 1 Strongly Agree; 2 Agree; 3 Neutral; 4 Disagree; 5 Strongly Disagree; NA Not Applicable

Job-Specific Questions

I would enjoy performing this work.	1	2	3	4	5	NA
This job relates to my career goals.	1	2	3	4	5	NA
I like my immediate supervisor's management style.	1	2	3	4	5	NA
The location of the job is good.	1	2	3	4	5	NA
There are opportunities for advancement.	1	2	3	4	5	NA
Continuing education will be provided.	1	2	3	4	5	NA
Salary is what was expected.	1	2	3	4	5	NA
The benefit package offered is appropriate.	1	2	3	4	5	NA
The company's mission harmonizes with my career goals.	1	2	3	4	5	NA
My lifestyle would not need to be changed.	1	2	3	4	5	NA
The company culture suits my personality.	1	2	3	4	5	NA
The office area where I will work is pleasant.	1	2	3	4	5	NA
The company maintains a smoke-free, clean, and healthy environment.	1	2	3	4	5	NA
The company rewards competence and accomplishments.	1	2	3	4	5	NA

Figure E-4.   Job Evaluation Rating

Table E-5.   Next Job Worksheet

Specify the Appropriate Response in One or Both Columns to the Right	**Essential**	**Desired**
Minimum acceptable salary:		
Benefit package:		
Level of management responsibility:		
Geographic preference:		
Degree of travel:		
Lifestyle necessities:		
Computer technology:		
Corporate culture:		
Functions to be performed:		

Table E-6.   Advanced Education Decision

Ratings you assign are from 1 to 5: 5 the best, 3 average, and 1 poor.

	Law	Informatics	Public Health	Business
		Degree Choices		
Enjoy subject matter				
Ability to afford:				
X University				
Y University				
Financial assistance				
Part-time work				
Job market for this degree				
Total (25)				
for X University				
for Y University				
Percent				

Calculate the percentage by dividing actual points into total 25 points (derived from 5 items × 5 maximum rating).

Appendix **F**

Learning Syllabus

Subject Outline

   I.   Health Information Management as a Profession
- A. Definition
- B. Educational Programs
- C. Function of Allied Health Professionals
- D. Career Opportunities
- E. Vision 2006
- F. Professionalism
- G. Success Cycle
- H. Values and Needs

  II. Searching the Job Market
- A. A Job or a Career
- B. Who Are You?
- C. Developing a Job Search Action Plan
- D. Agencies
- E. Computerized Job Searches
- F. Resources and References

 III. The Portfolio
- A. Definition
- B. How to Organize the Portfolio
- C. Appearance
- F. Contents
- G. Uses for the Portfolio
- H. Confidentiality Issues
- I. Mentors

    J. Networking

    K. Prospecting

IV. Professional Correspondence

    A. Definition

    B. Guidelines for Professional Correspondence

    C. Letter to Market Yourself

    D. Employment Applications

V. Resume Development

    A. Definition

    B. Resume Formats

    C. Elements of a Good Resume

    D. Order

    E. Home Page Resumes

    F. Applications

    G. Follow-Up Calls

VI. The Interview

    A. Purpose of Interviews

    B. Types of Interviews

    C. Interview Setting

    D. Preparing for the Interview

    E. Formats Used by Interviewers

    F. Steps in the Interview Process

    G. Strategies for an Interview

    H. Questioning

    I. Techniques for Making Lasting Impressions

    J. Answering the Interviewer's Questions

    K. Salary/Benefits

    L. Accepting the Job Offer

VII. Postinterview Strategies

    A. Items to Detail Following an Interview

    B. Interview Logistics

    C. Evaluating a Job Offer

    D. Tips to Follow When Starting a New Job

VIII. Opportunities in Health Information Management

    A. Definition of a Profession

    B. Career versus a Job

   C. Educational Opportunities
   D. Opportunities in the Field of Health Information
   E. Entrepreneurship
   F. Intrapreneurship

IX. Stress Management and Burnout

   A. Trends in Healthcare Enterprises
   B. Causes of Stress
   C. Stages of Change
   D. Methods for Coping with Stress
   E. Burnout
   F. Stages of Work
   G. How to Combat Burnout
   H. Stress Reduction Techniques
   I. Stress Associated with Job Change

Lecture Notes: Chapter 1

I. Health Information Management as a Profession

   A. Developed as information systems assumed greater importance in the processing and analyzing of patient-care documentation.
   B. Involved combining skills including computers, business, medical sciences, medicolegal aspects, and system for reimbursement and data processing.
   C. Broadened to include employers such as:
      1. Ambulatory surgery centers
      2. Behavioral healthcare facilities
      3. Clinics
      4. Computer companies
      5. Consulting firms
      6. Group practices
      7. Home health agencies
      8. Hospices
      9. Hospitals
      10. Insurance companies
      11. Managed-care groups
      12. Rehabilitation centers
      13. Subacute-care facilities

    D. Enhanced as professionals and future professionals (students) identify goals, values, and needs.

II. Educational Programs

    A. Accrediting agency: Commission on Accreditation of Allied Health Education Programs (CAAHEP).

    B. Essentials: the minimum standards of quality used in accrediting health information administration (HIA) and health information technology (HIT) programs.

III. Allied Health

    A. Function of allied health professionals and practitioners is to promote health and provide services associated with healthcare.

    B. Examples of allied health professionals include physical therapists, occupational therapists, dietitians, clinical laboratory scientists, nuclear medicine technologists, and physician assistants.

IV. Career Opportunities

    A. According to the Bureau of Labor Statistics, more than 47,000 additional health information management professionals will be needed by the year 2005.

    B. Emphasizing the various components of the HIA/HIT curriculum to employers is important as this may lead to and provide additional career opportunities. For example, list courses on the resume that support a position in quality assurance such as clinical medicine, anatomy and physiology, pathophysiology, and chemistry.

    C. Reviewing Appendix A with a listing of position titles and responsibilities can increase awareness of skills of the health information professional.

    D. Identifying those titles that appeal to you can assist in the job search and portfolio development.

V. Vision 2006

    A. Appendix A identifies existing roles that are being performed by health information professionals; new roles are envisioned due to the rapidly changing healthcare environment.

    B. Changes resulting from Vision 2006 incorporate:
      1. The shift in healthcare from the acute-care hospital to nonacute care
      2. Electronic systems for patient care and billing

3. A labor market with about 25 percent of all new jobs being in healthcare

C. AHIMA's Emergency HIM role diagram identifies six emerging roles in three clusters:

Clusters:	*Roles:*
Data management analysis	Clinical data specialist, data quality manager and research analyst
Patient health information coordination	Patient information coordinator
Information systems management	Security manager and document/repository manager

D. Seventh role is that of a health information manager, which is enterprisewide and includes working with the chief information officer.

VI. Positions in Times of Change

A. Changes in healthcare include managed care with capitated forms of payment, team approaches for problem solving, and consumers' involvement in managing their own health information.

B. Demands resulting from these changes that are anticipated for professionals who can function competently and effectively as:
1. Coding specialists
2. Clinical data analysts
3. Educators
4. Clinical data systems managers
5. Directors of health information management
6. Management consultants

VII. Professionalism

A. The transition from college student to professional requires you to do the following:
1. Commit to lifelong learning—your college education has prepared you for entry-level skills and competencies. Education should be continued either formally or informally to remain current.
2. Demonstrate credibility in job-related activities—invest whatever time is necessary to produce a quality product. Adhere to high standards.

3. Gain maturity—demonstrate composure in stressful situations.
4. Develop a winning attitude—believe in yourself. Know your strengths and weaknesses.
5. Demonstrate a consistent work ethic—adhere to the Code of Ethics of the American Health Information Management Association.
6. Belong to a professional organization—attend meetings and actively participate in the leadership of the organization.

B. Making a good impression is essential to career development. This includes being competent in your job, but also included are giving extra effort, being flexible, showing respect to others, listening, being prepared for meetings, maintaining a positive attitude, being punctual, returning borrowed items, and practicing good hygiene and manners.

VIII. Success Cycle
A. Attaining success involves finding and selecting a job that is compatible with your individual goals, values, and needs.
B. Figure 1-5 depicts the steps in the success cycle. The figure is circular indicating the flow is ongoing. Once a goal is achieved, new ones should be formed. The steps in the cycle are:
1. Decide your personal goals.
2. Act on the goals by outlining the course of action needed to meet the goals.
3. Achieve your goals.
4. Reward yourself when goals are achieved.

IX. Values and Needs
A. Job satisfaction will occur when your job is consistent with your values.
B. Value theorists:
1. Lawrence Kohlberg—three stages of value orientation:
(a) Preconventional—ages 2 to 7. Accepts whatever authority figure says. Responds to the cultural values of right, wrong, good, and bad.
(b) Conventional—ages 7–12. Conforms to expectations of society, family, and peers. Tries to win approval of authority figure.

(c) Postconventional—ages 12 and older. Individual begins to draw his or her own conscience to determine right and wrong. Begins to believe in humane treatment of others, respect for the dignity of others.

2. Morris Massey—we are shaped by events that occurred around us as we were growing up.

(a) Value cohort—events that happen to groups of people and shape an entire generation.

C. It is important to remember that your value system is shaped by your exposure to events that have occurred during your life. When your employer's values parallel yours, you will be on your way to satisfaction in the workplace.

D. Hierarchy of needs, developed by Abraham Maslow, support his theory that people work to meet their needs. Specifically the need for:

1. Clothing, food, shelter (physiological need)
2. Safety
3. Belonging
4. Self-esteem
5. Self-actualization

E. Health information management hierarchy of needs, Figure 1-6. This figure illustrates how Maslow's theory can be applied to the health information professional. A circular model is used to indicate that attainment of needs is ongoing.

Lecture Notes: Chapter 2

I. Searching the Job Market

A. Employers seek employers that "fit" into the organization. "Fit" is defined as an individual who accepts the mission and goals of the organization as well as the product or service being offered.

B. Know yourself before initiating a job search. This is accomplished through self-assessments and will enable you to optimize your time and effort.

C. A successful job hunt involves:

1. Determining if you are seeking a job or a career.
2. Assessing yourself.

3. Evaluating past work experiences.
4. Identifying desired attributes in the workplace.
5. Determining geographic boundaries.

II. A Job or a Career

    A. Job—a position that allows for a steady source of income but does not lead to achieving a career goal.

    B. Career—implies that you will progress through life with your work while earning a living in your chosen career path.

III. Who Are You?

    A. Performing self-assessments provides insight into your needs, likes, and dislikes. This will enable you to make better job or career choices.

    B. Once the student has completed Figure 2-1 and has analyzed the results, discuss the types of careers that are available. These are:

       1. Technical careers—focus on a specific competency such as coding. Normally, technical jobs/careers have little management component.

       2. Service careers—for individuals who have a commitment to a cause, for example, improving the environment. These careers provide health information professionals with an opportunity to enter nontraditional fields such as research.

       3. Entrepreneurial careers—for the risk takers. Those individuals interested in sales or owning their own business are best suited for entrepreneurial careers.

       4. Managerial careers—one attribute necessary for individuals seeking a management career is the willingness to accept total responsibility for functions within their span of control and authority.

    C. Evaluating past work experiences provides a means in determining what you liked and disliked about previous jobs. Knowing this will enhance your chances of not repeating a bad experience.

    D. Finally, determine the geographic boundaries in which you desire to work and live. Researching locations prior to initiating a job search refines your target area. Consider the following:

       1. Cost of living
       2. Proximity of affordable housing to work
       3. Commuting time from home to work
       4. Taxes

       5. Educational system

       6. Cultural activities

       7. Accessibilities to libraries

       8. Climate

       9. Primary industry

       10. Healthcare systems

E. New graduates should consider the following observations:

    1. The job market may be better in communities where health information programs are not offered in colleges or universities.

    2. Rural communities are underserved by health information administration or health information technology.

    3. Cities with a variety of healthcare systems provide more career opportunities.

    4. Employment in acute-care facilities located in cities outside a major metropolitan area often allows a faster track to management positions.

F. Demographic information about cities can be found by using the following resources:

    1. Public library

    2. Newspapers

    3. World Wide Web

    4. Chamber of commerce for the city being considered

IV. Developing a Job Search Action Plan

A. Once you have a better understanding of the type of career you are seeking, the type of organization, and geographic location, you are ready to develop a plan to facilitate an effective job search.

B. How long will the search take? A rule of thumb is one month for every $10,000 earned. Hourly positions take approximately two months, professional positions two to three months, middle-level positions three to six months, and executive-level positions six to twelve months.

C. Searching for a position is a full-time job. Listed below are tips for job searching:

    1. Remain employed throughout the search. A steady income removes the temptation to accept a position only for the paycheck.

    2. Designate a work space in your home. This will become the office from which you will make appointments, write correspondence, make telephone calls, and maintain search files.

3. Purchase a telephone answering machine.
4. Maintain a telephone conversation log to document to whom you have spoken and the topic of conversation, and to remind you of any follow-up activities.
5. Purchase an appointment book.
6. Use simple stationery and envelopes for correspondence.
7. Evaluate your wardrobe.
8. Familiarize yourself with the reference department in the public library. Review these references:
   (a) *U.S. Industrial Outlook*
   (b) *U.S. Dictionary of Occupational Titles*
   (c) *Encyclopedia of Careers & Vocational Guidance*
   (d) *Gale Director of Databases*
   (e) *Journal of the American Health Information Management Association*
   (f) *Advance*
   (g) *For the Record*
9. Subscribe to newspapers, professional journals, and publications as needed.
10. Purchase books to become knowledgeable in job searches and writing resumes and cover letters.
11. List with the appropriate search firms, employment agencies, alumni associations, professional organizations, and all other referral services depending on your potential employment level.
12. Recent graduates should attend college job fairs.
13. Be prepared for your interview by researching the organization with whom you will be interviewing. Two references that provide a historical perspective of a company's performance along with comments pertaining to the company's future outlook are *Moody's* and *Standard and Poor*. Annual reports are also available at public libraries.

D. Networking is the oldest and best method for securing a job. For networking to be successful, it is necessary to list all individuals whom you want to contact. Consider classmates, neighbors, friends, co-workers, and relatives.

E. Agencies—executive search firm vs. employment agency vs. outplacement firm.
   1. Executive search firm—identifies and appraises candidates for a specific position. This requires a contractual agreement be-

tween the search firm and the organization. The search firm receives payment from the organization to which it is contracted. Resumes are not acknowledged. Face-to-face interviewing and reference checking of all prospective candidates is completed prior to presenting the candidate to the organization.

2. Employment agencies—find jobs for people and for companies. Fees are paid by the individual seeking the job.

3. Outplacement firm—assists individuals in packaging resumes for perspective employers if you have been displaced from your position. These firms offer a wide array of services including assessments, career suggestions, resume preparation, interview training, and secretarial support.

F. Computerized job searches:

1. Searching for a job or a career has been greatly enhanced by using computers to access job databases.

2. Access to the job databases is achieved via the Internet. Through the Internet, the World Wide Web is where organizations store their information. A "navigator" such as Netscape enables the user to go from one Web page to another.

3. Job-searching Web sites change frequently. A starting place is:
   (a) HeadHunter (www.headhunter.net)
   (b) Monster Board (www.monster.com)

4. Computer job banks use a resume as a source document for a job bank database. Key words are abstracted from the resume and placed into the database. Some companies use an applicant tracking system to screen internal candidates for job openings within the organization. Filling the position from within provides the organization with cost savings since fees for search firms, employment agencies, and advertising are not incurred.

5. Problems with job bank:
   (a) The individual entering your resume into the system may not select the correct words.
   (b) Key words can be weighted by individual hiring. Your resume and qualifications may not match those desired.
   (c) The computer may not select your resume if you are making more salary than what the desired position pays.

6. When selecting an external computer job bank service:
   (a) Ask for a list of what will be abstracted from your resume.
   (b) Request names and addresses of companies that use their service.

(c) Request information on the number of searches that are made of the databases.
(d) Inquire about the number of placements that have resulted.
(e) Ask for a live demonstration of the system using your resume.
(f) Determine how often the database is updated.
(g) Get a fee schedule.
(h) Ask for references.

V.   Resources and References
   A. Chapter 2 provides you with a list of references to assist in the job search. Select some to discuss with the class.

Lecture Notes: Chapter 3

I.   The Portfolio
   A. A portfolio consists of documentation of various projects from college courses and work experiences. It is a creative document that highlights your strengths and accomplishments.
   B. Contents of the portfolio provide a display of the scope and quality of your education and experience. When developing the portfolio, try to include documentation from several positions that might start your career path.
   C. Benefits—developing a portfolio will enable you to:
      1. Examine your progress in your educational program by comparing portfolio contents over a period of time.
      2. Evaluate your growth and development over a period of time rather than single accomplishments.
      3. Compare achievements in light of your career goals.
      4. Provide prospective employers with concrete examples of work-related experiences performed during college years and in the work environment.
      5. Support your statements regarding your knowledge, skills, and abilities with specific examples.
      6. Document team experiences.

II. How to Organize the Portfolio
   A. Determining how to organize the portfolio requires you to review your course of study and work experiences. Since the portfolio is to "showcase" your abilities and accomplishments, highlight pro-

jects that demonstrate your knowledge, skills, and abilities and reflect your personality.

B. Compile your documentation in a three-ring notebook using tabs to divide the document into major headings and subheadings. Examples of major categories include:

1. Subject categories—group your achievements according to the following: Clinical Medicine, Coding, Computers, Health Information Systems, Human Resource Management, Quality Assessment, Record Retention and Retrieval, Release of Information, Research, Statistics, Transcription, Utilization.

2. Review. Select the subject categories that reflect the area in which you have had the most accomplishments. You do not need to address all these areas.

3. Refer to Figure 3-1 in the textbook for examples of what could be included under each of the subject headings.

C. Year and function—Actual years could be used for tabs when dividing by chronology, or if a new graduate, state the year as Freshman, Sophomore, Junior, or Senior.

D. Function—include categories such as planning, organizing, leading, controlling, and representing. Examples of projects that could be included under the function of planning might be a PERT chart developed for transitioning files from one area to another, policies and procedures developed, position descriptions, and a revised organization chart.

E. Location—organizing the portfolio by location would include examples of work or performance for different departments or work areas. Location could also be by the types of care and facilities such as Managed Care, Home Health, Long Term, Subacute, Mental Health, Acute, Hospice, Health Maintenance Organization, etc.

F. The portfolio should not contain everything you have done and every accomplishment made. It should include examples of successful past performance that document your skills and accomplishments.

III. Appearance

A. The portfolio is a professional document, not a scrapbook. Follow these guidelines for the development of a professional document:

1. Cover—soft and rich looking.

2. Page size 8½-by-11 inches, with each page encased in a transparent acetate jacket.

        3. Table of contents and tabs for easy referencing.

        4. Print is dark and laser quality.

        5. Key words and phrases are highlighted and bolded.

        6. Graphs and charts are incorporated when possible.

   B. Examples included should reflect only successful past projects and achievements.

IV. Contents

   A. The portfolio should contain:

      1. Cover sheet—should include the word "Portfolio" followed by your name bolded and capitalized, address, and telephone number. This information should be centered on the page.

      2. Table of contents—see Figure 3-2.

      3. Resume.

      4. Management philosophy statement—this statement will give insight into your leadership style and indicate how you perceive and judge the world around you. It also should indicate how you gain a sense of personal satisfaction and competence, how you handle conflict, and how you use power.

      5. Personal statement/summary—this statement will help the reader see you as a person. In developing your statement, consider the attributes an employer wants in an employee, such as you worked your way through college to pay tuition.

      6. Projects and visual presentations, charts, and graphs—can be summarized in a narrative outline. See Figure 3-1.

      7. Continuing education certificates and statements regarding the application of learning—this is important for individuals who have been in the profession for several years. Listing key points learned will enhance this section.

      8. Diplomas and results of certifying examinations.

      9. Statements from instructors, clinical supervisors, employers, officers of the organization—be sure to include commendations, awards, or scholarships received.

     10. Personal goals for the next five years—when listing your goals, make sure they match your prospective employer. Their needs should be consistent with your goals.

     11. References on one page, followed by the actual letters of reference if available—list three to five references, including name, organization, complete address, and telephone number.

   B. Uses for the portfolio:

1. The portfolio is a companion to the resume.
2. Do not show your portfolio to every prospective employer. If you find a job that you really want, showing your portfolio may contribute to the success in achieving the position.
3. The portfolio can also be used for career planning and advancement.

V. Confidentiality

    A. Issues to consider are content and reader.

    B. Content—if you are using material that identifies organization, permission from the organization may be necessary. If a simulation is used, permission is not necessary as the organization is not identified. If the document is for internal use, permission is not needed, for example, if you are seeking a promotion or a raise and you include a project to document your abilities or skills.

    C. Document from whom permission was granted and the date. This should appear at the bottom of the document.

    D. As a reader of a portfolio, reproduction of documents in the portfolio should not occur without the authorization from the author of the portfolio.

VI. Advantages of a Mentor

    A. Developing a portfolio can be an arduous task. A mentor is an advisor. A mentor can be a college professor or an experienced professional. Clinical supervisors frequently become mentors for students.

    B. Mentors assist in providing answers to questions such as why the portfolio is being developed, the kinds of information that should be included, and how the information can be improved.

    C. Ideally, a mentor has developed his or her own portfolio. This is not always possible, so it is important to find an individual with whom you are comfortable working.

    D. The process of selecting and organizing your portfolio requires you to reflect, self-assess, review your goals and accomplishments. This process will provide focus and positioning for entry-level or career advancement opportunities.

VII. Networking

    A. Networking involves building bridges throughout your career. This can be either formal or informal in nature. Formal networks are individuals with whom you remain in contact for a specific sit-

uation. Informal networks include those individuals with whom you remain in contact.
   B. Forty-six percent of individuals in non-acute care positions used acquaintance networking during their career to find new positions.
   C. Start early in your career to develop a circle of acquaintances who can assist you in advancing your career. Various methods can be used to organize networking contacts, for example, collecting business cards or maintaining telephone and address files.

VIII. Prospecting
   A. Prospecting is sending your resume to a wide range of companies and associates without knowing if any jobs are available.
   B. Sharing a job hotline telephone number or data regarding new markets is one way to help a job searcher.
   C. Career fairs are another form of prospecting.

Lecture Notes: Chapter 4

I.   Professional Correspondence
   A. Professional correspondence includes letters written for the purpose of:
      1. Requesting information.
      2. Accompanying a resume (cover letter).
      3. Showing appreciation for an interview.
      4. Rejecting a job offer.
      5. Accepting a job offer.
      6. Resigning.
   B. Every business letter you write is a way of marketing yourself.

II.   Guidelines for Professional Correspondence
   A. Structure of the letter—refer to Table 4-1 for details.
      1. Subject—What is the theme of the letter?
      2. Audience—Who are the potential readers of the letter?
      3. Purpose—Why am I writing this letter?
      4. Organization—How should the letter be organized?
         (a) State the reason for the letter.
         (b) Explain what you want to happen.

           (c) Provide supporting documentation.

           (d) Give a positive response—say thank you.

B. Style guidelines:
1. One main idea per paragraph.
2. Average seventeen words per sentence.
3. Use active voice.
4. Be specific.
5. Select positive words.
6. Put your reader first by using "you," not "I" or "me."
7. Be accurate. Read the letter out loud; check spelling.
8. Make sure all details are included in the letter such as your address and phone number.

C. Appearance:
1. Use good-quality paper measuring 8½-by-11 inches.
2. Avoid flashy colored paper. White is preferred.
3. Full-block or modified block is preferred. See Figures 4-3 and 4-4.
4. Most business letters are single spaced with a single line between paragraphs.
5. Leave at least a 1-inch margin on the left and right.

D. Major sections of a business letter:
1. Letterhead
2. Date
3. Inside address
4. Attention line
5. Salutation
6. Body of letter
7. Complimentary close
8. Signature
9. Your typed name and credentials
10. Enclosure

III. Letters to Market Yourself

A. Request letter:
1. Keep it short.
2. First sentence should state your purpose—why are you marking the request.
3. Emphasize the valuable service the reader would be rendering by cooperating with the request.
4. Clarify what action is needed at the end of the letter.

B. Cover letter—say enough about yourself to get the reader's attention. This may be the letter of application. Include:
   1. Highlights of your accomplishments.
   2. Information indicating you have researched the company.
   3. Indications that you have the right skills for the position.
   4. Reasons that will motivate employer to interview you.
C. Interview confirmation letter—purpose is to keep your name in front of potential employers. Include:
   1. What you are confirming.
   2. Place, time, and date of the appointment.
   3. Where you will be staying if from out of town.
D. Thanks for the interview letter—purpose is to show professional behavior and to say thank you for the interview. Include:
   1. When and where the interview was held.
   2. The position for which you interviewed.
   3. Something that occurred during the interview to remind the interviewer of you.
   4. Offer to provide additional information to validate your qualifications.
E. Job rejection letter—purpose is to express appreciation for being considered. Include:
   1. Why you are rejecting the offer.
   2. Thank you for making you the offer.
F. Acceptance letter—purpose is to confirm the details of the job.
   1. Be enthusiastic about the good news.
   2. Confirm the position, salary, date, and time of starting.
G. Resignation letter—purpose is to terminate employment.
   1. Keep it very professional.
   2. Make it short and honest.
   3. If leaving for another position, mention that is the reason for leaving.
H. Maintain a copy of all correspondence received or sent during the job search.

IV. Employment Applications
   A. All places of employment require an application. Try to request one ahead of time so you can complete it neatly and thoroughly.
   B. Refer to Figures 4-10 and 4-11 for sample applications.
   C. Reason for leaving on application—note positive reasons when possible such as to advance HIM skills.

    D. Salary—research sources to determine a salary range. Use "negotiable" if in doubt.

Lecture Notes: Chapter 5

  I. Resume Development

    A. Resumes are designed to summarize the highlights of your education, experience, skills, and other relevant information. A resume becomes a resource for the interviewer and if properly written, facilitates good communications. Other uses include a component of the documentation for advanced education and promotion portfolio.

    B. A resume is used to "sell" yourself to potential employers.

    C. Update your resume frequently.

 II. Resume Formats

    A. The format you choose should be the one that best presents your qualifications.

    B. Formats:

      1. Chronological—arranging education and experience in order of occurrence.

      2. Reverse chronological—most widely used format. This format lists the most recent events first. It is not recommended if you have an inconsistent work record or a history of job hopping.

      3. Functional/skill-based—recommended when your education and experience do not directly support your career objective. Emphasis is on your skills. This format is excellent for those who have no work history, are self-employed, or have worked as a consultant. One disadvantage of the skill-based format is it is difficult and time-consuming to read.

      4. Combination—involves integrating components from the formats discussed. Creativity can be an asset in developing the resume. The resume should reflect the type of person the employer is seeking.

    C. Curriculum vitae—used primarily for professionals in law, medicine, science, and academic fields. CVs blend chronological and functional resumes. They differ from resumes as they include published works, presentations, foreign travel, community and professional service, grants applied for and amounts secured, re-search funding, and other information that documents scholarly background and achievements.

III. Elements of a Good Resume
   A. Content—relate resume to career objective. Content should be concise, focused, and easy to read.
   B. Identifying information—include your name, address, telephone number for work and home, e-mail address is optional.
   C. Objective—also referred to as a professional goal, career focus, career objective, job objective, career statement, skill summary, and position desired. (Refer to Figure 5-2).
   D. Educational information—includes degrees, majors, months and years of graduating, names of colleges and universities granting your degree. Include GPA if 3.3 or higher on a 4.0 scale. Related course work can be listed, but list no more than eight courses.
   E. Experience—use the heading of either "Professional Experiences" or "Experiences." Include in this section the job title, employer, city, state of employer, month and year employment began and ended, and a brief description of the work using action verb phrases. If no work experience, include internships, volunteer service, and extracurricular activities.
   F. Additional information—information in this section should highlight special skills.
   G. References—include a statement at the end of the resume, "available upon request."

IV. Order
   A. Heading
   B. Objective
   C. Education
   D. Work experience

V. Miscellaneous
   A. Be accurate with information included in your resume. Don't misrepresent your qualifications and accomplishments.
   B. Proofread your resume for spelling errors.
   C. Always check to make sure words at the beginning of lists are parallel. If you start with a verb, continue with a verb.
   D. Appearance—a one-page resume is preferred; two pages maximum.

    E. Buzzwords—do not use them.

VI. Home Page Resumes
    A. Using a multimedia resume, that is, one that combines voice, video, text, and picture, is the newest way to circulate a resume.
    B. Disadvantages to using this format include:
       1. Employers are reluctant to know too many details prior to hiring such as gender or race.
       2. Not every employer has the time or equipment for previewing multimedia.
       3. Appearing before a camera is difficult for some.

VII. Applications
    A. A resume does not substitute for an application.
    B. When possible, type the application.
    C. Complete the application and cover letter and mail in a timely fashion.

VIII. Follow-Up Calls
    A. A follow-up call should be made between 5 and 14 days after the application has been submitted.
    B. Before making the telephone call, practice what you are going to say.
    C. Make a notation in a log book of the date of the follow-up call and what was discussed.

Lecture Notes: Chapter 6

I. The Interview
    A. The interview provides an opportunity to market yourself.
    B. To ensure your interview leaves a lasting impression, learn as much about the employer and position as possible.
    C. Practice your interviewing skills with a friend or family member.
II. Types of Interviews
    A. Informational—mainly for educational purposes and networking. Allows student to talk with a professional about the knowledge and skills needed for a specific position, to learn about the functions performed, and to determine if there are opportunities in this area.

B. Screening—usually conducted by a trained interviewer. It can take place over the telephone, in person, or on videotape. The purpose is to confirm the information on the resume and determine if the applicant has qualifications for the position. Tips in talking with a screener:
   1. Do not try to control the interview.
   2. Avoid volunteering facts.
   3. Respond in a straightforward manner to the question.
C. Selection—the interview focuses on your background, work experience, projects, previous responsibilities, personality, leadership experience, and achievements.
D. Hiring—purpose is to finalize the major responsibilities of the position, salary and benefits will be explained at this time.

III. Interview Setting
   A. One-on-one—frequently used with entry-level positions. Usually meet with the person to whom you would be associated.
   B. Panel/board/committee—meet with several individuals at one time. This method gives the feeling for group dynamics of the organization.
   C. Meal—a meal interview can be used in combination with other methods of interviewing, or merely to evaluate social skills. Remember, although the setting is relaxed, be sure to act professionally, never smoke, abstain from alcoholic beverages, and do not introduce politics or religion.
   D. All-day, on-site—this type of interview is used for higher-level positions and provides the interviewee with an opportunity time to meet various persons and observe a variety of functions.
   E. Telephone—screening interviews use this method. To prepare for a telephone interview, make sure an environment free from disturbances is created.
   F. Videoconferencing—this method is primarily used for the screening process. Tips:
      1. Project the best image through appropriate hairstyle, professional dress, and positive body language.
      2. Avoid broad gestures.
      3. Prepare strategies for difficult questions.
   G. Computer-assisted videoconferences—a series of open-ended questions or multiple-choice questions relating to employment history, background, and qualifications are asked. This method

assists the employer in developing questions for the face-to-face interview.

H. Test taking—used for skill positions such as coding and transcriptions. A one-on-one interview follows once the results of the test are known.

IV. Preparing for the Interview

    A. Research—Seek out as much about the facility as possible. Consult previous instructors, friends, or individuals employed by the facility to gain insight into the organization. The public library offers a wealth of information. Refer to Figures 6-2 and 6-3 for the types of information you need to research.

    B. Strengths and job functions—prior to the interview, list your strengths and compare them to the position you are seeking. Identifying these will help you focus on how you fit into the organization.

    C. Role-playing—practice being interviewed. Ask a classmate, parent, friend, instructor, or if possible, a human resource professional to do a mock interview. Through role-playing, you can refine your listening skills, eliminate unwanted gestures, practice speaking clearly, and determine if your responses are complete and accurate.

    D. Get to the interview on time.

V. Formats Used by Interviewers

    A. Direct—very structured. Interviewer is working from an outline.

    B. Indirect—loosely structured, used to bring out the candidate's personality.

    C. Stress—interviewer creates a stressful situation such as asking questions that focus on the negative. For example, did you receive any D's or F's in your college work?

    D. Problem solving—the interviewer presents you with a management problem and asks how you would solve it. Tips:

        1. Listen to the problem; restate the question to make sure you understood it correctly.

        2. Apply problem-solving techniques. Identify the problem, think about alternative solutions, and make a recommendation.

        3. Discuss techniques that will solve problems.

        4. Conclude with your solution.

E. Question-answer-question—using this method, the interviewer asks you a question, which you answer. Then you ask the interviewer a question. This type of format tends to build your self-esteem.

VI. Steps in the Interview Process
   A. Greeting and introduction
   B. Describing the position
   C. Answering the interviewer's questions
   D. Asking the interviewer questions
   E. Closing

VII. Strategies for an Interview
   A. Emphasize your strengths.
   B. Throughout the interview, structure your comments and questions to prove you are the perfect candidate.
   C. Be visionary. Take the organization and job into the future.

VIII. Questioning
   A. Be prepared for various types of questions. Review Figures 6-6 through 6-10.
   B. A knowledgeable interviewer will not deliberately ask questions that are discriminatory in nature. If a question is inappropriate or unethical, be polite and professional in your response.

IX. Techniques for Lasting Impressions
   A. Appearance—clothing, posture, and initial greeting are very important. Be sure to smile and make eye contact. Handshakes should be firm but gentle.
   B. Do not use the first name unless directed to do so.
   C. Be a good listener.
   D. Ask questions to show you are interested.

X. Answering the Interviewer's Questions
   A. Do not tell jokes.
   B. Do not introduce religion or political beliefs.
   C. Do not ask questions that show little interest in work, such as when is the coffee break.
   D. Never present a requirement that you are not going to observe.

XI. Salary/Benefits

    A. Salary—never bring up salary. Leave the subject to the interviewer. Never rush to accept the first salary offer.

    B. Benefits—the benefits for which you qualify depend on the type of job and the organization. The benefit package could add as much as 35 percent to your salary.

XII. Accepting the Job Offer

    A. If an offer is made, but at less salary than you expected, you can counter the offer, or accept the job for the experience. The decision on whether to accept a position or not is based entirely on your career goals.

    B. Once you have accepted the position, it is important to confirm, in writing, your title, salary, and start date.

    C. If you have been negotiating with other companies, it is important to notify them that you have accepted another position.

Lecture Notes: Chapter 7

I. Postinterview Strategies

    A. The initial interview can be helpful for future interviews. Documentation after the interview is essential.

    B. Among the details to be covered following an interview are:
1. Reimbursement for expenses
2. Writing the thank-you letter
3. Contacting references
4. Keeping in consistent contact through networking

    C. Reimbursement for expenses should be determined prior to interviewing. If the interview is in the city in which you reside, generally there is no reimbursement. If out of town, the airline ticket, hotel, and other related expenses could be covered. Do not accept an expense-paid visit if you are not interested in being employed by the organization.

    D. Thank-you letter—discussed in Chapter 4.

    E. Contacting references soliciting their permission should be accomplished prior to completing the application. This will serve as a reminder of who you are. For new graduates, instructors are usually the references. Also consider clinical supervisors.

F. Consistent contact—at the end of the interview, ask "About when can I expect a reply?" If you do not hear by the specified date, contact the interviewer and ask the status of the position. If using the telephone, Monday is generally not a good day to call.

II. Interview Logistics

A. Reflect on what happened during the interview. Write notes immediately after the interview to assist your memory. Record the date of the interview, contact's name, phone number, actions taken by the company, actions taken by you.

B. You may also want to record if the receptionist was friendly, while waiting did you read brochures on the company, was the interviewer friendly, and was the interview structured or unstructured.

C. Recap the questions that you were asked. Jot down your responses.

D. Record the positives and negatives about the position.

E. Make note of the corporate culture. Were the employees friendly? How were incoming calls handled? Was there a positive attitude?

III. Evaluating a Job Offer

A. Consider if the job can contribute toward your interests, values, and skills.

IV. Starting a New Job

A. Be a good listener.

B. Strive to be competent.

C. Be an advocate for the HIM profession.

D. Be flexible.

E. Contribute to the organization.

F. Be responsible, timely, and adaptable.

G. Always be a professional.

Lecture Notes: Chapter 8

I. Opportunities in Health Information Management

A. Extraordinary changes have occurred in the healthcare industry that have created exciting career opportunities for health information professionals. One factor necessitating change has been the transition from a paper record to an electronic patient record.

Refer to Figure 8-1 for a comparison of healthcare past and present.

   B. Profession—an occupation requiring advanced training and involving mental rather than manual work. A profession can be defined by a set of characteristics. These include:
1. Expertise that is gained from specialized training in a body of abstract knowledge.
2. Autonomy that is the perceived right to make choices that concern both means and end.
3. Commitment to the work and the profession.
4. Identification with the profession and other professionals.
5. Adherence to an ethical standard—refer to Figure 8-2 for the Code of Ethics of the American Health Information Management Association.

II. Career versus a Job

   A. Career:
1. Allows you to use your education, training, skills, personal qualities, and talents.
2. Produces an income commensurate with your talents and contributions.
3. Provides growth and a professional career path.
4. Gives you control, authority, and respect from management.

   B. Job:
1. Unrelated to your strengths, or is unsatisfying to you.
2. Results in being underpaid for your contributions.
3. Does not provide a career path.
4. Allows little or no control.

   C. It is recommended that you spend the first year impressing your supervisor and others with your performance and effectiveness. Make them aware of your accomplishments. Accomplishments are work completed successfully.

III. Educational Opportunities

   A. Accredited record technician
1. Continue education full-time for a bachelor's degree.
2. Work while enrolled in an external degree program.
3. Advance through accomplishments, relocating as needed for advancement opportunities.
4. Refer to Figure 8-6 for a listing of bachelor's degrees.

B. Registered record administrators:
1. Graduate education—MPH, MBA, MHA, for example.
2. Law, medicine, osteopathy, dentistry.
3. Refer to Figure 8-7 for a listing of postbaccalaureate opportunities.

C. Advantages for a graduate degree—to mention a few:
1. Provides an opportunity for self-actualization and the ability to use your talents to the fullest.
2. Prepares you for advancement.
3. Develops additional skills.
4. Demonstrates your professional responsibility for lifelong learning.
5. Facilitates your growth and development for more challenging work.

D. Selecting a graduate program—ask yourself:
1. Why do I want an advanced degree?
2. What resources are available to me?
3. Will there be jobs available following graduation?
4. Which undergraduate courses did I like?
5. Who are my role models?

IV. Opportunities in Health Information
A. According to AHIMA, the demand for health information professionals exceeds the supply.
B. AHIMA's Vision 2006 outlines emerging roles for health information professionals. These include (refer to Figure 8-9):
1. Health information manager
2. Clinical data specialist
3. Patient information coordinator
4. Data quality manager
5. Document and repository manager
6. Research and decision support analyst
7. Security officer

C. International opportunities will emerge as healthcare systems become linked globally. Health information professionals have served as consultants and have been employed around the world. (Refer to Table 8-2 and Figure 8-10.) Although international opportunities are exciting, it is important to familiarize yourself with the customs of the country to make sure they are compatible with your lifestyle. Also consider living conditions and climate.

D. The International Federation of Health Record Organizations brings together people dedicated to the advancement of the art and science of health records. You do not need to work in a foreign country to join this organization.

E. Coding and informatic technology opportunities—the impending implementation of ICD-10 will provide opportunities for those skilled in this system.

F. Entrepreneurship involves starting your own business. These individuals organize, manage, and assume the risks of a business. Coding, transcription, release of information, and consulting are businesses HIM professionals have entered.

G. *Micropreneurs* is a term used for individuals who have home-based businesses with just one employee. This type of venture can be started without quitting your present job.

H. Intrapreneurship is something all HIM professionals do automatically. This is accomplished by assuming personal responsibility for marketing the profession and others' skills and knowledge within your workplace.

Lecture Notes: Chapter 9

I. Stress Management and Burnout
   A. Rarely does a book targeted to individuals who are early in career development address the issues of stress and burnout. However, sometime in your career you will encounter both.
   B. Healthcare has not been isolated from the trend in business to do more with less. Downsizing or rightsizing of facilities and the evaluation of managed care are the products of cost-containment efforts. Workers in healthcare are seeing:
      1. Reductions in staffing, which necessitates longer workdays.
      2. Higher productivity expectations.
      3. Mergers of hospitals.
      4. Efforts by healthcare facilities to gain a larger share of the market.
      5. Purchases of physician practices by provider organizations.
      6. Measures implemented to decrease the length of stay for patients.

C. Everything can cause stress—work, debt, relationships, friends, change, not achieving your goals, and so forth. One uniform cause cannot be identified as stress differs for each individual. Sources of stress for health information professionals may include:
   1. Working with the medical staff.
   2. Lack of support or recognition by administration.
   3. Rightsizing of your department necessitated by organizational reengineering.
   4. Information systems that do not function as intended.
   5. Inability to obtain qualified employees.
   6. Decreases in the budget.
   7. Insufficient release time to attend continuing education opportunities.
D. A recent trend is for people to balance their work and personal lives. Corporations are aware of this trend and are offering more latitude for employees. Flex hours, job sharing, and compressed work weeks are just some of the innovations.
E. Change is a significant stressor. Learning to cope with change involves becoming a master of change, not a victim. There are four stages of change:
   1. Denial
   2. Resistance
   3. Exploring opportunities created by change
   4. Acceptance
F. If you become stuck in any of these stages, then chronic stress could result. When this happens, burnout occurs.
G. Causes of stress may not always be a single overt act, but a combination of incidents that "pile up." This is referred to as sneaking stress.
H. The best method for coping with stress is to try to prevent it from happening in the first place. Ask yourself:
   1. Can this be delegated?
   2. Is the deadline realistic?
   3. Is it imperative?
   4. Can something else be substituted?
   5. Should I say no?

II. Burnout
   A. Symptoms of burnout include:
      1. Fatigue

2. Emotional outbursts
3. Inability to make a decision
4. Irritability

B. Burnout is the lack of motivation to work. It does not occur overnight, but develops slowly.

C. The relationship between stress and burnout is close in that if stressors are left unattended, there is a greater chance for burnout. The primary difference is stressors can be changed, but once burnout has occurred, it is very difficult to reverse the situation.

III. Stages of Work

A. Honeymoon period:
1. Your job is challenging and exciting.
2. Possibilities for growth and learning are limitless.
3. You have endless energy.

B. Stagnation:
1. Your enthusiasm for the job wains.
2. You feel you have mastered all the skills needed for completion of your function.
3. You are overwhelmed and do not have the time to complete the tasks required in your position.

C. Frustration:
1. You begin to exhibit many of the symptoms found in the Burnout Inventory. (Refer to Figure 9-2.)
2. You are angry, irritable, and hostile with others.

D. Apathy:
1. You develop a "who cares" attitude.

V. How Can You Combat Burnout

A. Watch for signs and symptoms.
B. Find another way to perform your job.
C. Become a lifelong learner.
D. Think positively.
E. Balance your work and personal life.

VI. Stress Reduction Techniques

A. Breathe correctly.
B. Shut the office door and think about where you would rather be.
C. Close your eyes and concentrate on relaxing each muscle that is tense.
D. Build a support system in the workplace.

E. Pursue a job that meets your needs.

F. Learn how to meditate.

G. Develop outside interests.

H. Commit to not taking work home routinely.

VII. Stress Associated with Job Change

A. Develop a plan that addresses a "what-if" scenario.

B. Communicate with your spouse.

C. Involve your spouse in decision making.

D. Begin to network within the community to identify employment opportunities.

E. Involve the family in discussion to the extent they need to know.

F. Assist your spouse in identifying potential employers when requested.

G. Maintain a positive attitude.

Glossary

Accomplishment: The act of achieving and bringing a task to a successful conclusion.

Accreditation: A voluntary peer process whereby a private, nongovernment association grants public recognition to educational programs that meet or exceed nationally established standards. The process for the program of study generally includes these four steps: (1) a clear statement of goals and educational objectives, (2) a directed self-assessment focused on activities related to the objectives, (3) a site visit by peers, and (4) a decision by an independent body that the program does or does not meet the standards for accreditation. When the program is accredited, a given number of years are assigned until the process is repeated. The predetermined standards for health information administration and health information technology programs are termed **essentials.**

Accredited record technician (ART): An individual who graduated from an accredited program in health information technology and passed the national certification examination. A current listing of accredited programs in health information technology can be obtained from the American Health Information Management Association, headquartered in Chicago, Illinois.

Administration: The guidance of an undertaking toward the achievement of its purpose. Administration and management are so similar that they may be considered synonymous. Frequently, administration is applied to public activities and management to private.

Allied health practitioners: Specially trained healthcare personnel who assist, facilitate, and complement the work of physicians and other specialists and who are licensed or credentialed. Pharmacists, dentists, podiatrists, clinical psychologists, and nurses traditionally have preferred identities independent of allied health. Others may or may not regard themselves as allied health practitioners depending on circumstances. They include dental hygienists, nutritionists, speech pathologists, audiologists, public health specialists, licensed practical nurses, and medical research assistants.

Ambulatory care: All types of health services provided on an outpatient basis for patients who travel to locations other than their home to receive services and then depart the same day.

Associate-degree program: An educational program usually associated with a junior or community college.

Baccalaureate-degree program: An educational program combining liberal arts and specialized studies in a four-year college or university that awards bachelor's degrees.

Burnout: The lack of motivation to work.

Cancer registry: A system of identifying and keeping data on cancerous neoplasms. These data are gathered by healthcare institutions, compiled on a national basis, and used for research purposes.

Career planning: The process by which one determines career goals based on personal needs and values and specifies objectives or pathways to accomplishing those goals.

Certified coding specialist (CCS): A person who has passed a national examination that tests skills in assigning accurate codes to diseases, conditions, injuries, procedures, and treatments for reimbursement, research, and other purposes.

Commission on Accreditation of Allied Health Education Programs (CAAHEP): An allied health education accrediting agency that works cooperatively with external sponsored review committees to accredit educational programs in numerous fields of postsecondary allied health education. CAAHEP is recognized by the Council on Postsecondary Accreditation (COPA). The American Health Information Management Association is a sponsor of CAAHEP.

Computer-based patient record (CPR): Patient health information captured and stored electronically as a patient record. The CPR is a system designed to provide accurate, complete, timely, and comprehensive data to authorized users for patient care and to link financial, administrative, and clinical data for reimbursement, research, and other purposes.

Competent: Having the capacity to function in an approved way according to standards.

Concurrent review: A review of the medical necessity of hospital or other healthcare. This is conducted within a short period of time following admission of a patient and continues with periodic review of the services provided to the patient.

Confidentiality: The degree and circumstances in which information is kept private or secret. Information that is held confidential may include medical, financial, portfolio, interview, or other information obtained.

Conflict resolution: An action by managers to resolve disagreements through accommodation, force, compromise, and collaboration.

Consultant: One who advises professionally and provides services in specialized areas.

Continuing education: Formal education obtained by a health professional after completing entry-level degree and training requirements. The purpose of continuing education is to improve and maintain the professional competence of healthcare practitioners.

Council on Postsecondary Accreditation (COPA): A national, nonprofit, private-sector organization whose major purpose is to support, coordinate, and improve nongovernmental accrediting activities conducted at postsecondary educational levels in the United States.

Cover letter: An introductory document that accompanies a resume sent to a prospective employer.

Creativity: A thinking process that combines ideas in a unique way to produce new and original concepts.

Credentials: The recognition of professional or technical competence through a registration or other certifying examination. Credentialing assists in determining the quality of personnel by providing standards for evaluating competence for a specific role and for various functions.

Current Procedural Terminology, **4th edition (CPT-4):** A comprehensive listing of medical terms and codes for the uniform designation of diagnostic and therapeutic procedures.

Customers: Those persons who use the services or goods provided or have an investor's stake in the success of an organization.

Diagnosis-related group (DRG): A system used by insurance companies to classify illnesses according to diagnoses and treatments with a fixed amount established for each DRG. DRGs are used to determine reimbursement for hospitalized patients with healthcare coverage under Medicare.

Effectiveness: The degree to which actions achieve the intended result through a consideration of outcomes to be measured.

Efficiency: The relationship between the quantity of inputs or resources used and the quantity of outputs produced.

Electronic patient record (EPR): An electronic path toward the CPR that includes databases, integrated work flow, optical disk storage, and paper documents.

Employment agency: A company that finds jobs for people.

Empowerment: The process of increasing the decision-making discretion of employees.

Encoder: A computer program that assists those assigning code numbers to diagnosis and procedure codes.

Entrepreneur: A person who conceives a product or service idea, pursues opportunities for innovation, and starts an organization to provide the product or service.

Equal opportunity employment: The opportunity for all people to have a fair chance to succeed without discrimination.

Essentials: The minimum standards of quality used in accrediting programs that prepare individuals to enter an allied health profession. The extent to which a program complies with these standards determines the accreditation status.

Ethics: A system of moral behavior and standards of conduct for healthcare professionals.

Executive search firm: Identifies and appraises candidates for a specific position. This requires a contractual agreement between the search firm and the organization.

External degree: An academic award earned through one or more of the following means: prior learning, credit by examination, specially devised sponsored experimental learning programs, self-directed study, or satisfactory completion of on-campus or off-campus courses.

External environment: Outside forces that potentially affect a department's or an organization's performance.

Facilitator: A professional with expertise in leading group discussions, especially in quality improvement activities.

Facility: Buildings, equipment, and supplies used in providing healthcare. Hospitals, nursing homes, and ambulatory-care centers are considered facilities.

Faculty: Instructors in allied health programs who have faculty status referred to as rank. Responsibilities in addition to teaching may include academic advisement, curricular development and review, research and scholarly activities, and service to the educational institution, the community, and a professional organization through committee functions, presentations, and other activities.

Goal: A quantified or specific statement of a desired future state or condition. A goal differs from an objective by lacking a deadline and usually because it is for a longer period of time than a year or two.

Guidelines: Explanatory statements accompanying the essentials that provide examples intended to assist in understanding and applying the essentials for accreditation of programs.

Health information management: This profession focuses on the management of healthcare data and information resources. The translation of data into information is conducted for the advancement of healthcare.

Health information manager: A professional who plans, designs, develops, and manages systems of administrative and clinical data in all types of healthcare and health-related institutions, organizations, and agencies.

Health maintenance organization (HMO): A membership insurance company that provides payment for services at a fixed dollar amount.

Hospice: A program that provides both palliative and supportive care for terminally ill patients and their families either directly or on a consulting basis.

ICD-9-CM: A publication containing diseases and injuries and surgical, investigative, and therapeutic procedures with numerical codes assigned. A table of drugs and chemicals, an index to external causes of injury, and a table of neoplasms are included.

Informatics: The combination of technology and methodology that makes possible computer-assisted collecting, processing, retrieving, distributing, and managing of information.

Internal environment: Forces within the organization but outside the department that potentially affect the department's performance.

Internship: On-the-job training that is part of a larger educational program. For students in health information administration and health information technology programs, the educational experience in a healthcare facility is referred to as a practicum, clinical education, or management experience.

Interview: An opportunity to market yourself and to prove to a prospective employer that you are capable, competent, and qualified for a particular position.

Intrapreneur: A person who creates an entrepreneurial spirit within an organization.

Job description: The written statement summarizing the duties and expectations associated with a job to provide direction and to clarify roles. The following elements are usually included: title, responsibilities, duties, educational and job requirements, and accountability statement. Specifying the priority of duties is helpful to new employees.

Joint Commission on Accreditation of Healthcare Organizations: A private, nonprofit organization whose purpose is to promote the attainment of uniformly high standards. Self-assessments and surveyors assist in the determination of compliance with standards.

Leadership: The ability to inspire and influence attitudes and behaviors of group members in accomplishing objectives.

Licensure: The process by which an agency of government grants permission to persons meeting predetermined qualifications to engage in a given occupation and to use a particular title. Physicians, nurses, physical therapists, and others are licensed. Institutions, such as hospitals and nursing homes, are also licensed by an agency of government to perform specified functions.

Longitudinal health record: Documentation of a patient's medical information from date of birth to death.

Managed care: A general term for the systems or techniques that are used to control access to healthcare and payment.

Management: A process of activities for creating objectives and for teaming with people to meet these objectives through efficient and effective use of resources.

Management information system (MIS): An automated or computer-based system that collects and produces the necessary information at appropriate intervals and can measure progress toward achievement of objectives. Costs and problems needing attention can be identified.

Master patient index: A listing that helps locate and associate patients with medical records, charts, and computerized documentation.

Mentor: A trusted advisor, counselor, or guide who assists with special projects such as portfolio development and with advancing a person's professional career.

Monitor: A process of taking the action necessary to be aware of the quality and quantity of employee activities that may be performed by manual or electronic means.

Motivation: A willingness to exert high levels of effort to reach departmental goals, conditioned by the ability to satisfy some employee need.

Networking: Formal and informal contacts established to assist in identifying and providing information that will advance and enhance an individual's career.

Nondiscriminatory practices: Activities that prohibit discrimination with respect to race, color, creed, sex, age, handicap(s), or national origin.

Objectives: Statements that outline desired outcomes to give direction to an organization and its employees. At times it is used synonymously with goals.

Oncology: The branch of medicine that specializes in cancer diagnosis and treatment.

Outplacement firm: Assists individuals packaging resumes for prospective employment.

Planning: The management function concerned with defining goals, establishing strategies, and creating plans to guide efforts to meet goals and objectives. Planning is a conscious design of a set of desired future occurrences that are specified as goals.

Portfolio: Documentation of accomplishments to display the scope and quality of educational and employment experiences.

Position description: This has generally the same meaning as job description and can include a more professional approach to accomplishing specific duties. Instead of a job, a position implies being on a career track.

Power: The ability of one person in an organization to influence the behavior of another.

Practicum: An extended period of experience (weeks or months) during which a student reconstructs and applies the theory learned through classroom and laboratory experiences. During the practicum the student develops proficiency prior to entering the job market. The practicum is a type of internship providing opportunities for the student to assume responsibility for a full range of duties related to the profession being studied.

Process: Specific actions taken, events and interactions occurring, to achieve a specified outcome.

Professional: Although the term has no consistent or agreed-upon meaning, there are several characteristics associated with a professional. These are (1) formal and advanced education in a specialized field; (2) certifying examination or licensure to meet standards; (3) an association affiliated with the profession; (4) a code of ethics; (5) a body of knowledge, abilities, and skills; and (6) a degree of autonomy and authority to make decisions in the area of competence.

Program Evaluation Review Technique (PERT): A scheduling device and a system of diagramming the steps of component parts of a complex project. Preparation of the PERT network includes determination of a critical path, the longest route and estimated completion time for a given project.

Promotion: Movement of an employee from one job to another that has higher compensation and additional responsibilities.

Quality: The degree to which an activity produces a product or service that meets the standards set for that activity.

Quality assurance (QA): Programs within managed-care organizations that assess patient care against preestablished standards. QA includes peer review, utilization management, evaluation of patient satisfaction, review of medical protocols, and credentialing.

Quality improvement (QI): The philosophy that processes, management, and employees benefit from efforts to provide better service, products, and ideas focusing on the customer. The term is used by the healthcare industry to describe a constant cycle of improvement that is patient and employee focused.

Quality management (QM): Commitment to a higher standard of performance, service, and outcomes through the empowerment of all employees in a process of continuous quality improvement. Scientific methods of data collection, analysis, and interpretation are applied.

Quantity: The ratio between input and output.

Recruiter: A professional who is employed in the business of securing qualified individuals for vacant positions.

Recruitment: A process of finding and attracting capable people to fill jobs.

Reengineering: The process of changing business practices to maintain quality, reduce costs, and improve performance. Reengineering involves fundamental rethinking and redesigning processes.

Registered record administrator (RRA): An individual who administers medical record systems for healthcare facilities and organizations. The RRA has graduated from an approved program in health information administration and successfully written a national examination that indicates entry-level competence as a record administrator.

Registration: The process by which qualified individuals are listed on an official roster maintained by a nongovernment organization, such as the American Health Information Management Association, or a government agency.

Regulation: Dictates of agencies charged with enforcing and implementing legislation in a particular area.

Resume: A summary or brief account of one's background that includes work experience, education, and significant accomplishments.

Self-assessment: An individual's ability to assess his or her strengths and weaknesses and to take necessary action to continue to improve. Associated terms are *self-analysis* and *self-evaluation.*

Self-esteem: An individual's degree of like or dislike for himself or herself.

Standards: Criteria by which programs, institutions, and individuals evaluate performance.

Strategic planning: A planning process that documents long-range objectives, develops activities to achieve the objectives, and allocates resources to those activities.

Success: The attainment of goals; these may be personal, professional, spiritual, and/or emotional. The favorable accomplishment of predetermined goals is a cause for celebrating.

SWOT analysis: A process involving identification of strengths, weaknesses, opportunities, and threats.

System: Series of interrelated elements that are planned for achieving a well-defined goal.

Technician: One who specializes in the technical details of a profession and who has acquired the ability to perform a complex set of tasks.

The Diagnostic and Statistical Manual of Mental Disorders (DSM-IV): A statistical classification and glossary of mental disorders.

Transcription: Translation of dictation into written form.

Utilization review: An evaluation of the necessity, availability, appropriateness, and efficiency of the use of medical services and procedures.

Vision: An idealized goal that is seen as a new future for an organization.

Win-win: A bargaining process used to encourage an outcome in which both parties achieve net gains and experience satisfaction.

Index